D1282762

Chesapeake Sails

A HISTORY OF YACHTING ON THE BAY

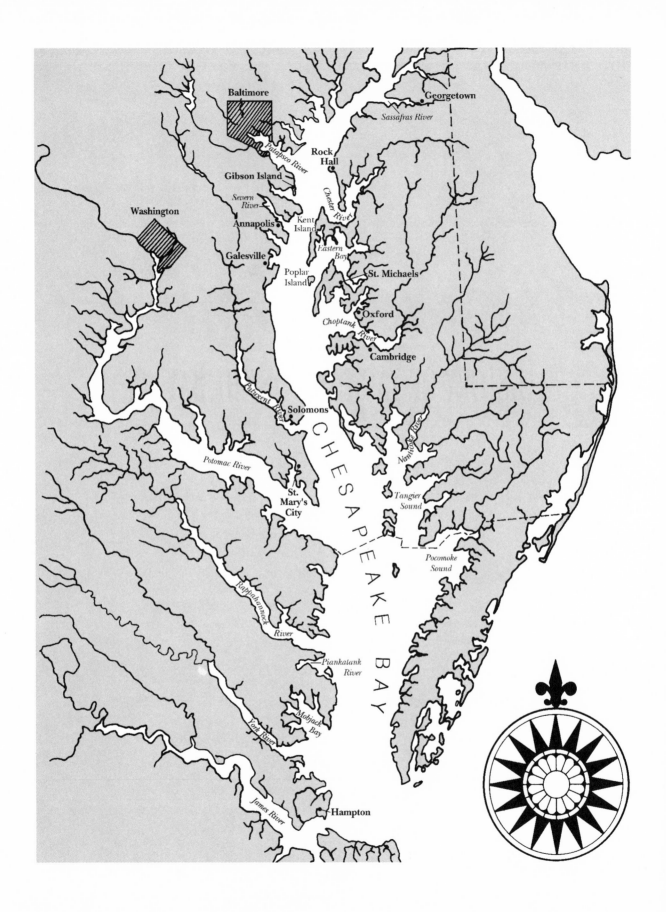

Chesapeake Sails

A HISTORY OF YACHTING ON THE BAY

RICHARD "JUD" HENDERSON

TIDEWATER PUBLISHERS
CENTREVILLE, MARYLAND

Library of Congress Cataloging-in-Publication Data

Henderson, Richard, 1924–
    Chesapeake sails : a history of yachting on the bay / by Richard
"Jud" Henderson. — 1st ed.
      p. cm.
    Includes bibliographical references (p.) and index.
    ISBN 0-87033-514-6
    1. Sailing—Chesapeake Bay (Md. and Va.)—History. 2. Yachting—
Chesapeake Bay (Md. and Va.)—History. 3. Sailboats—Chesapeake
Bay (Md. and Va.)—Design and construction. 4. Yachts—Chesapeake
Bay (Md. and Va.)—Design and construction. I. Title.
GV811.H3596 1999
797.1′246′0916347—dc21   99-31177
                             CIP

Photos
Page vi—The Luders yawl *Frolic* in Annapolis around 1953. Courtesy United States Naval Institute Archives.
Page viii—Fred Thomas photo of Thomas C. Gillmer–designed Seawind 30. Courtesy Katrina Thomas.

Manufactured in the United States of America
First edition

In memory of three Chesapeake sailing friends—
Art Sherwood, Ed Henderson, and Buzz White—
who have dropped their hooks in Kingdom Come,
described by John Masefield as that
"sunny pleasant anchorage . . .
where crews is always layin' aft for double-tots o' rum."

CONTENTS

PREFACE

Although a fair amount has been written about the Chesapeake's native working craft and the watermen who run them, relatively little has been presented in book form about the Bay's yachts and the sailors who race and cruise them. *Chesapeake Sails* attempts to fill that gap. A chowder of memoirs, ruminations, and history, the book describes the great sailing yachts of the Chesapeake Bay. It also introduces their designers, in some cases their builders, and in many cases, their colorful skippers and crews. The term yacht is used in its broadest sense—not to mean large, luxurious, expensive craft, but rather boats of any size that are used primarily for pleasure.

The yachts selected for coverage are those with which I am familiar and which are famous or, in my opinion, interesting. The hazard of this undertaking is that some good boats may have been overlooked (there has to be a limit), but I believe most of the important ones have been included. Although the primary focus of the book is on the vessels, I have also included their skippers and the sailing personalities who are well known on the Bay. I hope the reader will not be put off by this sprinkling of anecdotes and side remarks. As Richard Gordon McCloskey (founder of the Slocum Society at Shady Side, Maryland) advised, boat writing should contain "a touch of poesy here and there to leaven what would be a nourishing but too-solid hunk of hard tack."

For the most part, the personalities featured are corinthians (amateurs), although many of the best known professionals are at least mentioned. Of course, there are degrees of professionalism. This book considers those borderline sailors who are in the gray area between amateur and professional (such as yard owners and designers) to be corinthians when they skipper their own boats, offer clients the same services they provide for their own boats, and most importantly, sail primarily for pleasure rather than for business reasons.

A unique area for yachting, this Bay of ours offers protected waters, countless harbors, a soft bottom, moderate tides and currents, clear visibility, open roadsteads for racing, an abundance of seafood and wildfowl, and scenery of historic interest. The words "liquid delirium," used by E. B. White to describe ideal sailing waters in his *Essays*, certainly could be applied to the Chesapeake.

ACKNOWLEDGMENTS

By and large, yachtsmen are a cooperative lot when asked to share their knowledge and information. At least I have found this to be true, and in the preparation of this book, I owe much to many. Some of the most generous in giving me their time and help have been the yacht designers Edward Burgess; Thomas Gillmer; Worth Holden; Frank MacLear; Richards Miller; Norman Owens; the late Carl Alberg, Robert Henry, A. E. "Bill" Luders, and Rod Stephens; and especially Thomas Colvin and Karl Kirkman.

Also showing interest and supplying lore and/or photos or plans of value were the following yachting personalities (mostly former or current boatowners, club officers/officials, or crew): Paul Adamthwaite, George Bahen, George Blome, Virginia Brown, Howard Fawcett, Pat Brown Fitzgerald, Peter Geis, Morton "Sunny" Gibbons-Neff and his son

Mitchell of Sparkman and Stephens, Fred Hecklinger, Sally Henderson, Thomas Hunnicutt, Nicholas Iliff, Richard Jablin, Elwood Jennings, Claudia Jew of the Mariners' Museum, William Kouwenhoven, Carleton Mitchell, Dr. William Peach, the late Gifford Pinchot, Richard Schluederberg, Gaither Scott, Newbold Smith, Charles "Sunny" Smith, Charles Stein, Jack Strickland, Roger Taylor, Ronald Ward, John and Harriet White, James Wolfe, and Jack Zanks.

Enhancing my knowledge of early times were Geoffrey Footner, Thomas Martin, Frank Moorshead, Jr., Nancy Reeder, Charles Wheeler, John Wilbur, and especially Pete Lesher of the Chesapeake Bay Maritime Museum.

Others who contributed photos or plans were Norman Baldwin, Skip Barker, William Boykin, Skip Brown, Achsah H. Carrier, Buckey Clemsen, Mark Cramer, Edmund Cutts, Leo Flanigan, Joe Fuller,

Leonie Labrot Gately, Joseph Gregory, Phil Hamblett, Laurence and Totch Hartge, Rip Henderson, Bill Homewood, Preston Kelly, Jack Kunz, navy archivist Gary LaValley, Harry Lord, Sam Manning, Herb McCormick, Ian McCurdy, Dick Newick, Donald Parrot, John Reichenbach, Bill Schill, Don Sherwood, William Shvodian, Henry Strong, James Tazelaar, Katrina Thomas, Elliott Torn, Stuart Walker, Marion Warren, Sally Henry Willis, Alan Willoughby, and Eric Woods. To all of the above and others who have contributed in any way, my sincere thanks.

Research for this book has been both tedious and rewarding. Much of the Bay's yachting history has not been adequately recorded, and recollections of old-timers are not always reliable, but the discovery of a nugget of information that can be confirmed evokes a great deal of satisfaction. Sharing with me in the joys as well as the frustrations of the project has been my daughter Sarah Cramer, who has been an invaluable assistant. Without Sarah's help in the research, typing, and computer know-how, the project might well have been becalmed or even grounded on a lee shore.

Chesapeake Sails

A History of Yachting on the Bay

CHAPTER ONE

WAY BACK WHEN

In the August 1905 issue of *Rudder* magazine, editor Thomas Fleming Day wrote:

> The Chesapeake offers many inducements to the cruiser, which it only needs advertising to be taken advantage of. Such a splendid ground; there are few yachts, and lots of missionary work is wanted along its shores. The presence of a few Northern yachts will work wonders in rousing up the laggards. The clubs around the North end of the Bay seem to be semi-dead and to be doing nothing to encourage or spread the sport.

An occasional curmudgeon who sometimes used words like "idiots" and "ignoramuses" to describe those who were less at one with the sea than he, Tom Day did much to promote yachting and encourage offshore sailing in small boats. When he wrote these words about yachting on the Chesapeake, he might not have realized that countless informal and less-than-highly-organized yachting activities had been taking place on the Bay since colonial times, not so much in yachts or boats specifically used for pleasure, but rather in workboats.

Life on the Chesapeake's six-thousand-mile-long indented shoreline with its multitude of rivers, creeks, bays, and coves originally required a vast number of utility boats for transportation, fishing, hunting, shellfishing, and cargo carrying. Boats built only for recreation were exceedingly rare in early times, because workboats were the craft really needed; but often on holidays or special occasions they became dual-purpose craft and were raced just for the sport of it. A major factor in the relatively slow development of pleasure boating on the Bay was that the vast majority of Chesapeake residents lacked the financial means and leisure time enjoyed by wealthy yachtsmen in areas such as Boston and New York.

The workboat most commonly raced in early times was the sailing dugout log canoe. Used for crabbing, oystering, transportation, and fishing, this craft has been described as the "workhorse of the Chesapeake." First made by the Indians from single logs, the canoe was improved by the early settlers with increased beam, sharp ends, shallow keels (later centerboards), and the addition of sail. Beam was increased by fastening two or more logs together with trunnels and driftpins, thus increasing stability and carrying capacity. Different requirements and building methods led to variations in hull shape and rig, but three general types emerged: Poquoson, Pocomoke, and Tilghman canoes. Later, when competition became keen, yacht canoes were built especially for racing, one prominent type being the St. Michaels racing canoe.

In *Chesapeake Bay Log Canoes and Bugeyes*, noted historian M. V. Brewington tells us that "organized" canoe races were held at St. Michaels by 1840, particularly on the Fourth of July, sometimes with as many as thirty canoes. The starts were often made from shore with the canoe sterns pulled up on the beach. A popular rig for the St. Michaels racing canoe consisted of two raked

masts supporting a balanced jib (with pivot point abaft the tack) and two "goosewing" sails described by Brewington as "altering the sail from a perfect triangle to a triangle with one of the base angles . . . truncated parallel to the mast." Each of these sails was boomed with a sprit. Brewington continues: "The truncated [sail] was spread by a light spar called a 'club,' which was lashed at its center to the end of the sprit."

At any rate, these canoes carried a cloud of sail with extra light sails in the form of squaresails, topsails, "skys'ls" (later called kites), and spinnakers. With this much sail area and their narrow beams, the canoes were extremely tender and could capsize even at the dock with the sails down. They were held upright by distributing the weight of crew on springboards—planks extended outboard of the hull to support the constantly shifting weight. Still raced today, these canoes are among the most tricky and demanding yachts to sail, but they have the reputation of being the fastest (for their length) of the displacement (nonplaning) sailboats. At one time there was a tradition of presenting a ham to the boat that finished last in a race so her bottom might be greased with fat to increase her speed next time.

As the canoes got larger and more logs were added to their bottoms, they evolved into brogans—larger partially-decked canoes with cuddy cabins. Soon after the Civil War when oyster dredging under sail was legalized, there was a demand for larger, more powerful canoes, and this led to the development of the bugeye, a completely decked-over boat with adequate accommodation for crew. With three simple

The log canoe *Magic* built by Charles Tarr of St. Michaels in 1894. Courtesy Chesapeake Bay Maritime Museum, Collection of Pete Lesher.

triangular sails set on two raked masts of nearly equal size, the bugeyes proved to be very handy vessels that were also fast. They were prominent participants in the workboat races that were organized soon after the turn of the century. These races received a lot of publicity when they were sponsored by the *Baltimore Sun* newspaper between 1921 and 1931. The first of these,

held off Claiborne, Maryland, drew an estimated ten thousand spectators including the governors of Maryland and Virginia. A number of bugeyes were eventually converted to yachts, and an interesting match race between two of them is described in chapter 4.

Other popular sailing craft to compete in the workboat races were schooners and

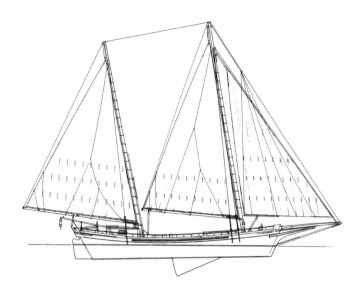

Last of the log-built bugeyes afloat, *Edna E. Lockwood*, built by John Harrison in 1889 and now owned by the Chesapeake Bay Maritime Museum. Courtesy Chesapeake Bay Maritime Museum.

especially skipjacks. The latter design evolved from the deadrise (V-bottom) skiff and originally was called a bateau. The typical rig for a skipjack is one raked mast with a jib and leg-of-mutton mainsail. Many of the skipjacks were home-built and are still dredging oysters under sail today. The creation of Chesapeake Appreciation Day in 1965 helped perpetuate the workboat races, in which the competitors now are almost entirely skipjacks.

Now an annual affair, Chesapeake Appreciation Day was the brainchild of Rolph Pottberg and was first promoted and organized by a group called the Windjammers of the Chesapeake, headed by veteran racing class skipper Marshall Duer. My own part in the project was to design posters and a fancy program that listed the competing skipjacks and charted the race course.

Some skipjacks were converted to yachts. In the late 1920s, my father owned one called *Pelican*. In *American Sailing Craft*, historian Howard Chapelle states that the famous *Sea Bird*, in which Thomas F. Day crossed the Atlantic, was a "skipjack yacht," although he admits she differed from the Chesapeake model. The most famous boat of this type was the *Islander* that was twice sailed around the world singlehandedly by Harry Pidgeon.

According to A.P. Middleton in *Tobacco Coast*, the earliest use of the word "yacht" on the Chesapeake occurred in 1676 when the term was used to describe Lord Baltimore's vessel *Loyal Charles*. She was completely armed and carried soldiers, however, and so would hardly be considered a yacht today. Middleton's first use of the term complying with our modern conception was in 1689, when Major Richard Sewall's vessel *Susanna* was described as "a small yatch [*sic*] or pleasure boate." As William P. Stephens, "the dean of American yachting historians," states in *Traditions and Memories of American Yachting:* "The first purely pleasure craft mentioned in American history is the sloop *Fancy*, built in 1717 for Colonel Lewis Morris." However, if *Susanna* preceded *Fancy*, the Chesapeake might claim to have had the first yacht in America or at least the first mention of a yacht. Although *Susanna* was considered a small vessel, she was large enough to carry a master and three crewmembers. Middleton points out that *Susanna* was exceptional at that time, for "There were so many kinds of boats and small vessels in the Chesapeake, that the need for special types to be used solely for pleasure was not yet felt."

By the middle of the eighteenth century, some vessels were advertised as "being fit for a gentleman's use." This generally meant that a dual-purpose vessel was finely finished and decorated. Indeed, a few gentlemen owned yachts that played a part in symbolizing their wealth and/or high positions in business or government. In *Tidewater, Maryland,* Paul Wilstach quotes a letter by Edward Lloyd of Wye House, the father-in-law of Francis Scott Key, ordering certain chandlery from London for his "Pleasure-Boat of about 60 Tons burthen." The order included a "compleat Sett of American Colours" and "Six Brass Guns with hammers, screws & c. compleat, to fix on Swivels, and to act in such manner as *to give the greatest report.*" Middleton writes that on gala occasions vessels were in the habit of dressing ship (flying all flags) and firing their guns, occasionally all afternoon.

Before the mid-1700s a successful type of pilot boat appeared in the Chesapeake. According to Howard Chapelle, this was the forerunner of all pilot boats along our coasts.[1] These vessels evolved into what were called "sharp-built" schooners (having fine waterlines forward), and they influenced the schooner yacht. As Chapelle wrote, "The pilot boat most closely approaches the yacht in her requirements, since she carries no cargo and has to be fast and seaworthy." A similar development was the rakish Baltimore clipper, the fine-lined schooner that was a forerunner of the clipper ships

and produced the handsome workboat schooner known as the pungy.

The origin of the Baltimore clipper is obscure. Chapelle and others have theorized that "the Baltimore Clipper descended from the Jamaica sloop, by way of Bermuda."[2] But historian/designer Thomas Gillmer, who has thoroughly researched the subject, wrote in *The Pride of Baltimore* that this theory is "poppycock." In his words, "The fast Chesapeake schooners were without immediate influential ancestors; it is best to see them as a natural growth from the Chesapeake sloops, which were simply found to be too small." Concerning the influence of the Baltimore clipper/pilot-boat-type on yachts, perhaps the culmination of this development was the schooner yacht *America,* which beat the best British yachts in the famous race around the Isle of Wight in 1851. *America* and her connection with the Chesapeake Bay is discussed later in this chapter and in chapter 7.

A most unusual early yacht was the 15-foot replica of an eighteenth-century vessel with a ship rig (three masts having square sails on each mast). This ornamental miniature ship named *Federalist* was built in 1788 by the merchants of Baltimore to commemorate Maryland's ratification of the Constitution. Before being launched, she was the centerpiece of an elaborate parade in Baltimore. Once afloat she was boarded and sailed by Commodore Joshua Barney, a naval hero of the American Revolution (dubbed the "prince of privateers"), who had supervised her building and ensured that the

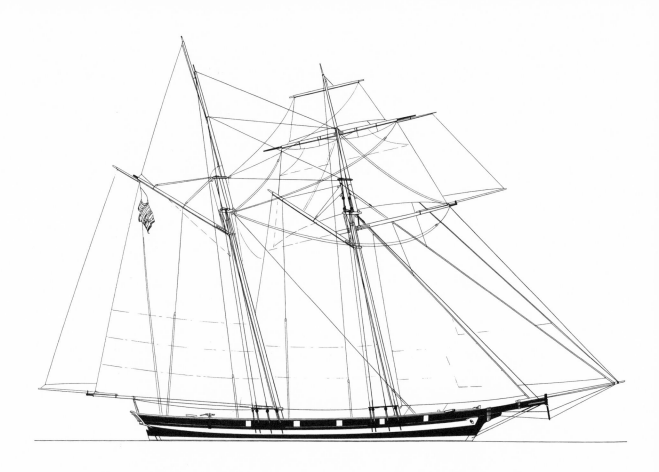

Plan of the Baltimore clipper schooner *Pride of Baltimore II* designed by Thomas C. Gillmer. Courtesy Thomas C. Gillmer.

rigging and sails were complete in every detail. *Federalist* was to be presented as a gift to George Washington, and Barney volunteered to sail her from Baltimore to Mount Vernon, far up the Potomac River. Even today it would be considered quite a feat to sail a 15-foot square-rigged powerless boat a distance of over 150 miles, singlehanded and often against the wind; much of the passage was in exposed and rough water, especially near the mouth of the Potomac.

Not many details of the passage are known, but in *Soldier of Fortune,* Hulbert Footner tells us that Barney stopped for two or three days at Annapolis, where *Federalist* drew crowds of spectators, and Barney was entertained by Governor Smallwood. After leaving Annapolis, he hugged the western shore until reaching Point Lookout, and then proceeded up the Potomac, reaching Mount Vernon eight days after leaving Baltimore. Washington graciously accepted the gift, and Barney stayed at Mount Vernon for about a week. Washington's stepson was fascinated with the boat, and Barney took him sailing. Unfortunately, *Federalist* was sunk during a hurricane three months after her delivery.

Two hundred years later, to celebrate the bicentennial anniversary of the Constitution, two replicas of *Federalist* were built. The Potomac Maritime Historical Society built one in Alexandria, Virginia; the other, a more elaborate replica, was an Annapolis creation spearheaded by marine artist/historian/builder Melbourne Smith.

After the War of 1812 (in which Joshua Barney served as leader in a plan to harass the British navy with shoal-draft

The *Maryland Federalist* under sail. Photograph courtesy of the Maryland State Archives. MSA SC 1863.

war barges), the principal sailboat yachting activity on the Chesapeake was log canoe racing. In addition, there were some fast sailboats called shooting yachts that were used for hunting wildfowl. Some cruising was combined with hunting and fishing as described in a journal written by Horatio Rideout, who took an ex-

tended cruise down the Bay with his brother-in-law John Gibson aboard the latter's sloop *Sea Gull* in 1824. Published in the Maryland Historical Society's magazine in June 1956, the journal was excerpted by my father as follows for a March 1966 article in *Yachting*:

It still continued blowing hard with rain, so that thirteen sail of sea vessels, bound out, were obliged to remain in the River [Severn River in Mobjack Bay]; besides five large ships at anchor under New Point [Comfort]. On this day one Jenkins came on board our sloop, and having heard him spoken of as "a very kind feeder," we had the curiosity to see a specimen of his talent and asked him to take dinner. He was helped literally to a Benjamin mess of pork and peas, cold boiled beef, and a duck pye—which he discussed in fine style, washing it down with a quart of strong grog and three quarts of cider—yet he remained quite sober. It seemed too that he had just before taken a damper on board some of the other vessels that he had been visiting.

Dad's response to the above was "Evidently the Chesapeake Bay country was a land of pleasant living even in those days." Rideout called the cruise a "voyage in search of pleasure." He commented that "There was some pleasure in sailing while the wind was fair and moderate, but the pain was greater, when it blew a storm in the night, and was dead calm in the day, or when it blew hard and rained at the same time."

Aside from the log canoe races at St. Michaels around 1840, there was little if any organized sailboat yachting on the

Lark, believed to be a shooting yacht (probably built before the sport became illegal), on the Miles River in the early 1900s. Note the five rows of reef points and balanced jib.

Chesapeake before the middle of the nineteenth century.

Concerning the national scene, W. P. Stephens wrote, "Prior to 1844 there were not more than twenty vessels about New York and Boston which could be classed as yachts."[3] These included the famous ornate hermaphrodite brig *Cleopatra's Barge* (launched in 1816 and owned by Captain George Crowninshield), which historian William N. Wallace considers "America's first Yacht."[4] Stephens's twenty yachts, some of which he describes, also include two yachts built in Baltimore. Information on these Chesapeake-built boats is sparse, but Stephens tells us that *Hornet*, "said to be a yacht," was built in 1819, while the other was a 46-foot 30-ton yacht named *Dream* (no date given). Both boats apparently went to New England soon after being launched.[5]

Formed by a small group in 1839, the Detroit Boat Club is sometimes called America's oldest (longest lasting) yacht club; however, the New York Yacht Club (NYYC), founded in 1844, is usually considered the first "proper," highly organized, continuing club with sizable yachts. Over the years this distinguished group set the standards for clubs that would follow in matters such as management, routine, rules, and etiquette. About a year after its founding, the New York Yacht Club held its first regatta, the centerpiece of which was a race for six sturdy schooners and three sloops. (The term regatta is said to have originated in Italy. My father called these often-chaotic nautical social affairs "regrettas.")

The Stevens family was a great force behind the NYYC—John Cox Stevens was the first commodore, and two Stevens brothers, John and Edwin, were involved when the club received a request from England to display an American pilot boat and a syndicate was formed to build the schooner yacht *America*.

Designed by George Steers, *America*'s form and rig show a heritage that started with the Chesapeake pilot schooners and Baltimore clippers. Everyone knows the story of *America*'s race around the Isle of Wight in 1851, but according to L.F. Herreshoff and others, her victory has been greatly overblown. The old story, told ad nauseam, of Queen Victoria asking

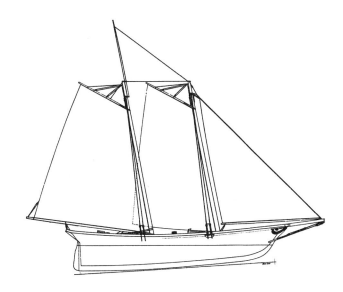

Sail plan of the yacht *America* by Howard I. Chapelle. From *History of American Sailing Ships* by Howard I. Chapelle. Copyright 1935 by W.W. Norton & Company, Inc., renewed © 1963 by Howard I. Chapelle. Reprinted by permission of W.W. Norton & Company, Inc.

about the next boat and being answered with "There is no second, your Majesty" doesn't seem justifiable when the second boat, much smaller and without a handicap allowance, finished only eighteen minutes behind in very light air. Nevertheless, *America* was the victor and thus started the highly publicized series of international contests that, of course, continue to this day. *America* lived a long, varied, and often adventurous life. She spent some time on the Chesapeake as a practice vessel for the navy and later, for nearly two decades, was on display at the U.S. Naval Academy. Her demise occurred in Annapolis soon after a snow-laden shed roof collapsed on her in 1942.

The Civil War brought an abrupt end to organized yachting activities in America, but almost immediately after

Stern view of *America* at the Annapolis Yacht Yard circa 1940. Courtesy United States Naval Academy Archives.

The Baltimore ketch *John T. Ford* before her Atlantic crossing in 1867. Courtesy The Mariners' Museum, Newport News, Virginia.

the end of hostilities there emerged two popular forms of pleasure boat sailing. W. P. Stephens calls this period the "big schooner era" because a number of wealthy New Yorkers and New Englanders built large yachts, mostly schooner-rigged, and raced them, usually with professional skippers and crew. The other popular form of yachting was the racing of sandbaggers—dinghy-type yachts with long bowsprits and large sail areas—that were kept upright by moving bags of sand to windward.

The concept of racing sandbaggers was not unlike racing log canoes on the Chesapeake since both craft used movable ballast to counterbalance unlimited sail. For the most part, both types were manned by ordinary folk (normally with considerable heft) and owned by working-class people of modest means, although sizable cash bets on the races were not uncommon. It has been written that a pi-

oneering Chesapeake yachtsman, Captain Jacob G. Morris, revived organized log canoe racing about 1870 when he brought two champion Delaware River racing craft to the Bay.[6] Exactly what kind of boats these were is not clear, but they were built by the famous Patrick McGiehan of Jersey City who specialized in producing competitive sandbaggers. It is known that Captain Morris owned a sleek cruising sloop, which he converted to a yawl named *Cora* in 1885 when he was a charter member of the Chesapeake Bay Yacht Club. He is credited by the magazine *Forest and Stream*[7] with popularizing the yawl rig on the Chesapeake and by the *Rudder*[8] for being "the prime mover" in popularizing log canoe racing. A canoe race off Claibourne in 1894 attracted more than seven thousand people.

Yachting on the Bay received some publicity in 1867 with a daring cruise that ended in tragedy. Perhaps inspired by the transatlantic crossing of the miniature ship-rigged boat *Red, White, and Blue* the previous year, a group of Baltimoreans built an even smaller boat for the purpose of crossing the Atlantic and being displayed in the Paris Exposition. The Baltimore boat, named *John T. Ford* after the major financial backer, was a 24½-foot double-ended ketch. Although a sketch of her in the *London Illustrated News* shows a rounded stern, a more detailed engraving in *Harper's Weekly* depicts a pinkie-type double-ended stern with pronounced sheer (but without the overhanging bulwarks and "tombstone"). It is interesting that Raphael Semmes in his *Captains and Mariners of Early Maryland* writes that pinks were built on the Eastern Shore in colonial times.

Skippered by Baltimorean Charles Gold and with three additional crew, *John T. Ford* sailed down the Bay and then up the coast to Nova Scotia. There, a crew substitution was made when a remarkable man named Armstrong shipped aboard for the Atlantic crossing. After mid-July the boat departed for Ireland. Encountering heavy weather, not unusual in those latitudes so late in the season, *Ford* was rolled over and lost her oil for lamps and cooking. To obtain heat and light, her crew made the serious mistake of ripping out and burning the floorboards that held her loose ballast in the bilge. Near the south coast of Ireland while running before a gale, *Ford* capsized and most of her ballast fell through an open hatch. The boat could not be righted and the crew desperately clung

Cora, owned by Jacob Morris, prominent Chesapeake yachtsman of the late 1800s. Courtesy Chesapeake Bay Maritime Museum.

to her bottom. One by one they were swept off and drowned—all except Armstrong, who tenaciously hung on for three days and four nights! With little if any food or water and in a near state of hypothermia, Armstrong nevertheless managed to upend an oar with a flag of canvas to attract the attention of a passing vessel named *Aerolite*. Miraculously he was saved, and *Ford* was washed ashore on the Irish coast. She made it across but very obviously far from successfully. In *Atlantic Adventurers*, Humphrey Barton, founder of the Ocean Cruising Club and record keeper for small boat passages, indicated that *John T. Ford* was the second small boat to cross the Atlantic and the first under 25 feet long.

Although local historian M. V. Brewington reports a boat club on the Bay existed as early as 1852,[9] and Frederick Tilp reports the Potomac Boat Club was founded in 1844,[10] the first bona fide yacht club on the Chesapeake seems to be the Baltimore Yacht Club of Baltimore City, with a charter date of 1880. There were five charter members: William P. Towles, Matthias Roberts, James Towles, William M. Busey, and J. William Middendorf, all of Baltimore city. Some of them owned the 74-foot schooner *Rena,* which was built by Beacham Brothers in Baltimore the same year the club was founded. A corporation was formed with the stated purpose of "building, owning and controlling one or more sailing or steam yachts to be used for social purposes and pleasure on the waters of this state and elsewhere and to encourage naval architecture and the cultivation of naval science."[11]

This organization was actually the first of three separate clubs having the name Baltimore Yacht Club. The second, formed eleven years later, was officially named "The Baltimore Yacht Club of Baltimore City 1891." Their flagship was the lovely Herreshoff schooner *Albatross,* which, judging from a photograph, seems to be about 72 feet long. In 1900 she won a 167-mile race from Baltimore to Norfolk, Virginia, competing against ten other entries, and, according to the Easton *Star-Democrat,* she equaled the time of the Baltimore to Norfolk steamer.

The original fleet of the second club had three schooners, two sloops, and five steam yachts including two paddle wheelers and Alexander Brown's 148-foot *Ballymena.* Later Henry Walter's 224-foot *Narada* joined the fleet. She was a steam-powered brigantine converted to a schooner, but it has been said that her sails were carried mainly for decoration. *Narada* transported a few art treasures to the Walters Art Gallery in Baltimore, in-

The second Baltimore Yacht Club in the early 1900s.

CHESAPEAKE SAILS

cluding an important Raphael painting. The third Baltimore Yacht Club, a carry-over of the second, was established at Sue Island in 1938.

Everyone agrees that the oldest *surviving* yacht club on the Bay is the Chesapeake Bay Yacht Club located at Easton on Maryland's Eastern Shore. Founded in 1885, its first commodore was William O'Sullivan Dimpfel, who has been called "the father of yachting on the Chesapeake Bay." Dimpfel was an amateur yacht designer, and the club was formed by nineteen Eastern Shoremen at the old port of Oxford aboard the 39-foot schooner *Gaetina,* which was designed by Dimpfel himself and built in 1883.[12] As a matter of fact, many prestigious yacht clubs were formed aboard boats: the New York Yacht Club, founded aboard the schooner *Gimcrack;* the Cruising Club of America, conceived in the cabin of the ketch *Typhoon* (still in a shambles after nearly capsizing in mid-Atlantic); the Capital Yacht Club of Washington, D.C., formed in the cabin of the naptha launch *Alert* in 1892; and the Corinthian Yacht Club of Washington, born in 1903 aboard the sloop *Janet.*

Gaetina, whose plans are reproduced here along with an attractive detailed profile drawing by C. P. Kunhardt (the editor of *Forest and Stream*), resembled in some respects a Penzance lugger with the rig of a pilot schooner. She must have been a handy boat, as Kunhardt reported that Dimpfel often sailed her singlehandedly between Baltimore and his residence "near the mouth of the Choptank, a distance of sixty miles." Actually, the residence was on Plaindealing Creek off the Tred Avon River, considerably past the mouth of the Choptank.

Another one of Dimpfel's many designs was the yawl *Panola,* which is mentioned a number of times by the Barrie brothers in their classic book *Cruises, Mainly in the Bay of the Chesapeake.* An amusing story about *Panola's* launching at Oxford was told to me by Dimpfel's grandson, Tom Martin. When she slid down the ways and met her element for the first time, presumably before a crowd of spectators, the handsome *Panola* promptly rolled over and swamped. Dimpfel had neglected to put any ballast aboard. When proper ballast was added to her bilge, however, the yawl proved adequately stiff, and Dimpfel did a lot of cruising in her on the Chesapeake.

Evidently, the founders of the Chesapeake Bay Yacht Club were a fun-loving group who did not take themselves too seriously. Although dedicated to yachting and to their considerable nautical skills, they also emphasized fine meals, good liquor, and lively social activities. An old gentleman who used to sail on *Gaetina* told Tom Martin in the 1930s that the CBYC was formed primarily so that its members could participate in the annual New York Yacht Club cruise. The same old gent confirmed that a newspaper account describing the first NYYC cruise attended by members of the CBYC was framed and hung on the wall of the barroom in the Easton clubhouse for many years. According to this newspaper account, the CBYC contingent picked up some dancing girls in Newport and, in

The schooner *Gaetina*, designed and owned by William O'Sullivan Dimpfel, as drawn by C.P. Kunhardt. From *Small Yachts* by C.P. Kunhardt, Forest and Stream Publishing Company (1885).

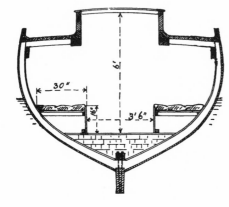

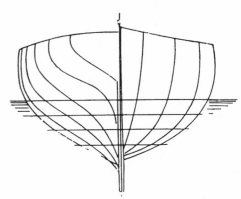

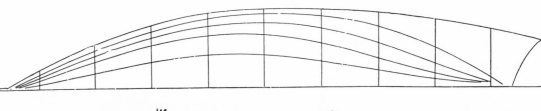

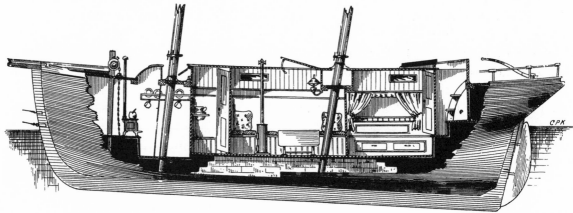

CHESAPEAKE SAILS

the words of Tom Martin, "had a noisy and scandalous evening aboard *Gaetina*."[13] An oft-repeated report, possibly apocryphal, was that a very scantily clad woman was hoisted up the mast. The next morning the commodore of the NYYC arrived in his barge to voice his disapproval in no uncertain terms. At any rate, a good time was had by the Eastern Shoremen, and the CBYC gained some recognition. At least no one could accuse the Chesapeake sailors of being stuffy.

A detailed report of CBYC's first regatta on June 10, 1885, was published in *Forest and Stream*. It was written by "Sinkboat," also known as "Sneakbox," the noms de plume of Jacob G. Morris, the previously mentioned charter member of the club and owner of the yawl *Cora*. This regatta consisted of the rendezvous (including "merry" parties aboard the participating yachts) as well as cruising, racing, and visiting waterfront homes of members. In addition to *Cora* and *Gaetina*, other yachts mentioned were *Zema*, a centerboard schooner owned by J. Chandler Roach; *Enchre*, a sloop; *Willie*, a yawl; and *Lulu*, a sloop (later converted to a yawl) owned by Francis C. Goldsborough. The latter was a particular rival to *Cora*, and, as Morris put it, the two speedy craft always "hunted" each other when they met.

One of many prominent members of the Chesapeake Bay Yacht Club was Colonel Oswald Tilghman, a flag officer in the early 1900s. My father used to tell the story about Colonel Tilghman crossing the Miles River bridge in his horse-drawn buggy. When the horse began rearing and bucking in the middle of the bridge,

the Colonel, being the consummate seaman, shouted to his steed, "Jump overboard, damn you, then I'll know how to handle you."

Other early yacht clubs on the Chesapeake include the Severn Boat Club formed in 1886; it evolved into the Annapolis Yacht Club, but its original boating activities were limited to canoeing and rowing. The Capital Yacht Club formed in 1892 has already been mentioned. It established a cruising station in Annapolis and in the early 1900s sponsored an annual long-distance sailing race from Washington to Annapolis. This race, which continued until World War I, was a real test of seamanship and endurance. In addition to the problems of shoals, strong currents, and frequent squalls, the competitors had to sail at night through numerous fishnet stakes and fleets of unlit fishing boats in the Potomac River, since the race didn't start until four in the afternoon.[14]

Miles River belles, one of whom was a Tilghman, sailing with the author's uncle and Graham Johnson in 1908.

In the lower Bay, early yacht clubs include the Virginia Yacht Club that was incorporated in 1907 according to *Chesapeake Skipper* magazine.[15] It dissolved and was replaced by the Hampton Yacht Club in 1926. A still-earlier club, the Hampton Roads Yacht Club (predecessor of the Norfolk Yacht and Country Club organized in 1896), held a Fourth of July regatta in 1905 that was described in *Rudder* magazine.[16] This event followed a pioneering ocean race, sponsored by the Brooklyn Yacht Club of New York with assistance from the Hampton Roads Yacht Club, having a course that ran between Brooklyn and Hampton Roads. The race was won by the famous 38-foot New York yawl *Tamerlane*, which, a year later, won the first Bermuda Race. Only one Chesapeake boat was entered in the 250-mile Brooklyn-Hampton Race, an ancient yawl named *Anna*,[17] owned by C. Lowndes Johnson, later a well-known Star boatbuilder/sailor and designer of the Comet class. But *Anna* never made the race. In the following regatta, however, many Chesapeake yachts competed against the Brooklyn visitors, and most of the class winners hailed from the Hampton Roads Yacht Club.

Handicap racing rules have always had a profound effect on yacht design. In England the Thames Measurement Rule, which penalized beam, produced the extreme in a hull form designed to cut through the water rather than ride over it. This was the "plank-on-edge" deep, narrow, heavily ballasted cutter that sometimes had a beam less than one-sixth the waterline length. On the

other hand, the designs of many American yachts were the opposite extreme: beamy, shallow, low-freeboard hulls with centerboards, a hull form encouraged by a Cubic Contents Rule. These boats proved practical for shoal waters, and they were good sail carriers, but two events in particular influenced the development of a more moderate, less extreme, middle-of-the-road type of hull somewhere between the British plank-on-edge cutter and the American "skimming dish." The first event occurred in 1876 when the 140-foot beamy centerboard schooner *Mohawk* capsized during a sudden squall while at anchor but with sails up in a New York Yacht Club anchorage and five people drowned. The other event was the 1881 appearance in American waters of the 46-foot Scottish cutter *Madge*, a relatively deep narrow boat, which, in six out of seven races, trounced some of the best American yachts.

An example of the newer, middle-of-the-road design was Ellis Ellicott's cutter *Binker*, which resided at Gibson Island in the mid-1930s to early 1940s. Designed by Henry Gruber of the Donaldson and Burgess Company, *Binker* could be considered a later moderate development of the plank-on-edge type. As Roger Taylor stated in *Still More Good Boats*, "The *Binker* has a fairly short bow and a longish, fine counter . . . somewhat reminiscent of British cutters, from which she may have received some rather distant inspiration."

At the time *Madge* was designed, sail area was not considered in the rating system, but the noted British designer/author Dixon Kemp suggested a rule that considered both length and sail area. A variation of Kemp's rule was adopted by the Seawanhaka Corinthian Yacht Club of New York, and in 1890 a further modification, which added the boat's waterline length to the square root of her sail area and divided the result by two, became known as the Seawanhaka Rule. The ingenious designer of Bristol, Rhode Island, Nathanael Herreshoff, took advantage of the rule's loopholes and designed the forerunners of modern American yachts: first *Gloriana,* with overhanging bow and cutaway forefoot, and then fin-keelers with spade rudders. In an effort to plug these loopholes, the Americans put forth the Universal Rule, originally devised by Herreshoff in 1901, which recognized displacement as follows: length times the square root of sail area divided by the cube root of displacement. The British took a different approach to discourage light-displacement fin-keeled skimming dishes (the kind of boat very much in evidence today, incidentally); they created the International Rule in 1909, using girth measurements to encourage deeper hulls with slacker bilges.

With the introduction of the Universal Rule that created class boats with letter designations such as R-, P-, Q-, and the enormous J-boats, and the International Rule that created numerically designated classes such as 6-, 8-, 10-, and 12-meter boats, a different concept of racing gained wide acceptance. These rules allowed boat-for-boat racing (with-

Binker, a modern representation of a design that was a compromise between the extremes of British and American yacht design trends of the late 1800s. Reproduced with permission from *The Best of Uffa,* International Marine, 1998.

out handicaps) in boats having some variation in design parameters. The designer could make trade-offs such as the reduction of sail area to obtain greater waterline length. A number of design variations were possible as long as the rating number resulting from the solution of the rating formula was not exceeded.

In the early 1900s it became quite popular on the Chesapeake to race and even cruise on Universal Rule boats. At the Jamestown Exposition in 1907, a sizable gathering of Q-boats, including some New England champions, were

The Q-boat *Eleanor,* which claimed more victories than any other Chesapeake racer from 1907 until about 1937.

there to race for the King's Cup, presented by King Edward VII. The cup was won by Sherman Hoyt's *Capsicum* after a controversial series in which the leading boat was protested and disqualified for an illegal rating.[18] Among the competitors was the Herreshoff-designed Q-boat *Eleanor,* which was brought to the Bay for

the exposition by Isaac E. Emerson of the second Baltimore Yacht Club. In a subsequent series off Norfolk, she defeated *Capsicum* for the President Roosevelt Trophy. *Eleanor* was still racing on the Bay in the mid-1930s, and, under the ownership of sailors like Dudley Williams and Maurice Skinner, Jr., claimed more victories than any other Chesapeake boat.

The popularity of Universal Rule racing on the northern Bay is illustrated by an article in the *Philadelpia Inquirer* (date unknown) describing the twenty-fifth annual regatta of the Chesapeake Bay Yacht Club held at Oxford, Maryland, in 1911 and attended by "several thousand persons." There was hot competition among the P- and Q-class sloops as well as Y- and Z-class yawls. *Eleanor* was competing, but on this occasion she did not shine, being defeated by Graham Johnson, brother of the previously mentioned Lowndes Johnson, sailing the Gielow-designed Q-boat *Vingt-Trois.* The article reported that the latter boat made the former "crack boat of the Baltimore Yacht Club look as though she was tied to a stake."

A favorite pastime for the racing skippers of those days was to participate in one of the annual cruising races, where members of the various yacht clubs (Baltimore Yacht Club, Corinthian Yacht Club of Baltimore, Capital Yacht Club, Maryland Yacht Club, Hampton Yacht Club, and of course Chesapeake Bay Yacht Club) would rendezvous and then proceed with competitive "squadron runs" to harbors of or near the various clubs. All of this activity took organization, so in 1908 the first Chesapeake Bay Yacht Racing

Left, Lowndes Johnson, and *center,* Graham Johnson, with Charles E. Henderson, the author's uncle.

Association (CBYRA) was formed. Even those Universal Rule boats without cabins, such as *Eleanor* and *Vingt-Trois,* would compete in these events, which included some overnight racing and often spanned a period of a week or more.

My father William L. Henderson and his older brother Charles E. Henderson were brought up on the Miles River at "the Rest," a modest estate formerly owned by Commodore Franklin Buchanan, commander of the *Merrimac* (of *Monitor* and *Merrimac* fame). The Hendersons were next-door neighbors of the Johnson boys, Graham and Lowndes, who were known far and wide for their sailing prowess. In sailing with and competing against the Johnsons, Dad and Uncle Charlie learned some valuable tricks of the sailing trade.

The Rest was not far from St. Michaels, a quaint waterfront town that had been a center of shipbuilding since colonial times. An oft-told tale claims that the town was cleverly saved from destruction from a night bombardment by British frigates during the War of 1812. St. Michaels residents extinguished all downstairs lights in their houses, illuminated the upper floors, and hung lanterns in the trees. The British gunners assumed the lights were at ground level and overshot their target; supposedly, the shots passed harmlessly overhead, and the town survived. Today, St. Michaels is the location of the Chesapeake Bay Maritime Museum and attracts many tourists.

As a young boy, Dad loved to visit the boatyards in St. Michaels. At least one, probably Thomas Kirby's yard, had a railway that hauled vessels with a horse treadmill. It was powered by an old mule named Henry that walked around in a circle to wind a cable around a large capstan, while Henry's owner, a black waterman, lay back on a mound of straw and made encouraging remarks to his four-legged source of livelihood. "Come on Henry. You're doin' fine. She's almost up now." One day, while Dad was watching, Henry stopped dead in his tracks; the concerned waterman jumped to his feet, and in a plaintive voice asked, "What's a matta Henry? Does you wants to pee?"

Yearning for his own boat, Dad asked his father to buy him a skiff. My grandfather agreed provided Dad could prove he was able to swim across the Miles River. Later in life a respected jurist, Dad showed the first sign of having a legal mind. He argued that it would never be necessary to swim across the river, because he would always be closer to one

Ojigwan on the railway at the Thomas Kirby yard at St. Michaels, 1913. Courtesy Pete Lesher (from his collection); photograph by C. Lowndes Johnson, 1913.

shore than the other unless he were in the exact middle, and then it would be necessary to swim only half the width of the river. He got his boat.

Uncle Charlie acquired the P-class sloop (later a yawl) *Ojigwan* before 1910 and had great success racing her. He had some exciting sails, as when he tried to sneak between some fishnet stakes at night and was holed by a broken stake.

The boat was kept afloat with a mattress and shoring poles. On another occasion, when carrying a spinnaker through a squall, the Hendersons almost drove *Ojigwan* under; she buried her bow and stuck her stern in the air. As my father described it, she then began to roll, shook the water off her deck, and took off on a screaming plane with her crew back on the fantail.

Aboard the Q-boat *Suelew* after Charles Henderson and Lowndes Johnson sailed her to the Miles River from New York.

Dad also recalled the time when Uncle Charlie, at the helm, was being beaten by the Johnsons in a light-air race. He gave up in disgust and turned the helm over to his kid brother. Soon after Dad took the tiller, he got a lucky puff and eased by the Johnsons. Graham called over saying, "Charlie, I think you should let the kid sail your boat all the time." Having built a reputation as an outstanding racer, my uncle didn't much like the remark, but thereafter Dad was allowed to steer more often.

In 1914 the Henderson brothers bought the Q-boat *Suelew* in Brooklyn, New York, and Uncle Charlie sailed her down to the Chesapeake with Lowndes Johnson. Their offshore passage down the coast was played up in the local papers as somewhat of a feat, as in those times Qs were not considered very seaworthy because of their low freeboard, long overhangs, and low buoyancy. There was some hot racing in the class right up to the advent of World War I. Even after World War II a few Qs, such as Harold "Buzz" White's double-ended *Gale,* were leaving their marks.

One of the Qs my uncle and father regularly raced against prior to the first war was *Mary* of the Cambridge Yacht Club. She won a hundred-mile race in 1914. Built in 1910, she was still going strong in the 1960s under the ownership of Martin Alvey. *Mary* was given an impressive fiftieth birthday party at the Potapscut Sailing Association and presented with a gold-colored cockpit awning. This boat should not be confused with another racing boat named *Mary* (later *Mary E.*), an R-boat successfully raced in the 1950s by Howard Jones.

A regatta scene, probably at Oxford in the early 1900s.

America's entry into World War I put a definite damper on yacht racing. The CBYRA dissolved and was not reformed until 1934. Sailing gradually picked up again after the war and was stimulated in the upper Bay when the Baltimore Yacht Club acquired a fleet of Larchmont Interclub one-designs that usually raced in the Baltimore and Annapolis areas. Then came the famous Star boats that proved most popular and are still raced today. I have always felt that most of the very best big-boat racing skippers are graduates of the Star class.

An enlarged version of the Bug class one-design, the Star was designed in 1911 by Francis Sweisguth of William Gardner's New York architectural firm. A fin-keeler, it has an arc bottom and hard chines that decrease leeway and help prevent pounding when the boat is well heeled in moderate choppy seas, such as those often encountered on the Chesapeake. Originally the Star was a gaff-rigged sloop, but by the time it reached the Bay it had a low jib-headed rig. The Star first appeared on the Chesapeake at Gibson Island, Maryland (located between Baltimore and Annapolis), in 1924. That was the year a formal charter was granted by the International Star Class Yacht Racing Association for the first Chesapeake Bay fleet. Charter members were Nathaniel S. "Cap" Kenney, J. Rulon Miller, Sifford Pearre, and W. Stuart Symington, members of the Gibson Island Club.

Founded in 1921, the Gibson Island Club grew from a golfing center and small assemblage of rowboats and canoes to one of the major East Coast yachting

Larchmont Interclubs racing from Baltimore to Annapolis in 1920.

centers in a few short years. Its first significant move in yachting activities was the
purchase of eight 24-foot centerboard
Fisher Island sloops. Two years later, in
1923, a strong interest developed in
strict one-design interclub racing, and
the Star class was selected. An order for a
dozen Star boats was underwritten and
all boats were bought by eager Gibson Is-

land Club members before delivery. The
early boats were named for fish, and a requirement that each be painted a different color led to the group being called
the "Rainbow Fleet." At first the boats
were kept at anchor moorings in the
Chesapeake Bay off Gibson Island's
causeway, but one morning after a northeast storm, owners were shocked to find

STAR Rigs

CHESAPEAKE SAILS

eleven of the twelve boats sunk; only the tops of their masts showed above the surface. The twelfth Star, Cap Kenney's *Porpoise,* remained afloat by virtue of having been protected by a cockpit cover. The sunken boats were all salvaged and thereafter were kept in Gibson Island's protected harbor.[19]

Porpoise was selected as the representative of the Chesapeake fleet at the Star Internationals on Long Island Sound in 1924. She was shipped there and back on the deck of a small bay freighter that lacked a reverse gear and had little more than two feet of freeboard. Skippered by Cap Kenney with Jay Miller as crew, *Porpoise* finished sixth out of ten boats, which was not too bad considering the caliber of the competition and the infancy of the Chesapeake fleet. *Porpoise* was again sent to the Internationals the following year, and this time she improved her position to fifth out of fifteen boats.

Chesapeake Stars gained further national recognition in 1927 when Harold W. Smith of the Gibson Island Club went to Providence, Rhode Island, to compete in the Internationals with my father as crew. Their boat *Mackerel* was given little chance of doing well against the hot competition that included two former world champions, but the series ended with *Mackerel* tied for first with two other boats. This required a sail-off which *Mackerel* lost to *Tempe III* of the West Coast, but Harold

was officially declared the Atlantic Coast Champion.

When only ten years old, I was fortunate enough to crew for Harold Smith in the 36-mile Bloody Point Race, the Chesapeake's long-distance event for Stars. Despite my light weight, a fresh breeze, and a borrowed boat, Harold won the race, leaving me with a most vivid memory of his brilliant sailing. He played the current to perfection, twice going so close to shore that we bumped the bottom.

That experience reminds me of another occasion when a Star skipper of my acquaintance was working the shore to escape the current and was uncertain as to how far inshore he could go before tacking out. His sharp-eyed crew observed a pair of swimmers with their shoulder tops just clear of the water, so he suggested going in a bit closer. He had assumed the swimmers were standing on the bottom, but unfortunately they had been sitting on it. When they suddenly stood up, it became painfully apparent that the Star was clear of the bottom only because she was well heeled. The skipper slammed over the helm, but it was too late; they were hard aground.

To illustrate the quality of the young Chesapeake Star fleet, the same year that *Mackerel* came within a whisker of winning the Internationals, she lost the Bay Championship to another Chesapeake boat named *Undine,* sailed by the Johnson brothers. She was the first Star built by Lowndes and Graham.[20] After an unsuccessful attempt at the World Championship in California, the Johnsons built with their own hands a new boat named

Facing page: A variety of Star rigs drawn by Richards T. Miller. Rigs on white boats sanctioned by Star Class. *Redwing* rig (far left) designed by Miller. Courtesy Richards T. Miller.

Eel, which proved as slippery as her namesake. In 1929, the Johnsons again earned the right to compete in the Star Internationals, so *Eel* was taken to New Orleans, venue of the World Championship series. Sailing against the likes of Arthur Knapp, the famous champion of Long Island Sound, the lightweight Johnsons did only moderately well in the first two heavy-weather races. The last three races, however, were light-air affairs more typical of midsummer drifters on the Chesapeake, and *Eel* showed her stern to the competition, winning the series by a comfortable margin.

Few Star sailors were more dedicated than Graham and Lowndes. Not only did they build their own boats, they regularly sailed more than thirty miles from their home on the Miles River to compete in races at Gibson Island. Sleeping and sometimes even cooking on their boat, they carried a finely crafted portable cabin trunk that was stowed under the foredeck when racing. Tragically, Graham died at the helm of a Star soon after the start of a race in 1931. Lowndes went on to become a locally famous small-boat designer/builder and creator of the Comet class, which was a sort of centerboard "baby Star."

Chesapeake Stars also gained the highest international respect in 1976 when James Allsopp of the Gibson Island Yacht Squadron won the World's Championship at Nassau. Like the Johnsons were, Jim is a mild-mannered, soft-spoken sailor with an inner intensity that belies his outwardly casual manner. He went on to win the European silver star that same year, and later became involved

with America's Cup racing. He was recently a coskipper of *Chessie Racing*, the Chesapeake's Whitbread racer.

In the early days before the popularity of boat trailers, most small racing boats were towed to regattas behind other boats, though the Johnsons preferred to sail there. Some yacht clubs had special tow boats such as Gibson Island's *Humdinger*, but most Stars were towed behind sizable mother yachts. In later years a well-known mother yacht that hailed from New Jersey but spent a lot of time on the Chesapeake was the 54-foot yawl *Zeearend* owned by Robert and Howard Lippincott. Those brothers were famous Star and Comet builders, and Robert won the Star World's Championship in 1950. I was told by Robert's son Richard that *Zeearend* once towed thirty Stars and Comets to a regatta and thirty-six people spent the night on board.

Later in the same year that the northern Bay received its charter from the International Star class, a second fleet was formed at the south end of the Bay in Hampton, Virginia. Prominent pioneers were the Miller brothers, Garland and Grady. It is a curious coincidence that J. Garland Miller of the south and J. Rulon Miller of the north each were called "the father of yachting" in their respective areas, and both were champion Star racers who later owned well-known yachts named *Tradition*. After all but dominating the Star class in his area, first with *Tomboy*

Facing page: Harold W. Smith, Star class Atlantic Coast champion of 1927 at the helm of his *Mackerel.*

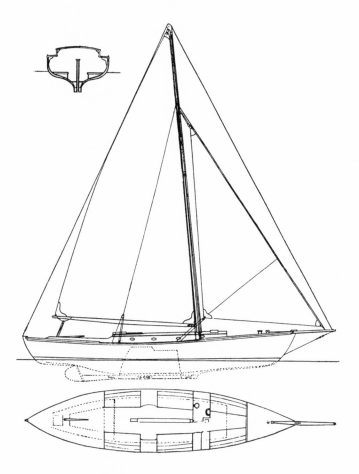

Plans of Garland Miller's *Tradition II*.

and proved extremely fast, winning the canoe title at Miles River Regatta in 1937 and repeating her performance the next two years at Oxford. Among the swift Tilghman Island canoes she defeated was the northern Bay champion *Flying Cloud* built by John B. Harrison.

Garland Miller's second *Tradition* was a double-ended centerboard cruising racer that showed a definite kinship to the log canoe. Forty-seven feet long overall with a beam of 10½ feet, she had a draft of only 4 feet with the board up and a tiny rudder. Her hull shape was determined by Miller, who carved a 47-inch model of her. Lines and offsets were done by a crewmember, Charles Cox, who was a naval architect. No rule beater, *Tradition II* rated well up in class A (for large boats), but she was a real speedster and often overcame her high rating.

Like his counterpart Jay Miller in the northern Bay, Garland was an aggressive sailor. One of his competitors told me that he was a threat on the starting line, almost appearing to fence with *Tradition II*'s long bowsprit. Up north, when a schooner poked her bowsprit between the shrouds of Jay Miller's *Tradition*, Jay took an ax and gave it several whacks before the two boats were untangled. So one could say that "bowspritting" was another thing the two Millers had in common.

During the early years of the depression, small inexpensive centerboarders were desired for racing. In the Norfolk area, a class of small catboats developed called DYs, the letters standing for "depression yachts." Of simple construction, a DY could be built for as little as forty

and then with *Flapper*, Garland sailed the latter in the 1930 Internationals at Gibson Island and did very well, finishing fifth in a sizable fleet of the best United States competitors plus a number of foreign champions. Stars began to fade in the lower Bay, however. Some attributed the decline to the need for centerboard boats for the shallow racing areas, and others blamed Miller for not giving the local competition enough opportunities to win.[21] Garland eventually went into log canoe racing with an old Poquoson canoe that he modernized with a one-mast, yachtlike rig. She was the first *Tradition* dollars. Then came the Scrappy Cats, larger catboats, first used in the Norfolk area in 1934 but designed and built by Ralph Wiley of Oxford three years earlier. The year 1935 brought the popular sloop-rigged Hampton One-Designs that would spread to most parts of the Bay. More about these handsome centerboarders is found in chapter 8.

Meanwhile up at Gibson Island, yacht racing had spread into big boats. In 1925 only four large yachts, including Jay Miller's Atkin-designed schooner *Harpoon* and my father and uncle's Herreshoff yawl *Vega,* graced the Gibson Island Harbor; but a decade later the fleet had grown to forty-two sailing yachts with cabins and these included some Universal and International Rule racers. Having gained some national recognition as a prominent yachting center with Harold Smith's good showing at the Star Internationals in 1927, the Gibson Island Club decided to sponsor an offshore race that would start at Cape May, New Jersey, follow a course around the Chesapeake lightship at the entrance to the Bay, and finish at Gibson Island. With a new Alden schooner named *Blue Water,* Jay Miller finished a close second, only ten minutes behind John Alden's *Malabar VIII.* This race was so successful that two years later, the club decided to sponsor a longer ocean race from New London to Gibson Island. It attracted forty entries, many of them famous yachts: the sleekest of all the Alden schooners, *Sachem,* first boat to finish; the legendary Burgess-designed schooner *Nina,* overall winner; and Olin Stephens's first racing

cruiser design, class winner *Kalmia,* skippered by the youthful designer.

Two other Chesapeake boats were class winners: William McMillan's *Merry Widow,* a sister of John Alden's *Malabar VI,* and my father's brand-new 35-foot yawl *Kelpie.* The latter was one of three Alden-designed sister yawls that had been sailed to New London from the builder's yard in Maine. I remember Dad telling a group of men how he had brought *Kelpie* down the coast to New London "singlehanded." My mother, who was his crew, overheard his remark from the next room; she stomped into the room where Dad was holding forth and screamed, "You did what?"

Described as "incredible" by *Yachting* magazine,[22] all three sisters, after 475 miles of racing in all sorts of weather vagaries, finished within a space of nineteen minutes. Rivalry was particularly keen between *Kelpie* and her sister *Merry Ann,* owned by Ellis Ellicott, because my uncle was crewing on the latter, and he was determined not to be beaten by his kid brother. The two boats converged at the Virginia Capes and traded positions all the way up the Bay. Uncle Charlie was acknowledged as the best helmsman on *Merry Ann.* He did the lion's share of steering, and according to one report, near the end of the race he was given coffee constantly and lashed to the helm to keep him upright if he fell asleep. Dad had no less than Harold Smith to help him with the steering, and *Kelpie* nipped *Merry Ann* at the finish line by just a few minutes.

A second New London–Gibson Island Race was held in 1933, and this time the

Ellis Ellicott at the helm of *Merry Ann;* C.E. Henderson to his left (port side) in the background.

overall award went to a Gibson Island boat, Eugene Du Pont's schooner *High Tide,* featured in chapter 5. Light air made the race extremely slow. One boat, an ancient Friendship sloop, took more than eleven days to sail the course. *High Tide* was first boat, finishing four hours ahead and beating a number of hot racers—including three 10-meters—boat-for-boat. *High Tide* was formerly owned by Jay Miller, who died in 1931. Fittingly, she won the prestigious J. Rulon Miller Memorial trophy.

Held again for the third and final time in 1937, the New London–Gibson Island event was called by no less an authority than British author/designer Uffa Fox, "the most important long-distance race in America."[23] It was won by a new Sparkman and Stephens yawl, *Avanti,* owned by Walter Rothschild. Although no Chesapeake boats were outstanding in this race, Dudley Wolfe's *Highland Light,* seemingly omnipresent on the Bay in later years under ownership of the U.S. Naval Academy, was the first boat to finish and corrected to third place overall. My father skippered Corrin Strong's new Rhodes cutter *Narada* to a respectable fifth out of fifteen boats in class B.

Two years later, the Annapolis Yacht Club took over running the event; it later became the classic Newport-Annapolis Race, and then, after the course was reversed in 1957, the Annapolis-Newport Race. In the 1939 affair top honors went to Spencer Berger's large yawl *Mandoo II*, which would later belong to the Naval Academy under the name *Royono*. Annapolitan William Labrot recently had acquired the famous yawl *Stormy Weather* and took third in class A. My father, who crewed for Labrot, had his moment of glory at the awards banquet when, before a large audience that included the governor of Maryland, he sang two rousing sea chanties, "Whiskey Johnny" and "It's Time for Us to Leave Her." The banquet must have been lively—according to the log of Corrin Strong, full drinks were being dropped from the second-story balcony near the bar to thirsty customers on the ground floor.

In 1941, under the auspices of the Hampton Yacht Club and Storm Trysail Club, a race was run from New London to Hampton, Virginia. *Blitzen,* from off the Bay, won the race, but the Naval Academy's *Vamarie* and *Highland Light* finished second and third in class.

William McMillan was a prominent Chesapeake ocean-racing skipper of the late 1920s and early 1930s. With his Alden schooner *Merry Widow,* he took a class third in the 1928 Bermuda Race, and, as mentioned, won his class with the

Corrin Strong's *Narada* with her original rig. Photograph by Morris Rosenfeld. © Mystic Seaport, Rosenfeld Collection, Mystic, Connecticut.

same boat in the New London–Gibson Island event the following year. With a new Alden schooner *Water Gipsy,* he

The crew of *Water Gipsy*, with Bill McMillan at the helm and famous yachting writer Sam Wetherill (in light shirt) and Bally Bailliere on his left. Second from the right is regular crew member C.T. Williams. Courtesy Gibson Island Historical Society.

sailed the 1931 Transatlantic Race, and then entered the British Fastnet contest known as the Grand National of ocean races. In the latter he was first around the Fastnet rock and finished second on corrected time. His *Water Gipsy* finished third in class and fleet and second in class and fleet respectively in the 1932 and 1934 Bermuda Races.

Big-boat racing on the Chesapeake received a stimulus in 1929 with the inauguration of the annual Cedar Point Race sponsored by the Gibson Island Club. The original conception was an overnight race 100 miles long, but the selected course turned out to be a slightly shorter distance, 92 miles, running from Baltimore Lighthouse off Gibson Island to the Cedar Point buoy off the mouth of the Patuxent River and return. Still held

today, this race created great interest, especially in the early days when there were detailed reports in the newspapers, bets on finishing times, and often all-night parties for the wives of crew. The first race was won by the yawl *Scarab*, owned by George Pulver of Philadelphia, and the second race was won by *Kelpie*'s sister *Merry Ann*, owned by Ellis Ellicott. In 1934 Dad retired the huge silver cup awarded to the first three-time winner.

Other annual big-boats races were started by the Gibson Island club in the early thirties. Lasting for a great many years were the Rhode River, Swan Point–Love Point, and Poplar Island races. The latter two, started in 1931, had courses that assured some variety in points of sailing, but wind direction was "potluck" for the point-to-point Rhode River to Gibson Island Race. The evening before the Rhode River Race, a well-attended rendezvous normally attracted the top racers as well as many cruising boats from the northern half of the Bay. The popularity of the Rhode River rendezvous cocktail party is illustrated by the following notice published in 1939 by Gibson Island's commodore Corrin Strong, who hosted the party that year on his 46-foot cutter *Narada*: "Warning—don't go aboard if less than 6 inches of freeboard exists on *Narada*—wait until someone falls overboard and then go aboard."[24]

Additional yachting activity was taking place on the Eastern Shore with the founding of the Tred Avon Yacht Club, originally called the Kap-Dun Club, at Oxford in 1931. One of the founding members was Maria Dimpfel Martin (later Mrs. Elliot Wheeler), daughter of William O'Sullivan Dimpfel. She raced the first Johnson-built Star *Undine* through the early thirties and in 1932 commissioned Lowndes to design a small Star-type centerboarder for her son Thomas Martin and his brother. This boat, built by Ralph Wiley in Oxford, became the first of the famous Comet class. Tom Martin wrote me that the Tred Avon Yacht Club "started life as a one-room shack (with bath) near the Oxford town wharf." In Tom's words, "It was a standard joke with family and friends that the real reason for its founding was to furnish the two women in the Star class a place to go to the bathroom! The other lady was Mrs. Hersloff, who used to crew for her husband." Tom went on to add, "The races were all started from Jerry Valiant's ferryboat. Jerry also had a hot dog stand at the wharf, and by coincidence, of course, the spectators who gathered on Sundays to watch the races had a place to eat and drink!"[25] Later Maria Martin had Fred Geiger design a 41-foot cutter for her that she named *Gaetina II* after her father's creation described earlier.

A prominent seaport in colonial times and even the site of an early naval academy, Oxford grew into a particularly popular yachting center in the thirties. "Free-for-all" races pitted log canoes against E-scows, Stars, and even schooner yachts. After the middle of the decade, the Tred Avon Yacht Club combined with the Chesapeake Bay Yacht Club to establish one of the major annual regattas, and it continues today. A race to the regatta from Baltimore Light

off Gibson Island was started in the mid-thirties and in 1937, my father won it with his Alden yawl *Kelpie*. An unusual strategy was used in this race. A fresh southerly gave the fleet a beat down the Bay to Blackwalnut Point at the mouth of the Choptank River. This gave *Kelpie* little chance to compete with the sloops and cutters that sailed closer to the wind, one of which was being crewed by my cousin Charlie Henderson, who was most anxious to whip his uncle. Sure enough, *Kelpie* had fallen far behind the single-masted boats by the time she reached Bloody Point at the south end of Kent Island, so Dad decided to take a desperate gamble. To escape the foul tide that was slowing the fleet, he ducked into the Poplar Island Narrows, a narrow channel that runs between Poplar Island and the Eastern Shore north of the Choptank. Having a boomed self-tending jib, *Kelpie* could be tacked with ease and little loss of speed. After a dozen or more short tacks through the channel, she emerged once again into the broad Chesapeake far ahead of her competition, much to the amazement of everyone. The weaker current and smoother waters of the narrows had helped *Kelpie* far more than anyone had imagined possible. She held her lead on a reach up the Choptank and the short run up the Tred Avon River to the finish line off Oxford.

The following year *Kelpie* again won this race when it was primarily a reaching affair more to her liking, and she was awarded the coveted Poker Bowl. On this occasion the bell buoy near the middle of the Bay off Poplar Island was a mark of

CHESAPEAKE SAILS

the course, eliminating any opportunity to use the narrows. The Poker Bowl, first donated in 1938 by members of the Chesapeake Bay Yacht Club, derived its name from the method used to raise money to pay for the trophy. The original bowl was lost overboard from the Dimpfels' *Gaetina,* and its replacement cost was raised over a period of many years mostly by club members who agreed to contribute 10 percent of their winnings at the poker table.

Another popular distance race, established in 1936, was the Hampton Race which ran from Baltimore Light off Gibson Island to Hampton, Virginia. Sponsored by the Hampton Yacht Club, it was conceived by Henry D. Baldwin, a prominent and colorful Bay yachtsman, whose home was in Chesapeake, Virginia, and whose business was in Baltimore. An unusual feature of this race was that there was no need to honor any buoys or channel markers, and that made it mighty interesting in Virginia waters, where there were forests of fishnet stakes. On the first race the yawl *Torbatross* became so surrounded by stakes after dark off Wolf Trap that she was forced to anchor until daylight. I remember losing one race to John Sherwood's Bounty sloop *Gibson Girl,* because my mother (in tears) was afraid to take a short cut inside the pound nets.

Henry Baldwin, a member of both the Hampton and Gibson Island Clubs, owned a well-known bugeye named *Bee* and was probably the only sailor who

Facing page: Kelpie beating to windward during the race to Oxford in 1937.

regularly raced an authentic bugeye (converted to a yacht) in sanctioned CBYRA events. As mentioned earlier, the CBYRA was formed in 1908 and reformed in 1934. Henry Baldwin was its chairman for three consecutive years, from 1935 through 1937, the only chairman to hold that office for such a period of time.

Rebirth of the CBYRA resulted from the need to coordinate interclub activities, to standardize rules and racing conditions at the growing number of regattas, and to develop a schedule that would avoid conflicts in race or regatta dates. R. Hammond Gibson, a Star champ and maritime historian from Easton, started the ball rolling. He suggested to Elliott Wheeler, then commodore of the Chesapeake Bay Yacht Club, that he set up a meeting of yacht club representatives to form a new yacht racing association. Representatives from nine yacht clubs (Chesapeake Bay, Hampton, Gibson Island, Miles River, Tred Avon, Chester River, Maryland, Havre de Grace, and even the Corinthian Club of Philadelphia) got together at Easton in late 1934. A new CBYRA was established, a committee to draft the bylaws was selected, and Elliott Wheeler was made the temporary chairman (Henry Baldwin took over that position about four months later).[26] The organization continues today and has been indispensable in establishing bay-wide regulations, schedules, championships, and general coordination of all racing activities.

It may be surprising to some that the Annapolis Yacht Club was not involved with the formation of the CBYRA. In

A regatta at St. Michaels, probably in the early 1930s. Courtesy Chesapeake Bay Maritime Museum.

formal yachting and big-boat racing Annapolis was a relatively late bloomer. Although the original club was organized in 1886 as the Severn Boat Club, it was devoted primarily to rowing, and it did not become the Annapolis Yacht Club in its present form until late 1937 when it was renamed and reincorporated. Under the leadership of J. Willis Martin, P. H. Magruder, and William H. Labrot, it quickly grew into one of the East Coast's premiere yachting centers, contributing to the often-heard description of Annapolis as the nation's "sailing capital." Annapolis was considered the ideal club to take over the New London–Gibson Island Race since Gibson Island was a private community with no commercial establishments, while the town of Annapolis had not only a first-class club and harbor, but also hotels, restaurants, boatyards, chandleries, and other facilities—thus the New London–Annapolis Race

of 1939. Bill Labrot bought the famous *Stormy Weather* especially for this race. The same year, the AYC put on a regatta that, a decade later, was said to be the largest ever held on the Chesapeake, with 238 entries.[27] This has become one of the Bay's most popular annual regattas. Chapter 2 includes some of the Annapolis club's important activities after World War II.

Meanwhile the U.S. Naval Academy had been building a fleet of excellent racing cruisers. The lovely 72-foot ketch *Vamarie,* finished bright and with her distinctive wishbone rig, had been donated by V.S. Makaroff in 1936. Then in 1939 came the first of a fleet of 44-foot Luders yawls. The following year a bequest from the estate of Dudley Wolfe brought to the academy the famous Bermuda Race record-holding 69-foot cutter *Highland Light.* That same year the 88-foot Alden schooner *Freedom* was donated by Sterling Morton.

With the exception of some Universal and International Rule boats, most of the larger racing craft of those times were dual-purpose boats; that is to say they were comfortable cruisers that were fast enough to race. Coupling this with the fact that the Chesapeake is an ideal body of water for cruising, it is not at all surprising that there developed a growing interest in exploring the myriad of rivers, creeks, and gunkholes of the Bay. In the early days cruises were sometimes combined with fishing and hunting expeditions, and boats were often left in commission throughout the winter. In contrast to modern boats of fiberglass that are often hauled in the winter in an attempt to avoid blistering, the wooden boats of early times were best left afloat to provide uniform support of the hull and to prevent drying out of the wood and the opening of seams. In many cases this encouraged extending the sailing season.

I was often taken cruising in the 1930s. I have many pleasant memories of poking into lovely rivers and ghosting past colonial homes, their broad lawns and stately trees reminding me of another era. The waters were uncrowded, and there were few motor craft to ruffle the surface or disrupt the quiet. We shared the Bay with picturesque sailing workboats: schooners, bugeyes, skipjacks, and even rams, the slab-sided three-masted schooners that were used to haul cargo. One of our favorite anchorages was the Poplar Island pot, where there were swimming "bogs" on the bayside, and the water was so clear that you could watch the crabs scurrying along the bottom. Este Fisher, owner of *Kelpie*'s sister *Cynara*, would recite the following ditty called "The Pot":

Have you ever been to that choice little
  spot
That's known as Poplar Island Pot?
If you've ever lain there all safe and
  sound,

Your anchor deep down in the cozy
  ground,
You surely will with me agree,
'Tis like an atoll of the Southern Sea.

Shaw Bay in the Wye River was another spot we liked to visit, and I'll never forget circling Wye Island and having to crank open the drawbridge ourselves manually because the bridgetender was nowhere to be found.

In hot weather, excitement was provided by the frequent late afternoon thunderstorms that were usually short-lived but fierce. Darkening skies and thunderheads building in the west usually gave ample warning, and most of the time we would reach a harbor and anchor before being hit by the squall, but then we would often drag. The old fisherman anchors then in use were not as effective in the soft mud of the Chesapeake as the modern anchors such as Danforths that are used today. On one occasion, when we were under sail and the skies were threatening, a nervous guest asked my father, "What do you make of that cloud in the west?" This was during the last days of Prohibition, and Dad was feeling no pain, having sampled some homemade peach brandy. He took a quick glance at the cloud and replied, "Cumulus Tumultuous—pass the peach."

CHAPTER TWO

YACHTING COMES OF AGE

During World War II, yachting on the Bay did not come to a near stop as it had during the first World War. It continued but naturally on a smaller scale. Certain races such as the Cedar Point Race were discontinued. Some yacht clubs awarded framed paper certificates for race prizes rather than silver trophies. Some regattas were consolidated, an example being the one held in July 1944 by the Virginia Sailing Association, which consisted of the Urbanna (later Fishing Bay), Rappahannock River, and Hampton yacht clubs, and the Norfolk Yacht and Country Club. There were ap-

proximately one hundred entries in this regatta.[1]

Many of the Bay's larger sailing yachts were donated to the U.S. Coast Guard for antisubmarine patrol. Known as the Coastal Picket Patrol or Corsair Fleet, these yachts conscripted into wartime service were mostly able sailing vessels that could stay at sea for long periods of time. They could not be detected by submarines from the turning of a screw. On the other hand, the sailing yachts, fitted with sonar and radiophones, could detect and report U-boats; they discouraged the German subs from surfacing near shore to use their deck guns or charge their batteries.

Offshore duty in the winter was incredibly rough at times, with frequent gales and freezing temperatures. All the boats were equipped with wooden mallets and baseball bats to knock ice off the decks and rigging.[2] The Corsair boats were also equipped with storm trysails and spitfire jibs or staysails, but these sails were nearly always found to be too large. Cabins were usually heated with coal stoves that often produced sickening fumes. A back draft down the Charley Noble (smokepipe) could drive the off-watch crew on deck. In bad weather everything was wet, and electrical systems would often short out. Some of the Chesapeake boats operating out of Norfolk, Virginia, carried homing pigeons in case the radio failed. A report in the *New York Times* (January 2, 1943) told of a pigeon, known only as number 1169, that was actually honored with an Army citation awarded by the commanding general of the Chesapeake Bay sector. After a Coast Guard schooner had lost contact with her home base, the pigeon carried an important message to its loft at Cape Henry.

During a notorious December gale in 1942, the famous yachtsman/designer Rod Stephens, driving a prototype DUKW amphibious vehicle that he helped develop, made a daring rescue of the crew from the stranded Alden yawl *Rose.* The Chesapeake schooner *Tradition,* originally owned by J. Rulon Miller, encountered the worst of this gale. She survived and eventually was towed to safety by a Coast Guard cutter. Corsair fleet researcher John Wilbur unearthed the log of *Tradition* written during the gale by her skipper Eugene Tompane. The following brief excerpts give us a hint of the appalling conditions:

13:10—Seas breaking over us badly, unable to heave-to properly due to confused seas and heavy gusts of wind causing ship to swing sharply, seas swept away ventilator over engine room, forward stateroom hatch cover, galley smoke head, tore life raft off rack. . . . Plugged openings with canvas etc. but water pouring in . . . rising faster than pumps can remove it. . . . Engine trouble, radio fading, gas in bilge, taking water, pumps inadequate, unless weather changes will require assistance.

After the radio died completely, distress flares were used, and eventually the schooner was taken in tow. It took forty hours to reach port, and Tompane wrote that *Tradition* suffered more strain and damage under tow than during the storm.

Some other well-known Chesapeake boats performing this rugged duty were the able Alden schooner *Fiddler's Green,* owned by Dr. Edmund Kelly and family (the "cruising Kellys") of Baltimore; the bugeye yacht *Brown, Smith, and Jones,* then owned by Harry Ogden; Donald Sherwood's Herreshoff cutter *Flying Cloud;* James Dunbar's Rhodes yawl *Dryad;* William Labrot's Stephens-designed yawl *Stormy Weather;* and Corrin Strong's Rhodes cutter *Narada.*[3] The latter was sunk following a collision off Hampton Roads in late 1942.

The Alden schooner *Fiddler's Green*, one of the Chesapeake yachts serving in the U.S. Coast Guard's antisubmarine patrol during World War II. Courtesy John G. Alden Naval Architects.

Many service veterans as well as stay-at-home civilians must have been dreaming about pleasure boating during the war, because soon after the end of hostilities there was a burst of yachting activity and creative boat designing by Chesapeake natives. Late 1945 and early 1946 produced many famous designs: the Owens cutter (created by the Owens Yacht Company of Baltimore) that had major racing victories almost everywhere in America; the fast and saucy Oxford 400 designed by Robert Henry; a revival of the lovely Tancook-whaler type created by Ralph Wiley of Oxford; the distinctive *Blue Moon* design by Annapolitan Thomas Gillmer; and an entire new line of Chesapeake sailing cruisers from Dickerson Boatbuilders, discussed in chapter 4.

The following year, the Mathis-Trumpy operation moved down to Annapolis from New Jersey. The com-

pany took over the Annapolis Yacht Yard and in later years, under the name John Trumpy and Sons, built some of the most elegant wooden power yachts ever produced. Frederick Geiger was brought from Philadelphia to Annapolis to take over the design work. He had previously designed the 38-foot shoal-draft Ranger class sloops that proved successful in racing and ideal for cruising the Chesapeake. Only five sailing yachts were produced by the Trumpys in Annapolis; two of them named *Sea Call* were built for John Trumpy himself. The first of these was the prototype for the Chesapeake 28 class (28 feet long on the waterline) designed by Sparkman and Stephens. The last of these, *Sea Call V,* was a 24½-foot waterline sloop designed by John Trumpy himself.

The other Trumpy sailboats built in Annapolis were *Sanban,* a handsome centerboard ketch designed by Geiger for George Johnson; the 49-foot sloop *Oceanus* for Charles (Chuck) Owens, formerly of the Owens Yacht Company; and the 62-foot motorsailer *Egret* for Porter Schutt, the next-to-last boat built by Trumpy before the yard closed in 1972.[4] Chuck Owens claimed that *Oceanus,* designed by William Tripp, was the prototype hull (minus appendages) for the Columbia 50. She had a good racing record that included a seasonal High Point win in Class A in 1968.

In 1947, the Annapolis Yacht Club, which had become an important yachting center, and the Naval Academy, whose boats had won most of the major CBYRA High Point awards during the war years, joined with the New York and Ida Lewis yacht clubs to begin the Newport to Annapolis Race. An outgrowth of the New London–Gibson Island Races held in 1929, 1933, and 1937, and the New London–Annapolis Race of 1939, the Newport-Annapolis Race became a biennial event run in odd-numbered years alternating with the Bermuda Race. Chesapeake boats did not fare too well in the 1947 race. Maria Dimpfel's *Gaetina II,* then owned by Charles Dell (later a prominent commodore of the Annapolis Yacht Club), went to the rescue of a dismasted boat that had become entangled in fish traps along the lower western shore. *Gaetina* stood by the stricken boat for twelve hours, but was not awarded any compensatory time.[5]

Both the inaugural Newport-Annapolis Race and the next race in 1949 were won by the New York 32 *Alar,* and her outstanding performance did nothing to discourage her sisters from racing on the Bay. The overall Chesapeake bigboat champion in 1948 was a sister named *Folly,* owned by A. J. Grimes of the Tred Avon Yacht Club. She later continued her winning ways as *Trig* under the ownership of Charles Dell. Thomas Closs of Annapolis and the Sailing Club of the Chesapeake collected 176 prizes over a lengthy time span in two New York 32s named *Fun* and *Raider.*

Besides the New York 32s, other boats that excelled in cruising division races on the Bay during the 1950s were the locally designed and built 40-foot Owens cutters, especially J. Miller Sherwood's *Rubicon* of the Gibson Island Yacht Squadron. Since 1939 the CBYRA has awarded the Labrot

The Sparkman and Stephens–designed Trumpy-built *Sea Call,* prototype of the Chesapeake 28. Courtesy Sparkman & Stephens, Inc.

Trophy (named after William Labrot) annually to the highest scoring yacht in the fleet. This coveted trophy, equivalent to a boat-of-the-year award, was won by *Rubicon* four times during the decade after 1948.

Less successful but with more than a few racing victories was another local design, the 35-foot cutter *Delilah,* designed and built by Franz Plunder at a small yard on Whitehall Creek near Annapolis. Owned by Arnold Gay, who had taken over the Thomas Langan yard in Annapolis, *Delilah* won High Points in her class three times during the 1950s.

By far the most famous racing cruisers of that period and later were two yachts owned by photographer/author

Teetotaler, one of the many successful Owens cutters racing on the Bay. Photograph by Fred Thomas, courtesy Katrina Thomas.

Carleton Mitchell of Annapolis. They were resident yachts, not designed or built locally, but hailing from the Chesa-

Facing page: The New York 32 *Folly* (later *Trig*), one of the Bay's most consistent winners, first under A.J. Grimes and later under Charles Dell. Photograph by Marion E. Warren.

peake. The first of these was the 57½-foot yawl *Caribbee*, formerly *Alondra*, a landmark design by Philip Rhodes. With her, Mitchell won not only two Labrot awards, but also two Southern Ocean Racing Conference (SORC) championships, and in 1952 he raced her across the Atlantic, finishing first and correcting to second in the fleet. His next boat

was the legendary 38-foot yawl *Finisterre*, the only boat to have three consecutive wins in the Bermuda Races.

In addition to the better-known local designs used for both racing and cruising such as the Owens cutter and Oxford 400 (discussed in chapter 4), several inexpensive hard-chine sailing cruisers were created by local designers in the early 1950s. The best known of these was the Quadrant, a 25-foot raised-deck cruising sloop designed by Laurence Hartge of Galesville, Maryland. Others were the Bay-Mate, a bugeye-rigged deadrise-type bateau yacht measuring 27 feet on deck, designed by Edgar Van Dyke of Cambridge, Maryland; the Simplisma, a somewhat similar 34-footer designed by William Dickerson of Church Creek; and the Cruisken, an arc-bottom plywood fin-keel sloop, 30 feet overall, designed by J. R. Speer of the Oxford Boat Yard. My wife and I owned one of the latter boats for several years and were right proud of her until Harold "Buzz" White, who later became one of my very best friends, made the cruel though witty remark that the Cruiskens would look much better when they were taken out of their boxes.

One of the prettiest of the smaller local designs was the 23-foot double-ended sloop *Persephone* designed for William Greene by Annapolitan Edward Burgess, nephew of the world-famous designer Starling Burgess. Ideal for the Bay, this was a shoal-draft centerboard boat with a huge forward hatch for ventilation, a large self-tending rig for easy handling, and pronounced sheer for dryness in the Chesapeake chop. Ed Burgess wrote me that *Persephone* was not designed with racing in mind, but she did extremely well competing in the Delta class. This class, first sanctioned by the CBYRA during World War II, was originally intended for small seaworthy cruisers under 30 feet.

Local yachting events had been well reported in the *Chesapeake Skipper* magazine under the editorships of Thomas Eddy and Harrison Roberts, but in the mid-1950s H. K. "Bunny" Rigg took over as editor and made the magazine national in scope. A keen sailor who was a regular crew for Carleton Mitchell on *Finisterre,* Bunny Rigg was also a talented writer and a former yachting editor for the *New Yorker* magazine. With the help of Victor Jorgenson, he injected a literary quality into the *Skipper* that made it what many sailors considered the finest yachting journal of its time.

About 1951 the magazine started the Skipper Race, the seasonal windup 100-mile race held in early November. This became an annual event and attracted some northern yachts that were passing through the Chesapeake headed for southern waters. Often sailed in cold and boisterous conditions, the Skipper Race

Freedom boiling down the Bay during an early Skipper Race. Photograph by Marion E. Warren.

had no upper size limit and allowed boats over 70 feet, such as the Naval Academy's schooner *Freedom,* a chance to compete for silver. Crews accustomed to gentler summer breezes were sometimes unprepared for the rugged conditions of the Skipper Race. My cousin told me how he suffered on one cold race when he made a last minute pierhead jump aboard a small racer with little more than "a skimpy sweater, a pair of wet sneakers, and a hangover."

After the unfortunate demise of the *Skipper* magazine in the early 1970s, local yachting has been well covered journalistically by *Chesapeake Bay Magazine* and a revival of the *Chesapeake Skipper*. In addition, two less-expensive publications, *Rags* and now *Spin Sheet* (available free) have concentrated on local sailing.

Not well known among Chesapeake sailors is the Slocum Society founded at Horn Point in Annapolis in 1955. Litterateur and small-boat historian Richard Gordon McClosky published a journal called the *Spray* (named after Joshua Slocum's famous boat) that was the best source of information on solo and double-handed voyaging. Known as "Two Reef" McCloskey, he sailed his skipjack yacht *Hope* with a deep reef even in calm weather because the foot of the sail was rotten. Under McCloskey's leadership, the Slocum Society had a prominent hand in starting the 1960 singlehander's transatlantic race which involved such famous British sailors as war hero H. G. Hasler, Sir Francis Chichester, and Dr. David Lewis. The latter, who is the only person to have circumnavigated Antarctica singlehandedly (close to land in a small boat), attended the Slocum Society's thirtieth anniversary rally in Annapolis.

During this period, the Newport-Annapolis Race was held every other year, alternating with the Bermuda Race. Chesapeake boats fared well in most of these races. After the tedious light-air race of 1955, described as the "slowest of the slow," the race was given new life two years later when the course was reversed and it became the Annapolis-Newport Race. Outstanding Chesapeake fleet and class winners in these races were Newbold Smith's *Reindeer*, Clayton Ewing's *Dyna*, and A. E. Van Metre's *Running Tide*. Additional Chesapeake class winners from 1951 through 1995 include the following boats:

Egret, Porter Schutt
Swift, navy yawl
Altair, Bradford Smith
Southern Star, James Mullen
Prim, Morton Gibbons-Neff
Fleetwind, Raymond Brown
Lancetilla (also a fleet winner), Juan Cameron
Ill Wind, Charles Ill
American Eagle and *Tenacious* (also fleet winners), R. E. Turner
Harpoon, Mark Ewing
Fling, Henry Chance
Little Babe, Arnold Gay
Merrythought, John King
Lightnin', R. E. Turner
Yellow Jacket, Bulman/Scholz/Winston
Gaylark, Kaighn Smith (MHS winner)
Dandy, navy yawl
Sugar, Scott Allan and Brad Parker
Donnybrook, James Muldoon
Gator, Thomas Wheatley
Blue Fish, Alan Harquail
Snow White, Edwin Shuman
Swift, Navy 44
Nicole, Coleman Du Pont
Reindeer (IV), Newbold Smith
Crescendo, Stephen Hiltabidle
Javelin, Lawrence Bulman

Javelin, Swift, and *Snow White* were also the Performance Handicap Racing Fleet (PHRF) winners.[6] In 1997 Arthur Birney of Washington, D.C., topped the PHRF fleet with his Gulfstar 44 *Adventurer*.

Start of the Newport-Annapolis Race in 1951 with *Royono* (64) in foreground and *Vamarie* (32) to windward of *Nina* (2) and *Highland Light* (34). Courtesy United States Naval Institutes Archives.

Although not in chronological order, this is a good place to call attention to *Donnybrook*, said to be the same boat that set the time record for the Annapolis-Newport Race in 1987 when named *Starlight Express* (then owned by B. A. Eissner). She was brought to the Chesapeake and named *Donnybrook* by James Muldoon, who became the president of the United States Sailing Association and is the founder of a sailing program for children with learning disabilities. A light-displacement Santa Cruz 70, *Donnybrook* was not a consistent corrected-time winner in standard races but often took line honors as the first boat to finish. While racing in the 1996

Antigua Sailing Week, she was totally destroyed after being nearly cut in half in a collision with a boat on the port tack. Muldoon now has a new, slightly larger *Donnybrook*, not unlike the one she replaces but highly customized and a bit faster upwind.

The 1960s decade was very special for me, as I managed to persuade my father to purchase a new Ohlson 35 yawl, which we coskippered the first year before he suggested my taking charge. Selling our beloved 30-year-old Alden yawl was painful, and I literally had tears in my eyes when she departed, but she was suffering from serious old-age problems and was no longer competitive on the race course. With our new *Kelpie* we joined a growing fleet of Ohlson 35s, most of which had names that ended in "ity" (*Temerity, Serendipity, Intrepidity,* and *Veracity*). In certain quarters we were known as the "ity" class, and I felt somewhat apologetic for not having named our boat *Kelpity.* Skippers of our sisters were a great bunch, and lasting friendships developed despite our rivalry. Most O-35 sailors such as Harold "Buzz" White, Donald Tate, Richard Schluederberg (and later James Wolfe and Marbury Fox) were very talented skippers.

After a slow start, we managed to get *Kelpie* tuned and had some especially tight racing against Buzz White, who had dominated Class C earlier. In the popular Annapolis Fall Series, Buzz's *Temerity* won the coveted Viking Trophy for fleet first, and *Kelpie* was runner-up. We had beaten Buzz two out of three races, but *Kelpie* had a less favorable rating than *Temerity* because of my stupidity (maybe

Donald Tate's Ohlson 35 *Intrepidity* alongside sisterboat *Kelpie* during a race in the early 1960s. Photograph by Sally Henderson.

that's the "ity" name we should have given our Ohlson) in not taking advantage of obvious allowances in the rating rule. We had no black bands on our spars to limit measured sail area. Nevertheless, the close racing had been fun, and *Kelpie* was moving well. Her success may have been due in part to a "secret weapon." The Ohlsons had deck-stepped masts with inadequate support that prohibited setting up the rigging tight. My solution to the problem was to use a pipe and screw jack under the mast; the headstay could then be set up taut in a fresh breeze, thus permitting higher pointing. When we'd raft up at a rendezvous, I'd naturally remove the pipe and stow it under the forward bunks. Buzz had his "secret weapons" too, for example, trying to intoxicate our crew on the evening before a race. He right well succeeded on one occasion and nipped us at the finish line when our hungover foredeck man fouled up a spinnaker jibe.

Of all the exciting races in the Ohlson yawls, the one I remember best is the Cedar Point Race of 1961. Most of the nearly 100-mile race was a steamy hot-weather drifting match, but near the finish we were struck by the fiercest squall I've ever experienced. As a cold front approached from the northwest, a line of thunderheads with an ugly black roll cloud leading the way gave us plenty of warning, but many of the racing boats were trying to finish before the squall and were caught with their sails up. Clocked at over 70 knots, the initial downdraft tore through the fleet, shredding light sails and causing beam-end knockdowns. The Coast Guard was out in force rescuing small craft.

We had an English artist onboard, Cavandish Morton, who was accustomed to the most rugged offshore sailing in the North Sea and elsewhere. I spent much time apologizing to him for the calm Chesapeake weather, saying that the wind really did blow at times and the Bay was noted for its summer squalls, but Cavy's facial expression revealed his skepticism. During the squall, however, when the Bay had turned to what looked like an Alabama cotton field (to use an Eastern Shore expression), I yelled to Cavy that this was a typical Chesapeake squall. He was suitably impressed and later said he'd had "the experience of a lifetime." He depicted that blow in a series of dramatic paintings, and we have one of them hanging in our home in a prominent spot (near the bar).

The Ohlsons got stiff competition from Raymond Brown's *Fleetwind*, a sloop-rigged Invicta from Hampton. In 1961 she came north for the Annapolis Yacht Club Fall Series and accumulated enough points to win the seasonal fleet award, thereby denying us the Labrot Trophy. *Kelpie* was once again the bridesmaid. From that year until 1966, *Fleetwind* all but dominated the cruising division, winning the Labrot Trophy four times in five years, tying the record set by Miller Sherwood in *Rubicon*.

This was the beginning of the plastic decade when most boats were built of fiberglass rather than wood. Ray Brown's Invicta was fiberglass, and one of the early "class" racing cruisers to be made of

The Ohlson 35 *Cricket* during a breezy AYC Fall Series race. Photograph by Henry Strong.

this relatively new material was the Alberg-designed Triton. Several Tritons did well racing, particularly Ridgely Melvin's *Gem*, but the most outstanding record for this design was compiled by *White Shadow III*, owned by William Myers of the Tred Avon Yacht Club. She won the Labrot Trophy in 1962. A Triton Cruising One-Design class was eventually formed that is still in existence today. Another early fiberglass design was the successful Tripp-designed Block Island 40 (originally known as the Vitesse class). In 1961 Newbold Smith's *Reindeer* was the overall winner of the Annapolis-Newport Race and the Northern Ocean Racing Circuit. Another outstanding Chesapeake Block Island 40 was Dr. Charles Iliff's *Alaris*, which raced successfully for more than three decades on the Bay.

Aluminum was another material that, to a lesser degree, was replacing wood as the building material for yachts.

A famous Chesapeake aluminum yacht was the 45-foot yawl *Loon* owned by Dr. Gifford Pinchot. *Loon* took a class second in the 1962 Bermuda Race and was the northern ocean racing champ in 1963. She also made an outstanding cruise to the South Seas a year later. Prior to sailing *Loon*, Sally and Giff Pinchot had distinguished themselves with a transatlantic passage and class win in the 1950 Bermuda Race in their engineless yawl *Loki*.

Another famous aluminum boat arrived on the Chesapeake in the early 1960s—Clayton Ewing's 58-foot Sparkman and Stephens–designed *Dyna*. Having been victorious in Mackinac races back to back in 1957 and 1958, it is not surprising that *Dyna* excelled in racing on her new home waters. Her debut in a CBYRA event was the 1962 AYC Fall Series in which she won Class A. She then proceeded to take fleet firsts in the 1963 and 1965 Annapolis-Newport Races.

Fleetwind, on a very rare occasion, finishing just behind *Kelpie*. The dark-hulled powerboat on the left marks one end of the finish line. Photograph by Henry Lord.

Other Bay boats that did particularly well in the latter two events were *Reindeer*, *Fleetwind*, and Morton "Sunny" Gibbons-Neff's home-rebuilt *Prim*, each with class wins. In the 1963 race the well-known conservative political writer/author William F. Buckley, who has written extensively on navigation, made a fetch that was too perfect. His *Suzy Wong* made contact with the Chesapeake Lightship, and he had to drop out of the race for "touching" a mark of the course.[7]

By far the most rugged Annapolis-Newport Race was the stormy one in 1967 in which thirty-four boats dropped out, seven were dismasted, and one sank. The latter was the 36-foot sloop *Vignette*, designed for his own use by Arlington, Virginia, naval architect Roger McAleer, who also designed the Raven class and the light-displacement ocean racer *Dirigo*. After being dismasted *Vignette* grounded and broke up at the mouth of the Chesapeake; the crew was rescued by the Coast Guard. Faring well in the heavy weather, Chesapeake boats won in four of the five classes. They were *Prim*, *Fleetwind*, *Ill Wind*, and fleet winner *Lancetilla*, a Cal 40 owned by Juan Cameron of Washington, D.C., who had finished last in the 1963 Annapolis-Newport Race. Although the crew reported she "pounded like a drum," *Lancetilla* held together and suffered only from electrical problems and slack rigging.[8]

R. E. "Ted" Turner became conspicuous on the Annapolis scene when he won the race to Newport in 1969 sailing the Luders-designed 12-meter *American Eagle*, a former contender for the America's Cup. Turner joined the Annapolis

An amazing photograph by the late Fred Thomas of a Cruising Club of America raft-up in 1965. The entire raft with such well-known boats as *Dyna*, *Vixen*, and *Gesture* is being propelled down the Chester River by one spinnaker (and a tiny riding sail). Courtesy Katrina Thomas.

Yacht Club and participated in some racing on the Bay, especially the popular AYC Fall Series, which often attracted more than a few competitive northern boats on their way south for the SORC. Arnie Gay liked to tell about the time when he crewed for Turner on a Cedar Point Race. The crew was all male except for one attractive woman who signed on as cook. Ten years after his triumph in the Annapolis-Newport race with *American Eagle*, Turner again won fleet first in this race with the 61-foot Sparkman and Stephens–designed *Tenacious*. Later that year, he skippered the same boat to victory in the stormy British Fastnet Race.

Despite a number of severe knockdowns, he and his crew, which included Annapolitan Gary Jobson, kept *Tenacious* moving under greatly reduced sail. After the race, Turner was quoted as telling British reporters, "If it hadn't been for a blow like that some years ago, you might all be speaking Spanish now."

In the classes for smaller boats, a great rivalry existed between William Myers and Douglas Hanks, expert sailors from the Tred Avon Yacht Club. With his Columbia 31, *White Shadow IV,* Myers won the Labrot Trophy in 1966 and 1967, while Hanks won this top seasonal award with his Cal 29 *Outrage* in 1971 and 1973. Prior to that, Hanks had won the AYC Fall Series Viking Trophy two years in a row—no mean accomplishment—with his Cal 28 *Rumpus.*

Handicap racing changed tacks early in the 1970s with the adoption of the International Offshore Rule (IOR). Before that, handicap racing operated under the Cruising Club of America (CCA) Rule, a base-boat concept, meaning that an ideal boat is conceived and speed enhancing or retarding measurements are added or subtracted to obtain a rating. The IOR, essentially a compromise between the CCA and the British RORC Rule, was intended to improve the fairness of handicaps in international racing. Many sailors, including me, were opposed to adopting the IOR on the Chesapeake, fearing that it was more of a development rule and would make most existing boats obsolete. I was a member of a committee that managed to forestall adoption of the rule for one year, but the IOR was being accepted universally, so

the Chesapeake began using it in 1972. Sure enough, a lot of racers became dissatisfied with the rating system and began to move into the Delta Class, which had its own handicap system (Delta had been expanded to accept larger boats). Later came the adoption of the PHRF system, a method of handicapping a boat according to her observed performance, rather than having her measurements applied to a rating rule. PHRF worked quite well for popular stock boats that raced in all parts of the country, but was very arbitrary for one-off designs. By 1981 there were over a thousand Chesapeake boats registered in PHRF.[9]

In my humble opinion, early IOR boats with their better balanced hulls were the more wholesome type of IOR designs. Later, as designers began to exploit loopholes in the rule, hulls were distorted to gain the advantage of optimal measurement points; sail-carrying power was achieved with broad beam rather than ballast, at the expense of ultimate stability. The disastrous Fastnet Race of 1979, in which seventy-seven boats capsized (or nearly so) and fifteen sailors lost their lives, clearly showed the wrong turn yacht design had taken under the influence of the IOR.

One of the very best of the early IOR designs came to the Bay in 1972—the 61-foot Sparkman and Stephens–designed aluminum sloop *Running Tide.* Actually, this graceful yacht might be considered a pre-IOR boat, but her designer, Olin Stephens, was the person largely responsible for drafting the original IOR, so not surprisingly the boat conformed very well to the original rule. Under the ownership of the A. E. Van Metres, *Running Tide* won fleet first in the 1976 Bermuda Race and firsts in the 1981 and 1983 Annapolis-Newport Races. She also took three AYC Fall Series and won her class in the SORC three times.

I had great fun racing in Class C in the early 1970s; a number of well-sailed Cal 2-30s, Morgan 30s, and Cal 29s made the class very competitive. At first there were some rating discrepancies among the former boats, but our Cal 2-30 *Kelpie* was made the "guinea pig" test boat by North American Racing Union's chief measurer Robert Blumenstock, and eventually our boat and all sisters were fairly rated by Blumenstock himself.

At the end of 1973, we purchased a used Ohlson 38, which was (and still is) my all-time favorite boat. My wife, two children, and I had the pleasure of sailing her across the Atlantic to the Azores in 1975. This was done very economically with no electronics, not even a sending radio, although we did have a couple of EPIRBs (emergency position-indicating radio beacons).

Among the most consistent High Point winners of those times was Charles Stein, who topped his class seven times in boats named *Snallygaster*, the first being a souped-up Owens cutter (formerly owned by Arnie Gay), the next a C & C (Cuthbertson and Cassian) 35, and the last a Douglas Peterson–designed Islander 40. The remarkable thing about Charlie's success is that he was severely disabled from polio, yet he did not hesitate to go on rugged overnight races and on two occasions even skippered boats in the

Decorating the cover of the *Dolphin Book Club News* in 1978, the author's daughter Sarah at the helm of the Ohlson 38 *Kelpie* in mid-Atlantic. Photograph by Rip Henderson.

Bermuda Race. During heavy weather his crew would sometimes lash him into the cockpit. On several occasions I had the opportunity to sail with him and found him to be an excellent helmsman and tactician with great ability to concentrate on sail trim and other details.

When I think of well-known Chesapeake sailors with disabilities, two others

Ernest Tucker, Chesapeake designer/sailor at the helm of his *Half Pint*. Courtesy Chesapeake Bay Maritime Museum, Ernest Tucker Collection.

immediately come to mind, Ernest Tucker and Charles Price. The former was not a racing sailor but a Chesapeake cruising enthusiast, a fine seaman, and talented naval architect who designed a number of Dickerson sailing cruisers as well as other good yachts. Despite having lost the use of his legs from polio, he often cruised his little double-ender *Half Pint* singlehandedly, sometimes in company with other cruising buffs such as

Lowndes and Clara Johnson or Charles and Betty McComas.[10] With great admiration, I once observed Tucker singlehanding his boat in the crowded harbor at Oxford during a regatta.

Not only a splendid seaman but a skilled racer as well, Charlie Price has won numerous awards including six first-in-class High Point awards in boats named *Proton*. His early prominent racing boat was a lovely 8-meter converted to a cruising racer. Then came a New York 32, in which he made a transatlantic passage, and a speedy C & C 35. Despite having only one hand, Charlie hardly seems disabled at all. On one occasion, I was told, a young athletic football player was struggling to position the spinnaker pole; Charlie left the helm, quickly moved forward, eased the foredeck crew aside, effortlessly positioned the pole with one hand, and returned to the helm with hardly a word spoken. Later he owned a Gulfstar 41 on which he sometimes cruised alone, singlehanding the boat in the most literal sense of the word.

While on the subject of sailors with disabilities, I should mention the organization CRAB (acronym for Chesapeake Region Accessible Boating), which is dedicated to providing sailing opportunities to disabled persons. Located at Sandy Point State Park near Annapolis, the nonprofit organization offers sailing and training for the disabled in specially equipped Freedom 20s designed by Gary Mull. One of the founders of CRAB, Annapolitan Chris Murphy, won a medal in the highly competitive international Paralympics.

Among the most consistent big-boat High Point winners was naval architect Nils Salvesen of the West River Sailing Club, who won his class five consecutive years beginning in 1978. I very much enjoyed sailing with him on his Peterson 34 *Streaker* in 1982 during a team race. The boat was certainly fast and sensitive, but I was somewhat surprised by a few obvious deficiencies in the Douglas Peterson design such as the lack of a proper keel sump to collect bilge water.

The record for seasonal High Point wins is held by a cruising one-design sailor, Steven Bandy. He has ten consecutive wins in the Cal 25 class and another seven wins in the Pearson 30 class. I've never met him and have no inkling of why he has been so successful, but his wife provided a clue. She explained that Steve is a nice, easygoing guy in everyday life but turns into an intense, totally focused demon when he races. In fact, his boats have been named *Mr. Hyde* after the transformed central character in Stevenson's classic horror tale.

During the mid-1970s two Chesapeake sailors were awarded the Blue Water Medal of the Cruising Club of America. Arguably, this is sailing's most prestigious award. Personally, I would rather earn a Blue Water Medal than win the America's Cup, although I'm sure a lot of sailors would not share that preference. An earlier Bay recipient was Carleton Mitchell for his racing and distance cruising prowess mainly in *Caribbee* and *Finisterre*. In 1974 the award went to James Crawford, whose home in later life was Easton, Maryland. His medal was awarded primarily for an earlier circumnavigation in an Alden schooner as well as ten Atlantic crossings, seven in the cutter *Angantyr* (one made singlehandedly). Two years later the medal was awarded to Newbold Smith for an outstanding voyage to Arctic waters in his Swan 43 *Reindeer*. If you count the famous world cruiser and solo circumnavigator Hal Roth, who has lived many places but whose present residence is at St. Michaels, Maryland, the Chesapeake can boast of having had four Blue Water Medalists.

In the heyday of the IOR, the epitome of international competition for racing cruisers was in the Ton Cup classes, especially the One Ton class. Named after a historic trophy, this is a type of level racing that pits boats of the same design (or various designs with almost identical ratings) against each other boat-for-boat. Just prior to the IOR in 1966, Annapolis Yacht Club member Edward Stettinius had won the European One Ton Cup with a sloop named *Tina,* which was designed and sailed by the New England designer Richard Carter. The Bay, however, has its own One Ton design, created by prominent native naval architect Karl Kirkman and designated the "Chesapeake One Ton." Only two of these boats were built, Thomas Lucke's *Muskrat* and David Saunders's *Spindrift,* but they did well in fleet racing, especially the latter boat, which won her class in a CBYRA Race Week and took a class second in High Points in 1975.[11] Kirkman also designed two boats named *Anthem* for Peter Geis, who built both boats himself. The second

Anthem won her class in the 1988 Bermuda Race.

Of the many sailing families produced by the Chesapeake, the Scotts (Gaither and his sons Jimmy and Charlie) from the Annapolis area are probably the most conspicuous for their racing prowess. Especially talented is Charlie, who, after all but dominating local junior sailing, won the Sears Cup national junior championship in 1971. The following year the Scott family's PT 30 *Mist,* usually skippered by Charlie, won the Chesapeake fleet championship (Labrot Trophy). Moving into the highly competitive J/24s, he won the North American Championship in 1978 and the World's the following year. Charlie had a very impressive year in 1984 when he won both the MORC (Midget Ocean Racing Club) Internationals and One Ton North American Championships. He brought more fame to the Chesapeake by winning the SORC the following year and the popular Block Island Race Week two years after that.

Many veteran sailors feel that long-distance singlehanded sailing demands the highest level of seamanship. The Bay has had a number of blue-water singlehanders. In addition to Jim Crawford and Charlie Price, some notable Chesapeake solo sailors are Moulton "Monk" Farnham, Bill Homewood, Judy Lawson, Paul Anderton, Philander Wallace, George Stricker, and Jim Dickson. Formerly from Annapolis, Judy Lawson had the misfortune of being dismasted in her BB 10 during the 1980 transatlantic race for singlehanders when she was almost

home. Another Annapolitan, Paul Anderton, has sailed alone to Bermuda four times, and, after an early aborted attempt, crossed the Atlantic to the Azores in a 25-footer named *Constant* in 1993. A solo circumnavigation of the world via the Panama Canal and Cape of Good Hope was completed by Philander Wallace when he sailed his 30-foot *Lady Jane* into Baltimore harbor in 1989. A remarkable solo passage was made by Washingtonian Jim Dickson, who was almost totally blind when he sailed his Freedom 36 *Eye Opener* from Rhode Island to Bermuda in 1987. George Stricker, a veteran singlehander now with a residence at Gibson Island, Maryland, recently competed in one of the most demanding sailing challenges, a globe-girdling solo race called Around Alone. In his Schock 50 named *Rapscallion III,* he completed the first of four legs, but was then forced to retire after suffering rigging and sail damage as well as a broken boom in a Force 10 gale.

Monk Farnham from Preston, Maryland, appeared in *The Guiness Book of World Records* for being the oldest solo sailor to cross the Atlantic. In 1981 at the age of seventy-two, he sailed alone on his Shannon 28 *Seven Bells* from Oxford, Maryland, to Falmouth, England. Although the Guiness claim was not quite right (Frank Casper had sailed across the Atlantic alone at the age of seventy-four), Farnham tied the record when he sailed home solo in 1983. This was no mean feat for a septuagenarian, especially since he had to steer by hand most of the way because of the malfunctioning vane-type self-steering gear. Although some boats can be made to steer themselves by connecting sheets to the helm, this could not be accomplished on *Seven Bells.* Rough weather was encountered both ways, and Farnham broke four ribs on the first crossing and three ribs on the second. A doctor told him he was fortunate that his lungs weren't punctured. Monk remarked that he could go on sailing solo forever as long as he didn't run out of ribs.

As this book goes to press, another solo circumnavigation has just been completed by Washingtonian Archie Wainright, who keeps his 34-foot Crealock sloop, *Aeolus' Tryst,* in Annapolis. This boat's track followed the usual trade wind route via the Panama Canal and on through the South Pacific, but then, instead of rounding the Cape of Good Hope, Wainright sailed north and through the Red Sea. The adventurous voyage lasted for about three and a half years.[11]

Bill Homewood singlehanding *Third Turtle* at the start of the 1984 OSTAR. Courtesy William G. Homewood.

Bill Homewood, an Englishman transplanted to the Annapolis area, first began singlehanding on a Ranger 26 named *Union Jack,* which he entered in the Bermuda One-Two, a singlehanded race to Bermuda with the return race doublehanded. Then he switched to a small Newick-designed trimaran named *Third Turtle* and completed two OSTARs (Observer Singlehanded Transatlantic Race). During the first in 1980, he weathered a severe storm lying to a sea anchor and nearly capsizing. Four years later he won his class and set a new transatlantic record for a 31-foot boat with a time of twenty-one days, five and a half hours.

Possessed with a great sense of humor, Bill sent me a suggested training program to follow in preparation for small-boat ocean sailing: "First, at home, you should go into the bedroom fully dressed and pour a bucket of water over your head. . . . Prop up one side of the bed to an angle of 20 degrees, then pour a bucket of water over the pillow and bedding. . . . Engage the services of a forklift (and operator) who will lift one corner of your house up into the air six feet and then let it drop down with a bang. He should do this all night, intermittently without warning. . . . A well-hidden friend should club you over the head with a two-by-four. This simulates head blows from bulkheads. . . ."

With *Third Turtle,* Homewood set a new course record for an unusual Chesapeake competition called "the Great Ocean Race," which involved a circumnavigation of the Delmarva peninsula. Although its title may seem a bit overblown in light of the far more demanding transoceanic and around-the-world races, the Great Ocean Race can have its own special challenges and tribulations. (One boat took over five days to finish the 360-mile course). Conceived in 1975 as a partial rounding of Delmarva for MORC boats, the race was later opened to other craft, and the course was extended to make a complete circle of the peninsula. On the extended course, the boats must motor through the Chesapeake and Delaware Canal. A unique aspect of the race is that when the canal exit is reached, each skipper is allowed to choose the time—within certain limits—to resume sailing down the tricky Delaware Bay toward the ocean.[12] The strategy, obvious but not easy, is to pick the time most advantageous with respect to wind and current.

A friendly rival of Homewood was Francis Stokes, one of America's best known oceangoing singlehanders. Although he is not a native of the Bay, for several years Francis was a yacht broker in Annapolis. Not only did he enter a number of Bermuda One-Two races and a couple of OSTARs, but also the 1982 BOC Challenge, a three-stop, around-the-world race for singlehanders. During the BOC he made a spectacular mid-ocean rescue of a competitor whose boat was sinking after it had pitchpoled.

Another relatively modern race that has become extremely popular is the Governor's Cup Race from Annapolis to St. Mary's City. Originating in 1974 with St. Mary's College as the sponsor, the 70-mile overnight contest had 470 partici-

pants in the history-making race of 1986. As with any point-to-point course, wind direction is potluck, but quite often there is a "smokey" southerly coming up the Bay emanating from the normal summertime Bermuda High, which, of course, gives the racers a long beat to windward and plenty of opportunities to run aground when hugging the shore to escape a flood tide. Historic St. Mary's City, site of the first permanent settlement in Maryland, is near the head of the beautiful St. Mary's River, and it has a large semicircular anchorage to accommodate a lot of deep-draft yachts. A lively party is held at St. Mary's College after the race.

An excellent sailing program is operated at the college, by the way, and it has produced some skillful sailors. Not long ago, St. Mary's won the prestigious McMillan Cup, awarded to the winner of the eastern U.S. Offshore Collegiate Championship. Recently a nineteen-year-old St. Mary's student, Danielle Brennan, was elected the Rolex Yachtswoman of the Year, and the college was ranked number one out of twenty-four sailing colleges by *Sailing World* magazine.

Mid-Bay yachting centers tend to attract boats from both the north and south. Such is the case with Solomons Island near the mouth of the Patuxent River. Two modern regattas that are very popular are the Screwpile Regatta and Solomons Race Week. Both are commercially sponsored and offer festive entertainment as well as keen racing. The Screwpile derives its name from the construction method used for the base of the historic lighthouse that formerly marked the entrance to the Patuxent at Drum Point.

Near the end of the 1970s, a new handicap rule made its appearance. It was originally called the MHS (Measurement Handicap System) but after international acceptance, its name was changed to IMS (International Measurement System). The most scientific rule to date, the MHS-IMS uses a velocity prediction program (VPP) that calculates the thrust of sails versus hull drag at various angles of heel, yaw, and leeway as measured in a towing (testing) tank. Hull measurements involve the entire hull rather than measurements at particular points as with the IOR, thus helping to eliminate bumps and distortions. At first, the MHS favored many of the older heavy boats, and partly as a result, Arnie Gay of Annapolis won the 1978 Bermuda Race sailing a classic Concordia yawl with a sister in second place. For a while, the new rule seemed the best answer to handicapping problems, but it is inevitable that designers will find ways to exploit loopholes (and no one can blame them), so the PHRF, based on performance alone, has become increasingly popular. Handicapping in the future may find increasing use of a new system called Americap, which combines certain elements of PHRF and IMS and considers the time spent racing as well as the length of the course.

When mentioning outstanding Chesapeake offshore racers, one cannot overlook Jack King from Fairfax, Virginia,

who has done very well with his various boats named *Merrythought*. He has excelled in numerous important events such as SORCs, Block Island and Edgartown Race Weeks, and also Halifax, Bermuda, and Annapolis-Newport races. In 1980 he was a member of the winning U.S. Sardinia Cup Team and was captain of the U.S. Admiral's Cup team in England four years later. Perhaps Jack King's best-known victory came after his highly modified Frers 45 (with new stern, thinner keel, new rudder and mast) topped the seventy-three boat IOR division of the 1984 Bermuda Race.

The Chesapeake has been blessed with a number of talented yacht designers, but not all of them are well known except locally. Names that come to mind are Jay Benford, James Brickell, Edward Burgess, Howard Chapelle, Thomas Colvin, Edmund Cutts, William Dimpfel, Frederick Geiger, Thomas Gillmer, Ernest H. Hartge, Laurence Hartge, George Hazen, Robert Henry, Leavenworth Holden, John Horner, Lowndes Johnson, Michael Kaufman, Karl Kirkman, Robert Ladd, Roger McAleer, George Meese, Richards Miller, Roger Moorman, Norman Owens, Robert Peach, Franz Plunder, Samuel Rabl, Linton Rigg, Mandell Rosenblatt, Vincent Serio, James Speer, Eric Steinlein, Ernest Tucker, Peter Van Dine, Ralph Wiley, and Charles Wittholz. William Lapworth has retired to the Bay but has done no design work here.

In 1981 a world-famous designer named Bruce Farr moved from New Zealand to Annapolis, where he set up a state-of-the-art design office specializing, for the most part, in offshore racers and performance cruisers. Farr boats have excelled all over the world in top-flight competitions including the Southern Cross series in Australia, Ton Cup Racing, the Admiral's Cup races in England, America's Cup racing, the SORC, the Transpac, and the Whitbread round-the-world race. In fact, Farr and Associates has produced more than thirty world champion offshore designs. A few years after settling in Annapolis, Farr designed two medium-sized cruising racers that were closely identified with the Chesapeake, the Farr 37 and 33. Both were built by local yards—Dickerson and Annapolis Custom Yachts—and both were successfully sailed by local clients, Scott Allan, Bert Jabin, Steve Hiltabidle, and Charles "Sunny" Smith. Another local sailor, Peter Gordon, has been very successful with his Farr 44 *Gaucho.* One of the most interesting Farr designs, in my opinion, is the Concept 80, a fast world cruiser with many innovations including a transom "garage" for a sizable tender. Commissioned by my friend and former Ohlson 35 rival Donald Tate, the Concept 80 was built in Taiwan and sailed by Don halfway around the world to her home port on the Chesapeake. Another interesting Farr design, described in chapter 4, is the 44-foot *Reindeer,* which Newbold Smith sailed to Hudson Bay in 1994.

Thus far I have not written much about small-boat racing on the Bay, with the exception of Stars, but many of the best local designs in this size range are

described in chapter 8. Two of the most famous are the Comet, designed by Lowndes Johnson in 1932, and the Hampton, designed by Vincent Serio two years later. The popular Penguin is usually considered a Chesapeake boat, although it was created by Philip Rhodes, who was not a local designer, and the protype Penguin was not first used on the Bay.

A host of talented small-boat skippers hail from the Chesapeake. With the possible exception of the Johnson brothers and perhaps one or two others, the Bay's most famous corinthian small-boat racer is probably Dr. Stuart Walker of Annapolis. I say corinthian because his profession was medicine, and he always sailed his own boats (although he does derive income from his books and articles about sailboat racing). Walker first achieved world yachting recognition when he raced International 14-foot dinghies and became the first American to

Famous small-boat champion Stuart Walker. Courtesy Stuart H. Walker.

CHESAPEAKE SAILS

win the coveted Prince of Wales Cup in England. After competing successfully on the Chesapeake and in many foreign countries in dinghies, he switched to 5.5-meter boats and then Solings and continued his winning ways. A long-time columnist for the magazine that was first called *One-Design Yachtsman* and is now *Sailing World*, Walker wrote extensively about his racing experiences, including losses as well as wins, and specialized in analytical studies of tactics and coastal (or inshore) weather. In the midfifties Dr. Walker helped organize and for many years has led (along with the likes of Margery Donald and George Brown) one of the top small-boat racing clubs on the Bay, the Severn Sailing Association. At the time of this writing, Dr. Walker has been selected as a member of the U.S. Sailing Team that is preparing for the Olympics in the year 2000. This is quite an honor considering his age of seventy-four. He hopes to compete in Solings with his grandson as crew.

And speaking of older Chesapeake sailors who are still racing, I should mention Edgar Hoyt, who, at the age of eighty-two, is still competitive in the Tempest Class. Another ancient mariner is John Aufhammer, former Alberg 30 racer and past president of the CBYRA. At ninety, John is actively racing a San Juan 21 in Florida. Austin "Jack" Penn is not a racer, but he was singlehanding his Alberg 30 at the age of ninety-two.

In recent years another doctor/sailor has been dominant in Chesapeake racing, this time in big boats on the southern Bay. With a pair of C & C de-

Revenge 2 skippered by southern Bay champ William Peach, who in recent years won three Labrot trophies. Photo by Elliott Torn, Creative Photography, Newport News, Virginia.

signs named *Revenge* hailing from Newport News, Dr. William Peach has won numerous southern regattas and High Point awards and, more impressively, three Baywide seasonal Labrot Trophy championships. The first *Revenge* was a 33-foot 3/4 Ton Cup boat and the second a C & C 37R. A former commodore of the Hampton Yacht Club and chief handicapper for MORC of the southern Bay, Dr. Peach was over thirty years old when he sailed his first race. He attributes much of his success to "having a crew of mature adults (average age over forty) who enjoy sailing and each other's company." Particular credit for *Revenge 2*'s success is given to tactician Mark Wheeler (former navy fighter pilot and 505-class racing champ) who Dr. Peach modestly calls his "mentor."

With regard to the best modern big-boat sailors on the southern Bay, Dr. Peach feels that the most outstanding include Ray Brown, Jack Zanks, Sledd Shellhorse, and Vernon "Bumps" Eberwine. Of the latter Peach writes, "[He] is probably the best seat-of-the-pants sailor on the Bay and our greatest 'tightwad,' i.e., he wins more races spending less money than anyone I know."[13]

The CBYRA Yearbook of 1989 states: "1987 also saw another aspect of the sport that kept rearing its head, and that is professional racing. Most of the signs have been pointing in this direction for some time, and this has been approached more openly and aggressively in other parts of the world. We are just scratching the surface of what appears to be a long road in reaching a solution." By the turn of the decade, professionalism in various forms was having a definite effect on handicap yacht racing. It almost seemed as if we were taking some first steps in returning to the early days of yachting, before the formation and domination of corinthian yacht clubs, when men of wealth bought state-of-the-art yachts and hired professional crew and captains to race them.

Modern counterparts are ultralight boats built of exotic materials, equipped with all manner of gadgets and sophisticated electronics and manned by sail-

makers or so-called "factory teams." An attempt to discourage this movement has been to specify that some classes be "owner-driven," but very often the owners have professionals by their sides telling them exactly what to do. All of this, combined with inequities in the rating systems and complicated by racing lightweight "sport boats" against displacement racing cruisers, has been discouraging to many of the less-than-totally-dedicated racers with limited time to sail who wish to compete in a relatively informal inexpensive way just for the fun of it.

Another aspect of professionalism, which cheapens the sport in the opinion of some traditional yachtsmen, is the emergence of commercial sponsorship. Olin Stephens recently said, "Sponsorship has damaged the sporting aspect of racing."[14] After the professional skipper of a sponsored Whitbread 60 refused to give out information about the loss of his mast, the well-respected publication *Practical Sailor* opined, "Don't look for sportsmanship in the Whitbread Race."[15] On the other hand, there has been universal approval of fundraising regattas such as the Hospice Cup, Leukemia Cup, Sail for Sight Race, and St. Brendan's Cup events. These relatively modern regattas contribute to worthy causes, and most have been steadily growing in popularity.

Despite its being highly commercial and strictly professional, the enormous publicity surrounding the recent Whitbread Race—a nine-legged, round-the-world race for 64-foot light-displacement skimmers—has stimulated a lot of public interest in yacht racing. Chesapeake residents were especially interested, since nearly all of the racing boats were designed by Annapolitan Bruce Farr, and for the first time since the inception of the race in 1973, a local boat was competing. Named *Chessie Racing*, she was financed by George Collins of Gibson Island, who also led her team. She was manned by professional sailors, some of them Annapolitans, but she was the only boat in the race without a major sponsor. Despite a disappointing sixth place in the overall standings, *Chessie* finished third in four legs of the race.

The Chesapeake has had its share of career racing sailors who are considered professionals by most people. Some might be called "rock stars" in the modern vernacular. A few of the best known are sailmakers Larry Leonard, Jim Brady, Greg Gendell, Terry Hutchinson, Al Girard, and recent Rolex Yachtsman of the Year Chris Larson; Gary Jobson, formerly an America's Cup tactician and a sailing commentator with ESPN; Gary Bodie, a noted sailing coach; match-racing ace Gavin Brady; and Geoff Stagg of Farr International. Over a period of time, other sailmakers such as Scott Allan, Jim Alsopp, Glen Housley, and Jim Scott have campaigned their own racing cruisers, so perhaps they are professional to a lesser degree. Then, too, I should add that Gary Jobson has in recent years taken up cruising and has had some exciting experiences sailing in remote places such as Antarctica. He is also co-owner with Jack King of a traditional cruising schooner named *Silver Heels*, which he uses for less adventurous cruising.

Efforts to restrict or ban professionals in certain races have been frustrated partly because of the difficulty in defining the term professionalism. The United States Sailing Association (formerly the USYRU), the national authority, has struggled with this problem. In *The Racing Rules of Sailing, 1997-2000*, published by the association (commonly called U.S. Sailing), "Appendix R—Definitions for Competitor Eligibility" originally contained examples of professional competitors, but these were deleted by the association's board of directors in March 1997 after a lively debate.

For a while, in the early and mid-1990s, big-boat racing was declining in almost all regions of the Chesapeake, with the exception of Annapolis. The March 1996 issue of the CBYRA publication called the *Traveler* contained an editorial on the subject. It opened with the question, "Will the racing sailboat become

Chessie Racing port-tacking the fleet at the start of the eighth leg of the Whitbread Race in 1998. Note the man up the mast on the boat to windward. Photograph by William A. Boykin III.

a dinosaur, found only in the confines of the waters off Annapolis?" Bemoaning the decline, the editorial pointed out that skippers who had been going out to race found fewer and fewer boats on the starting line. It went on to say: "After all the crew calls, buying food, ice, fuel, etc.—to say nothing of all the boat prep—it's a letdown to show up and race against two or three other boats. . . . The bottom line for us is that, unless we—the sailors who care about racing—take some action to get new people involved, the sport will continue shrinking, until we're reduced to a Jurassic Park of racing sailboats in Annapolis."

By no means has professionalism been entirely to blame for the decline. The sport has become very expensive, many individuals have less leisure time, racing boats have become less suitable for cruising (and less beautiful), and more people have been turning to motorboats and other sports such as golf. Recently, however, we may be seeing a reversal in the trend, and the future looks brighter. Corinthians are having fun in less formal Wednesday and Friday evening "beer can" races; there has been growing interest in nonspinnaker racing, which offers surprisingly keen competition without the hassle of lining up large crews; and club cruising races seem to be thriving. Another factor is that, while many of the most serious racers are migrating to the

The author's grandson Ned Cramer (age ten) receiving his prize from Robert Price at the CBYRA Bay Open Regatta in 1997. Note that his hand is going for the prize rather than the handshake (first things first). Photograph by Barbara Mersereau.

"skimming dish" sports boats, they are leaving behind many handsome, smart-sailing displacement boats that can be obtained at reasonable prices. The primary reason for hope, however, lies with the youngsters in the Bay's many excellent junior sailing programs. The many children who are introduced to the sport in Optimists and other small craft—those who are given a chance to have fun and "mess about" in their own boats—will be the ones who move to bigger boats and carry on the great tradition of yachting under sail, racing or cruising on the yet idyllic waters of the Chesapeake.

CHAPTER THREE

HALCYON DAYS AT GIBSON ISLAND

Soon after rounding the right-angle bend in Mountain Road near Pinehurst, Maryland, on the way to Gibson Island, a great feeling of excitement would well up inside of me, caused by the anticipation of once again viewing the lovely Chesapeake. This happened in the 1930s, during my family's annual trek, when we left our inland home to spend the summers on my father's 35-foot yawl moored in Gibson Island's harbor. Even before clearing the clump of trees that shielded our view of the bay, I could detect the fresh but slightly tangy smell of the water. The first one in our car to catch a glimpse of the silvery bay through the trees would shout "quack, quack." Our ducklike appreciation of the water equaled that of Ernest Shepard's much quoted rat who said "It (life on the water) is the only life."

At the end of a winding road that was once an Indian trail, a dramatic scene would suddenly burst into view. An ivy-covered brownstone gatehouse guarded a narrow causeway leading onto Gibson Island. To the left of the causeway was the broad Chesapeake with oceangoing ships in nearby Craighill Channel, a couple of lighthouses, and a

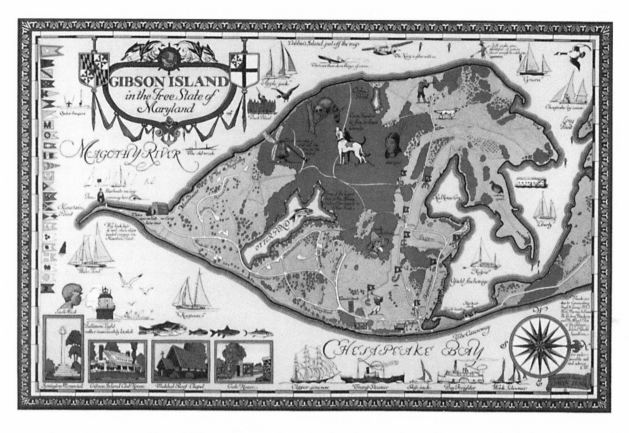

A map of Gibson Island circa 1931 drawn by Edwin Tunis. It shows *Kelpie* moored in the harbor and various yachts belonging to members surrounding the island. Courtesy Gibson Island Historical Society.

few boats under sail. To the right was a perfect harbor sheltering a fleet of anchored yachts, their reflections gently shimmering on the protected water. Lining the harbor's south shore was a group of attractive white cottages with smooth green lawns sloping down to the water's edge. Further to the west, a point marking the entrance to Red House Cove shielded our view of a small yacht yard and marine railway.

Other shores around the harbor were mostly wild: marsh grass, low banks, and a woods of scruffy pine, tulip poplars, gum, oak, and the occasional dead tree bleached white by the sun and capped

with the nest of an osprey. In the middle of the causeway was a low shingled building, an annex to the Gibson Island Club known as "the boathouse," where most yachting activities were conducted. My father's handsome yawl *Kelpie* was moored in the middle of the harbor opposite a marsh and golf course water hole on the south shore.

Despite the great economic depression of that era, which my parents and most Gibson Islanders were feeling, those were halcyon times for a preteenager like me who had a genetic predilection for boats and the water. A typical day of the mid-1930s began when I woke up to the gentle sound of rope halyards slapping against the solid spruce mast next to my bunk. Occasionally I could hear a crab scraping along the bottom of the boat. For a while I would lie there gazing up at the massive oak partners, an intricate arrangement of horizontal knees supporting the mast where it penetrated the deck. Then I'd check the shelf above my bunk, which housed my treasures: a miniature ship's clock, a Johnson and Johnson first-aid kit, a metal flashlight, notebooks for sketching, and some "Big-Little" books. A small portable windup Victrola on the opposite bunk held a few jazz records—Artie Shaw, Raymond Scott, and Bob Crosby.

When my parents awakened, all of us would take a dip over the side and then have a delicious breakfast which, in those precholesterol days, consisted of bacon and eggs. I could hardly wait to finish eating and board our sailing dinghy, a little clinker-built half-dory named *JT* (standing for *Jesus Tender*). She was my first boat, and it didn't take me long to learn how to sail her downwind. I'd run off before the wind, then lower sail and row back against the wind. After returning to *Kelpie,* I'd announce to my parents that sailing was easy—"nothing to it." Later I would meet my chums at the boathouse, and we would row, swim, "sail," and explore the island. One of our favorite spots was the yacht yard where we would watch the boat repair and servicing activities and build model boats or rafts.

I can still recall the redolent odors of that yard—the acrid aroma of copper bottom-paint blended with the mellow

The author as a young boy, looking less happy than he really was, aboard the cutter *Tejeria* with his mother and owner Ted Hoster, who later was a commodore of the Annapolis Yacht Club. Courtesy Leo Flanigan.

smell of cedar shavings. There was a wooden wall where the painters would clean their brushes: the accumulation of years of splattered paint and overbrushing had produced a work of art that would rival a masterpiece by Jackson Pollock, rich in color and texture.

The yard was run by Ed Lusby with the assistance of his brother Phil. They had migrated from the famous Davis yard at Solomons, Maryland, where their older brother Barnes Lusby was the foreman. In fact, the Gibson Island facility, founded around 1928, originally was an annex of the Solomons yard. In *The Last Generation,* Geoffrey Footner wrote about a formal testimonial banquet that was given by the Gibson Island Yacht Squadron to honor Clarence Davis, owner of the Solomons yard. After numerous speeches by yachtsmen praising Davis and his craftsmen for their excellent work in yacht building and maintenance, Davis was expected to say a few words. However, being a very shy man, he had departed unnoticed, slipping out through an open window at the back of the banquet hall.

The Lusby brothers and their head carpenter, "Skipper" Dixon, were extremely tolerant of us kids as we wandered through the yard, often barefooted, watching their work and borrowing tools to make boat models. From Skipper I eventually learned not only how to use a knife and gouge, but also some elementary naval architecture such as the value of overhangs and symmetry in hull form, qualities that are often overlooked today. Some of the sailing models made by the older children were surprisingly sophisticated, and races for them were held at the end of the summer.

Often I would eat lunch with the yard workmen in the commissary, a slightly weathered white two-story building perched on a bank facing the harbor. It was operated by a wonderful black couple, Mac McWilliams and his wife, who specialized in southern "country" cooking. Mac also ran the tender that delivered newspapers and picked up garbage from those living aboard yachts moored in the harbor. As he approached a boat, he'd call out "One gahbich man—one paipa man."

In the late afternoon my parents would often invite one or two of their harbor-dwelling neighbors over to *Kelpie* for cocktails. Those were the days immediately after Prohibition, so there were

more than a few imbibers. Among the most colorful was a fun-loving handsome man named Lawrence Bailliere whom everyone called Bally. He had owned the skipjack *Pelican* and the schooner *Harpoon,* but in 1934 he ordered a lovely 47-foot cutter named *Aweigh,* designed by Sparkman and Stephens and built by the Davis yard at Solomons. In her first year *Aweigh* was taken south to compete in the SORC and with some help in one or two races from Bally's friend Rod Stephens (of Sparkman and Stephens), she took second overall in the St. Petersburg to Havana Race and first in the Havana–Key West and Miami-Nassau races, bringing some fame to the Chesapeake and to Gibson Island in particular.

A bon vivant and impish prankster, Bally's activities were especially mischievous when he got together with John W. "Monk" Foster. The two were sometimes called the Katzenjammer Kids, after the then popular comic strip characters. Although frequently in hot water, Bally was a fine sailor. His stepson, "Tinky" Orrick, recalls the time when he, Tink, was steering *Aweigh* while she was running before the wind. Bally was below shaving under an open hatch and yelled a warning to Tink that he was sailing by the lee. Soon after, a flying jibe occurred as the boom slammed across the boat. Bally had sensed it from below, in the cabin. After *Aweigh's* triumph in southern waters, Bally would brag that she could "sail rings around *Kelpie,*" so I was delighted when our smaller boat sometimes beat *Aweigh* boat-for-boat in the local races. Obviously, *Aweigh* was underrigged for the light midsummer winds of the Chesapeake.

Some of the cocktail parties on the various Gibson Island yachts were lively affairs where the liquor flowed freely and everyone seemed to be celebrating the end of Prohibition. On one such occasion a prominent Eastern Shoreman, Harry Galligher, attended a party on my uncle Charlie's schooner *Sunshine* and awoke the next day with a hangover that helped inspire the following poem:

Gibson Island Harbor

There are men who face the Arctic
There are addicts of narcotic
There are men who've had their throats
    cut by a barber
But for sheer courageous splendor
Get the palm prepared to tender
To the guy who visits Gibson Island
    Harbor.

He can be an iron-willed dandy
or a drab Mahatma Ghandi
With sufficient will to lead the war-like
    Axis
But if he boards a yawl or schooner
Maybe later . . . maybe sooner
He'll get drunk as sure as we'll get death
    and taxes.

One or two have brought their women
Just for lunch or maybe swimmin'
And they've made it off the Island still
    untankered
They deserve a world of credit
And it's only fair they get it
But they never got on board tied up or
    anchored.

Makes no difference what the reason
Makes no difference what the season
Anytime I've tried, from April to October

Anytime—and I've been trying
And I'd say it were I dying
Have I ever called a tender and stayed
    sober.

There are buns you get and show it
You are pretty full and know it
You may fight and have to face the local
    jailor
Such severe police arraignment
Is but pleasant entertainment
When it comes to crossing goblets with a
    sailor

We who've faced this trial by fire
Have a strong suppressed desire
To a man we ask you grant our one
    ambition
When the palm is to the fearless
To the courage that is peerless
May we have a just and hard earned
    recognition

Supper was often late after a cocktail party, but my mother could always turn out a hasty but tasty meal cooked over our Primus stove. Being the shortest member of our family, I was seated at the dining table next to the bulkhead under a gimballed kerosene lamp that had a heavy round weight on its bottom to keep it upright when the boat heeled. Many were the times I bumped my head on that weight. Dinner was always pleasant in *Kelpie*'s cozy cabin except on a calm night when the mosquitoes arrived in force. In the early days we had no screens, and our only defense was a repellent called citronella. How well I remember its pungent odor dominating the blended smells of food and kerosene.

Usually we would turn in after supper, but one night a week my mother

Aweigh, Lawrence Bailliere's Sparkman and Stephens–designed 47-foot cutter, in southern waters during her first SORC in the mid-1930s.

and I would row over to Doctor William Roland's yawl *Alana* to listen to the Bob Crosby orchestra on the radio. The Crosby theme song was George Gershwin's "Summertime," and I'll never forget one particular evening rowing along the reflected path of the full moon while listening to the lilting strains of that theme.

Bill Roland was an associate of the well-known eye doctor Alan Woods, and *Alana* was named in his honor. Doctor Woods was a sailor also. He had owned a local Seabird yawl, which later became the workboat for the Gibson Island Yacht Yard. A good raconteur, the doctor liked to tell about the time when he and a wise old black employee named Horace were in a cabin cruiser drifting past an immersion ceremony of a Negro Baptist church on the shores of Mobjack Bay, Virginia. While Doctor Woods and his companion were observing the ceremony through the cabin portholes, Horace exclaimed, "Say, I know that preacher! Him and me used to oyster together. Why he ain't no better preacher than he was a waterman. Look at him washin' the sins away on a flood tide, and them sins is washin' right back agin."

Bedding down on *Kelpie* was always a ritual with my father neatly making up berths in the main cabin for my mother and himself while cheerfully singing a tune called "Here Come Those Pullman Porters." My bunk was in the forward cabin, and when I turned in, I would often lie down with my head at the foot of the berth so I could observe the canopy of stars through the open hatch directly above. Before falling asleep I'd listen for a while to the sweet songs of the whippoorwills on shore and the background symphony produced by a chorus of frogs in the marsh. So ended a typical day.

When I was old enough to join the Junior Fleet, the local sailing and seamanship training program for youngsters, I was provided with a so-called "kid boat," one of a class of deadrise skiffs rigged with a single spritsail. There seems to be no record of where these boats came from, but they were very similar to those made by Captain Ed Leatherbury at Galesville, Maryland. My first year with a kid boat was 1933, the same year the area was blasted by a hurricane, the most destructive storm ever experienced in the Chesapeake. The storm passed over Norfolk, Virginia, and then headed toward Washington, putting Tidewater areas in its most dangerous sector and pushing an enormous storm surge up the Bay.

At the first storm warning, I was sent ashore to spend the night at my aunt and uncle's home on the island. My parents stayed on board Kelpie, and Dad spent the night reinforcing Kelpie's mooring line, adding antichafing gear, and fending off drifting wreckage and boats that had broken loose. With the storm surge above the causeway, little protection was afforded for yachts moored in the harbor. The boathouse was nearly destroyed, and many of the cars parked there, including ours, were washed into the harbor. An enormous steel barge was stranded on the beach in front of and practically touching the Gibson Island clubhouse. When the surge reached the base of the clubhouse, someone inside the building observed the rapidly approaching barge and exclaimed, "This is another great flood, and thank God the Ark is coming to our rescue!" My uncle's home was inland, so I didn't witness the waterfront destruction while it was taking place, but I was very worried as I

A "kid boat" first used as the junior trainer in the late 1920s and early 1930s. Courtesy Gibson Island Historical Society.

watched trees bend and branches break, for a Junior Fleet race was scheduled that day, and my older cousin Charlie Henderson taunted me with "They'll never call off a race because of a little wind."

After the storm subsided, everyone came out to survey the damage and to look for lost possessions. Many boats were washed ashore including my kid boat which was named *Gnu.* During our search for her we would ask people if they had seen her, and they would reply, "No we haven't seen a canoe." We eventually recovered from the hurricane; the boathouse was rebuilt and a higher stronger bulkhead was added all along the causeway. Since then, no tide or surge has climbed above the improved bulkhead and hopefully Gibson Island harbor will always be one of the safest havens for yachts.

The Junior Fleet was founded by Nathaniel S. "Cap" Kenney in 1924. For more than twenty-five years, he gave it his full attention and produced one of the best junior training programs in the country. The original training craft were kid boats, but in 1935 they were replaced by small sailing scows called LJs in honor of their designer, Lowndes Johnson, who donated the design to Gibson Island. I had one of the first, number seven,

Sunny McKnew on the bow of the LJ *Curlew* in front of the Gibson Island boathouse. Photograph by John H. Reichenbach.

named *Swift.* All were named after birds. *Swift* was built by the Lusby brothers and was painted a medium blue with a pale blue deck.

Cat-rigged with a Marconi mainsail, the early LJs had no shrouds, but after a few masts jumped out of their steps and tore up the decks, shrouds were added. My first and so far only dismasting (knock wood) happened when I ducked astern of a yawl moored in the harbor and caught *Swift*'s shroud on the end of the yawl's overhanging mizzen boom. I'd forgotten that the shrouds had been added.

The LJs were superior to the kid boats in that they were faster, more responsive, and far more stable. When the junior sailors would bring their boats into the docks at the boathouse, they would shoot into the wind and land bow first. This meant that, when no one was on the pier, each sailor had to rush forward just before landing in order to fend off. It was difficult getting around the mast on the sharp bow of a kid boat without capsizing her, but the LJ's broad square bow allowed a young sailor to easily pass the mast and fend off. It was also easier to board an LJ. Of course, scows are more subject to pounding in a chop, but LJ's were nearly always sailed in protected waters.

The older and more advanced Junior Fleet members sailed Barnegat sloops. These were modeled after the Barnegat Bay "sneakboxes" that were originally gunning boats used for hunting waterfowl, primarily ducks. I graduated to a Barnegat in 1937 and was thrilled with the roomy cockpit that had benches, an aft locker, and room to sleep on the cockpit sole. All the boats in this class were named after ducks; mine was christened *Scaup* (often misspelled *Scamp*). Built a few miles north of Gibson Island at the yard of Rogers and Townsend, *Scaup* was sluggish at first, but she was vastly improved with a new suit of sails made by McClellan in Baltimore.

After winning the fleet championship in 1938, my crew and I were feeling pretty cocky, so we entered *Scaup* in a free-for-all race at Rock Hall across the Chesapeake. There we learned a lesson in humility when we were beaten by an older cat-rigged sneakbox with a gaff mainsail. To this day I still have great respect for the gaff rig on every point of sailing except beating and sometimes even then, when a gaff vang can be properly rigged.

Junior races at Gibson Island were started and finished in front of the boathouse, which had a long porch facing the harbor. There was always a large gallery of spectators, mostly parents, seated in a row of chairs along the porch. A few parents would stand on the docking float and shout instructions to their children. One such person was Colonel Gaillard, whose equipment included a pith helmet, camera, and megaphone. The gallery got a treat one day when the distinguished Colonel, with megaphone to his lips, stepped backwards off the float and into the drink, for a moment leaving only his pith helmet floating on the surface.

Another time was not so amusing. The racing fleet was caught in a violent squall and the parents were most worried

about the Barnegat fleet that had sailed out of the harbor into the Magothy River. All of the Barnegats, including my *Scaup*, capsized except for one that was "manned" by a pair of girls. Everyone in the fleet had seen the storm approaching in the classic form of the roll cloud that precedes a cold front, but none of us wanted to risk losing our position in the race by being the first to lower sail. As a result, we all waited until the first downdraft whipped across the water before attempting to douse sail, and by then it was too late. Sail slides were jammed by the force of the wind, and boats were heeled to the point of no return. In those days, before boats were fitted with flotation, self-rescue was slow and difficult, but we had been trained to stay with our boats, which, being unballasted, would float semisubmerged. We hung on, soaked and shivering, for what seemed an eternity until rescue boats came alongside. The girls who managed to stay upright

Barnegat sloops racing in Gibson Island's harbor. Photograph by John H. Reichenbach.

had lowered sail early and run off under bare pole, giving all of us a valuable lesson in seamanship.

In the evenings after a race, there would be a meeting in the boathouse presided over by Cap Kenney. He would lecture us on the racing rules, tactics, and basic sail trim. Climax of the junior sailing season was a gala banquet at the Gibson Island Club, where winners were awarded real silver (not pewter) prizes and were required to make acceptance speeches. Most recipients modestly gave credit for their success to their crew, but a winner once proclaimed "I owe it to my Daddy's bottom" (referring to the replacement of the plywood bottom on an LJ).

Along with our junior training in sail, we had lessons in basic marlinspike seamanship from George R. "Salty" Marks, a craggy-faced old navy veteran, who was Gibson Island's rigger and harbormaster. Formerly a chief bosun's mate who had served in the Spanish-American War, in World War I, and on the China coast, he was an excellent rigger who installed and serviced the rigging of most boats in the harbor. At that time, before the almost universal use of stainless steel wire and terminal fittings, shrouds and stays were often made of hot-dipped galvanized steel, then of superior quality, with spliced eyes at their ends. Salty Marks, with fingers like marlinespikes, spliced the galvanized rigging, and some of it lasted for almost thirty years.

He was a patient teacher but took no nonsense from the Junior Fleet kids. They all respected him and never dared

Right, Cap Kenney conferring with Salty Marks. Courtesy Gibson Island Historical Society.

to cause the slightest trouble. Under his tutelage some beautiful macrame was produced, and one large work of art still hangs in the club room at the boathouse.

Captain Marks lived in a small cottage on the south shore of the harbor directly across from the boatyard. His work room was always a fascinating place to visit with its long work bench, rigging tools and vises, canvas and rope, yacht fittings, boat models, and faded photographs of old navy ships. The building is now owned by the Gibson Island Historical Society and appropriately named "the Salty Marks House." In 1963, at the age of eighty-three, Salty died by falling on an anchor. My father said it was the most appropriate way for a mariner to die since Jason was killed by a beam falling from the *Argo.*

My nautical education was augmented by sailing and racing aboard *Kelpie* with my father, who had learned so many tricks of sailing from his Miles

River neighbors, Lowndes and Graham Johnson. Dad seemed to share the philosophy of the famous author/sailor Arthur Knapp, who once said, concerning junior instruction, "Start 'em young and tell 'em absolutely nothing." Consequently, I learned from Dad mostly by osmosis. Occasionally, he'd make such a remark as, "This wind is a typical dying norther, and when it can't make up its mind what to do, it'll come in from the south." But he wouldn't explain what I later learned: when a high-pressure system approaches from the west, its clockwise-turning winds produce a northerly that will die as the high passes over; then the wind will turn into a southerly when you are exposed to the backside of the high. After a great many years on the Chesapeake, Dad developed an instinct for predicting the local weather, and several experienced sailors, even the well-known yachting writer, Alf Loomis, said they used the actions taken on *Kelpie* as a guide when a thunderstorm was threatening. One of Dad's gems of advice was "never start a race without a hangover."

I was allowed to crew on *Kelpie* at an early age, and the details of many races still stick in my mind. My godfather, George Blakiston, would often crew; he was a delightful character but seldom exerted himself except for asking me to fetch him beers and once in a while offering advice. On one occasion Dad became exasperated and exploded, "For God's sake, Blakiston, can't you do anything? Trim that jib." George slowly put down his beer, stood up, rolled up his sleeves, and gave a mighty heave on the watch tackle attached to the jib sheet (we had no winches in those days). The old cotton sail split in half and immediately flapped itself to shreds. George turned around with a proud grin on his face and exclaimed, "Damn! I didn't know my own strength."

High point of the sailing season was the 100-mile (actually 92-mile) Cedar Point Race that took place over Labor Day weekend and attracted the top boats from all over the Bay and occasionally even from New England. These races were thrilling to me, especially the night sailing when *Kelpie* seemed to pick up speed, and the decreased visibility was offset by the increased awareness gained through sound and touch. The latter came from a greater sensitivity to the feel of the wind on your skin and the pull of the helm against your hand. Predominant sounds were the slosh of the bow wave, the hiss of the wake, the creak of straining lines, and the soft sigh of wind in the rigging. From my bunk in the forward cabin when I was off watch, I could hear the muffled talking of the crew, the metallic clatter of the sheet blocks on the bar travelers when we tacked, and the murmur of water moving past the hull only inches from my ear. I could almost judge *Kelpie's* speed by those watery sounds that Joshua Slocum once described as the "gossiping" of the waves.

Excitement would mount as the racers approached the Cedar Point turning mark flashing brightly in the dark. The boats seemed to converge in groups. First, you would see running lights and an occasional flash of light on the sails;

Some of Gibson Island's prominent yachtsmen of the 1930s onboard the schooner *Ataloa. Left to right:* Bill Henderson, author's father; Bally Bailliere; Corrin Strong; *foreground,* Ellis Ellicott; *at the helm,* Don Sherwood. Courtesy Gibson Island Historical Society.

then as they neared the turning buoy, there were shouts and orders for trimming sheets and setting new sails. Another climactic moment occurred at dawn when there was just enough light to spot your rivals. On Gibson Island at that time, it seemed that every resident was interested in the race. There were many bets and a cash pool for picking the time of the first boat to finish. A lively all-night party was attended by the wives of most crewmembers. Spectator boats were often waiting at the finish line, and the crews were greeted like heroes whether they won or lost. Coverage of the race sometimes appeared on the front page of the *Baltimore Sun's* sports section.

A few Cedar Point races really stand out in my mind. When we were returning home after rounding the Cedar Point

buoy in 1937, the wind died and a cold front moved in from the north. Its passing produced a steady 45-knot norther that soon kicked up a wicked chop. Having reduced sail to working jib and mizzen, we were splitting tacks with another yawl, the Rhodes-designed *Dryad,* under the same combination of sails. She was beating us until we set the storm trysail, which really gave us the power to slam through those choppy seas. *Kelpie* drove ahead and before long was leading her class by miles, but one of the crew was seriously seasick and another had a bad back. As we approached Sandy Point lighthouse, not far from the finish line, Dad decided, for the sake of the crew, to withdraw from the race and run off for the shelter of Annapolis harbor. I was deeply disappointed, even more so because I had to sleep in the same narrow berth with Dad, which I could only manage to do by removing the doors from the lockers behind the bunk, thus making room for my arms and legs. It turned out that the only boat in our class to finish was *Jemra* owned by Judge R. P. Melvin, who collected not only the first prize but silver for second and third places as well. Fourteen boats withdrew from that race, and some were so late in returning that the Gibson Island commodore, John Sherwood, arranged for a navy plane to search for the missing boats.

How well I remember running home from Cedar Point in 1939 when we were alongside a rival boat that had (would you believe it?) a radio onboard. Her excited skipper told us he had just heard that war had been declared in Europe. This was particularly meaningful for us, as my sister was residing in England. However, the news did little to distract Dad from his concentration on the race. He said, "Is that so—ease that jib a little more."

Being a one-night affair during which there was little opportunity to set up a routine watch system, the Cedar Point Race could be exhausting for the crews. Corrin Strong wrote in his log that on the 1933 race, which must have been exceptionally slow, he had no sleep for thirty-eight hours. Of course, fatigue leads to errors, and the boats that did well were usually the ones with the least mistakes. On one race when *Kelpie* finished under spinnaker miles ahead of her competition, the crew was exhausted but elated at the sound of the victory gun. The glory was only momentary, however, for in the process of lowering sail, one of the crew released the jig on the main halyard and the end of the halyard went aloft. Then the engine was started and a trailing spinnaker sheet wrapped around the propeller. Just a few minutes after her glorious finish, *Kelpie* was crippled and was forced to accept an ignominious tow back to her mooring.

A fun-loving but cautious sailor was Corrin Strong, owner of the lovely Rhodes cutter *Narada*. He founded the Timid Skipper's Union in 1934. The member's oath was: "I solemnly swear that I am a timid skipper; that I truly fear wind, waves, and clouds."[1] One of the charter members, skippering a Gibson Island yawl on the 1934 Cedar Point Race, could not find the turning mark and sailed all the way to Point Lookout, fifteen miles too far south, before discov-

ering his error. After turning back and reaching the Patuxent River, he and his crew were so exhausted that they put into Solomons. Leaving the boat there, they went home by automobile. Later the skipper was called on the carpet of the Timid Skipper's Union and, amid great applause from its members, was awarded a gold medal, the only one ever awarded by the union.

The unofficial chanty man of the Gibson Island Yacht Squadron, my father was a gifted vocalist. As a young man he had sung in many a barbershop quartet, but then he got serious and began studying at the Peabody Institute in Baltimore under the noted concert pianist and voice coach Frank Bibb. After meeting Bibb, one of Dad's cronies told him, "I doubt that you can teach Henderson anything, but if you can you'll probably ruin one of America's finest bar-room and back-alley singers." At nearly every Gibson Island banquet, Dad would sing some sea chanties; he even sang at the Annapolis Yacht Club at the awards banquet following the 1939 New London–Annapolis Race. Always included was the rousing chanty "Whiskey Johnny," with Dad singing verse after verse and everyone joining him in a thunderous chorus after each verse. In his history of the *14 West Hamilton Street Club*, author Walker Lewis had this to say about Dad: "Bill always had to encore 'Whiskey Johnny.' His rendition became so famous that Dr. Hugh Hampton Young got him to sing it at a kickoff party in the 'Ritchie for President' campaign. Later, Bernard Baruch came up to him and said, 'If Ritchie wins,

"Whiskey Johnny" will become the national anthem!'"

Dad loved to sing the songs of John Masefield such as "Sea Fever," "Mother Carey," and "Port of Many Ships." Inspired by our living aboard *Kelpie*, he made up a wonderful parody on "Sea Fever":

I must go down to the seas again, to the life of the canned sardine,
To the bilges stink and the wet clothes stink,
and the reek of the gasoline,
And all I ask is a stormy night, with the wild wind shrieking,
A sick child and a cross mate, and the damned decks le-e-e-eaking.

By the mid-1930s Gibson Island had become one of the leading yachting centers on the East Coast. As previously stated, the well-known British designer/author Uffa Fox called the 1937 New London–Gibson Island ocean race sponsored by the island's yacht squadron "the most important long-distance race in America." Many well-known yachts such as *Edlu, Highland Light, Kirawan, Mandoo II, Sirocco, Teragram,* and *Malabar XI* sailed in that race, and most were anchored in Gibson Island's harbor (or at Mountain Bar Point) for several days after the finish. Instant fame came to *Avanti,* the overall winner, and *Golden Eye,* the winner of Class B. Also seen in

An aerial view of Gibson Island's harbor in the late 1950s. Photograph by David Q. Scott.

the harbor and at the boathouse were some legendary sailors such as Rod Stephens, John Alden, Sherman Hoyt, and Gordon Raymond.

A lot of activity took place on the boats: drying sails, climbing aloft to check the rigging, and, of course, partying. Of the mast men going aloft there were, of course, Bally and Monk; Harold Smith, who, I was told, could climb hand-over-hand up a headstay and come down the backstay; and the ever-present Rod Stephens, who was called "Tarzan." Rod was sleeping at the Bailliere's house on the south shore of the harbor, and he told me years later that Bally's stepson Tinky Orrick had sneaked into his room to take a peek at him. After all, Rod was the famous sailor who had been given a ticker-tape parade in New York City.

The Stephens brothers aboard *Aweigh*—Olin in suit and tie, and the youthful-looking Rod seated in the right foreground. Others are *at helm,* Bally; *in apron,* Sam Thomsen; *seated left,* Andy Trippe; and Dick MacSherry. Courtesy Gibson Island Historical Society.

Known for his youthful appearance most of his life, Rod was awakened by Tinky exclaiming, "My God, he's only a kid!"

I was fascinated by the activities at the boathouse. Here, all the crews met to talk over the race; supplies were ordered and delivered, gear was given to Salty Marks for overhauling or repair, and a continuous party seemed to be going on. A buffet and bar was set up on the long boathouse porch. A notice was posted on the bulletin board: "Please instruct stewards not to throw garbage in the harbor." At times Bally and Monk, the Katzenjammer kids, would hose down the entire wooden porch floor (painted with a high-gloss paint), affix flypaper (sticky side up) to the bottoms of their feet, and proceed to "skate" up and down the entire length of the porch, while some of us kids manned the hose to keep the floor wet.

I don't mean to imply there was only carousing. Those sailors took their racing, cruising, and seamanship seriously, but they also knew how to relax and enjoy themselves. I'm not sure just how seriously a few of them took their navigation. Some were experts, of course, like George Mixture of the schooner *Teragram,* who wrote *the* yachtsman's book on celestial navigation. Others, however, were "naviguessors," as illustrated by the following story: Aboard one racer coming down the coast, the skipper asked his navigator where they were, and the latter answered without hesitation, "About ten miles off Atlantic City." The skipper raised his eyebrows and asked, "How do you know?" The navigator replied, "I just got a real good fix. I was bitten by a New

NEW LONDON – GIBSON ISLAND OCEAN RACE – 1937

CLASS A CRUISING

Entry List and Time Allowances

Code Letters	Name of Yacht	Length Overall	Owner	Rig	Sails	Net Rating Feet	Time Allowance Hrs.	Min.	Sec.
AB	Mandoo II	71.05	D. Spencer Berger	Yawl	M.	53.13	Scratch		
AC	Nordlys	71.05	Chester Bowles	Schr.	M.G.	52.01	0	24	47
AD	Highland Light	61.55	Dudley F. Wolfe	Sloop	M.	50.12	1	9	21
AW	Valkyrie	72.84	Cummins Catherwood	Ketch	M.	49.03	1	36	21
AE	Vixen III	58.55	John D. Archbold	Sloop	M.	48.19	1	56	27
AF	White Cloud	59.88	Geo. A. Whiting	Cutter	M.	47.41	2	17	22
AG	Elizabeth McCaw	62.65	Richard J. Reynolds	Yawl	M.	47.38	2	17	22
AK	Tradition	59.05	Dr.Frank A.Calderone	Schr.	G.G.	44.48	3	36	46
AN	Edlu	55.43	R. J. Schaefer	Yawl	M.	43.19	4	15	09
AO	Teragram	58.33	Geo. W. Mixter	Schr.	M.G.	42.38	4	39	28
AP	Spindrift	55.00	W.Wallace Lanahan	Cutter	M.	42.01	4	51	58
AQ	Sonny	53.40	Albert E. Peirce	Cutter	M.	40.60	5	37	01
AR	Alelnansr	57.16	Sayre M. Ramsdell	Ya					
AS	Avanti	55.56	Walter N.Rothschild	Ya					
AU	Vryling II	53.60	L. B. Dunham	Ya					
AV	Kirawan	53.00	Robert P. Baruch	Cu					
AX	Nam Sang	65.37	Dr.Philemon E. Truesdale	Ke					

Entry list and time allowances for class A in the 1937 New London–Gibson Island Race, with design sketches on the back by John G. Alden. Given to the author by Carl Alberg.

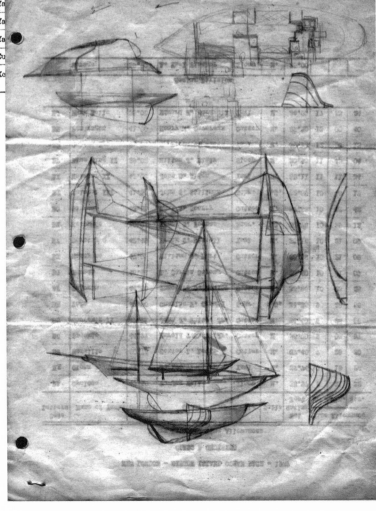

82

Jersey mosquito, and I saw a condom floating in the water."

The 1937 New London–Gibson Island Race marked an end to Gibson Island's preeminence as an ocean racing club, as the Annapolis Yacht Club took over running the event two years later. It made sense for the race, with its many off-the-Bay entries, to finish at a town such as Annapolis, because Gibson Island was and still is a private community with no commercial establishments. That is not to say that Gibson Island did not continue on for a great many years as a major yachting center. It sponsored or cosponsored several minor ocean races such as the Cape May and Lightship races, and ran four important events sanctioned by the CBYRA: the Rhode River, Swan Point–Love Point, Poplar Island, and Cedar Point races. It also hosted two popular annual yachting parties including what some sailors called the Rhode River "rendezbooze." Soon after the death of J. Rulon Miller in 1931, the Gibson Island Club inaugurated the annual Miller Series—still the premiere event for Stars on the Chesapeake. In 1951 the club hosted the Star Internationals and in 1990 the J/22 World Championship Regatta. Despite Gibson Island's continuing participation in modern yachting, however, the 1930s are the standout years for yachting at the island. For me those are the years most rich in memories that I'll cherish forever.

CHAPTER FOUR

NATIVE BOATS MAKE GOOD

Sailing yachts identified with the Chesapeake Bay can be grouped into two broad categories: native and resident yachts. When I say "native" I mean yachts that are designed by Chesapeake designers. Very often, but not always, these craft also have been built locally. Resident yachts, presented in the next two chapters, are those designed by off-the-Bay designers but owned by Chesapeake residents, sailors who live in tidewater Maryland or Virginia or at least have spent considerable time sailing, cruising, or racing on the Chesapeake.

Workboat yachts: Many of the early native yachts were workboats converted to yachts or pleasure craft having lines similar to workboats. These craft were seldom designed by naval architects, as is the case with most modern yachts; instead, they were derived from a carved model and built by eye or, in the early vernacular, by "rack of eye." A skillful builder could use his experience and memory to interpret the model without elaborate plans and lofting. Shapes were often derived from bending planks around midship section molds.

In the late 1920s my father owned an old skipjack yacht named *Pelican*. Howard Chapelle used to claim that many workboats could outsail yachts. There are a number of stories about their sailing abilities, one example being J. T. Rothrock's description of sailing alongside a working bugeye in 1883.[1] He wrote, "We were laboring; she was moving along without effort, going not only faster, but working more to the windward." Well, *Pelican* was not of this ilk. I remember Dad talking about beating down the Bay against a strong flood tide and a fresh southerly wind. From the western shore he took a long tack across the Bay to the Eastern Shore, then tacked again and, working upwind as best he could, returned to the exact same spot where he'd originally come about. He hadn't gained a foot to windward.

Being a small child at that time, I have only faint recollections of *Pelican*. I do remember the musty smell of dry rot down below, and the rusty iron beds (rather than built-in bunks). She leaked like a sieve, and Dad would sleep with one arm hanging down from his bed so that the rising bilge water would awaken him when it reached his hand. He then got up to pump and cuss. *Pelican*'s keelson was riddled with wormholes. Dad used to say that when he stomped his foot on it, water would squirt up from the vermiculated wood. He finally managed to unload the boat to a preacher, and after we got our Alden yawl *Kelpie*, he would marvel at how that preacher kept *Pelican* afloat. Was it prayer? One day he rowed over to examine the skipjack, and found that her new owner had installed an automatic electric bilge pump that was activated by a float switch, in much the same way as he had been activated by the wetting of his dangling hand.

Another skipjack yacht of my acquaintance was the one owned by my

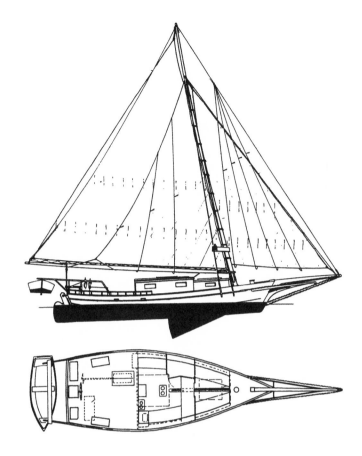

Roger Taylor's yacht, originally a working skipjack named *Sister* (then *Daisy B.*). Drawings by Samuel F. Manning, courtesy S. F. Manning and Roger Taylor.

friend Roger Taylor, the nautical publisher and author of four books entitled *Good Boats*. Originally she was named *Sister*, then *Daisy B.*, but Roger and his family simply called her *Skipjack*. She was 37 feet long on deck and had a generous beam of more than 14 feet with a stern deck broad enough to hold a set of lawn furniture including a chaise lounge. In 1968 I had a delightful sail on her and was impressed with the way she sailed under Roger's expert hand. She handled the choppy seas easily; she had a bit of weather helm but resisted yawing, and she had almost the initial stability of a multihull. When returning to her home berth, I was amazed at how fast Roger approached the dock, but at the last moment before landing he used the centerboard as a brake. The bottom of the board dropped into the soft mud and brought the heavy boat to a well-timed stop. Being a former oyster dredger with a lot of sail area, she had great power under sail. Roger once towed a broken-down 25-foot powerboat to her home dock some distance up the South River at a speed of about four knots without ever starting the skipjack's engine.

A well-known pungy conversion that cruised the Bay extensively for many years was *Kessie C. Price.* An evolutionary relative of the Baltimore clipper, the pungy model is one of the most handsome of workboats. With its fine lines, low freeboard, rakish schooner rig, and usual color scheme of pink and watermelon

The pungy yacht *Kessie C. Price,* a familiar sight on the Bay from the late 1920s until well after World War II. Courtesy Frank Moorshead, Jr.

green, the early pungy made a striking appearance that seemed incongruous with some of the cargoes it often carried such as firewood or fertilizer. The 61-foot *Kessie C. Price,* designed and built by Captain Rome Price at Rock Creek, Maryland, in 1888, was known as a "she" pungy, that is to say she had a centerboard and drew only 5 feet with the board up. A workboat until 1915, she was then bought by a Belgian lady and converted to a yacht. A long low cabin trunk with nine portlights on each side was added by the Smith and Williams yard at Salisbury. Later a huge icebox that held 650 pounds of ice was installed.

After being taken to Florida, the pungy experienced a two-hundred-mile-an-hour hurricane in 1926. She dragged her anchors, but fortunately they hooked on a coral head, and *Price* survived. Following that experience she was brought back to the Chesapeake by Edward Teesdale, who made the passage outside along the coast. At times it was rough offshore. On one occasion the boat was swept and Teesdale washed overboard, but he was saved because he was tethered to the boat with a 75-foot line.[2]

In 1928 *Kessie C. Price* was bought by Frank Moorshead, Sr., and she was widely seen on the Bay for the next twenty-six years. With her shoal draft and roomy accommodations, she was a great boat for cruising the Chesapeake. According to Frank Moorshead, Jr., she was also a fine sailer. She had a three-bladed prop that would be devastating to the speed of a modern yacht, but the pungy was powerful enough to overcome its drag. I was told that in her working days she could drag two dredges and still make good progress to windward.[3]

Another pungy that was converted to a yacht was the 54-foot *Wave*, built in Accomac County, Virginia, in 1863. A number of detailed photographs of her are in M. V. Brewington's book *Chesapeake Bay, A Pictorial Maritime History*. She became a yacht in 1937 and was taken to the Great Lakes in the 1950s.

A workboat type that was often converted for yachting purposes was the bugeye. Over the years there were at least four bugeye yachts in Gibson Island's harbor alone. These were Sam Thomsen's *Applejack*, Abner Sayler's *Florence Northam*, Henry Baldwin's *Bee*, and the well-known *Brown, Smith, and Jones*, owned by Harry Ogden when she hailed from the island. Also, yachting journalist N. T. Kenney, the son of Nathaniel "Cap" Kenney, who founded Gibson Island's Junior Fleet, owned the bugeye yacht *Colonel R. Johnson Colton*.

Just after World War II, my father was pointing out *Florence Northam*, moored in Gibson Island's harbor, to Bill Leader, my English nephew, then a young boy on his first visit to America. Dad said, "Billy, there's a bugeye." Bill's eyes opened wide, and with a shocked look on his face he replied, "Oh, we're not allowed to use that word in England."

Descending from the log canoe by way of the brogan, the bugeye has been called by designer/historian Eric Steinlein "the most distinctive and perhaps the only purely American vessel."[4] The vast majority of bugeyes were double-enders with well-balanced hulls having

fine quarters, although a few had round sterns. I use the past tense, because hardly any authentic bugeyes are left today. The distinctive bugeye rig with three sharp-headed sails of similar size set on two well-raked masts is a cross between the schooner and ketch rig. It is easy for a small crew to handle and easy to reduce sail while maintaining balance in a blow.

The purpose of the pronounced mast rake is partly to allow use of the halyards to lift cargo or heavy gear; it also takes away the need for backstays, and minimizes leech rollover, thus lessening the need for battens. It is interesting, however, that some sailors from former times attributed the bugeye's windward ability to her mast rake, and today we are seeing increasing rake in many small racing class designs. This practice is in accordance with the "lift line theory," which predicts greater thrust from a sail when the lift line (the imaginary line connecting all centers of lift from head to foot) is vertical rather than leaning forward, as would be the case for a mast with no rake. Another argument for rake was made by L.F. Herreshoff when he wrote, "It has been the common knowledge of sailor men for centuries that a lifting sail (as they used to call it) is much more efficient than a depressing sail."[5]

Two of the best known and fastest bugeye yachts were *Bee*, formerly *Carrie Moore*, built by Harry Skinner in Baltimore in 1893, and *Brown, Smith, and Jones*, built the following year by George Johnson in Cambridge, Maryland. The latter was never an oyster dredger but was built for the Maryland Oyster Navy, a

The famous bugeye yacht *Brown, Smith, and Jones*. Courtesy Chesapeake Bay Maritime Museum, Frank Moorshead Collection.

policing agency for the Chesapeake. In the words of yachting journalist Peter Chambliss, "Of necessity she (the *Brown, Smith, and Jones*) had to be a fast boat in order to cope with the oyster pirates and craft that broke the oyster laws. It was said at the time she was built nothing could outsail her."[6] At least one person, however, disagreed, and that was Henry Baldwin, a member of both the Gibson Island and Hampton Yacht Clubs, who owned *Bee*. To my knowledge, Henry was the only owner of a bugeye yacht who raced in CBYRA events, and he knew damn well that his *Bee* could beat *Brown, Smith, and Jones* even though the latter was four feet longer than his 66-foot craft. A match race took place in 1935 after Baldwin issued a formal written challenge to Linton Rigg who owned *Brown, Smith, and Jones* at the time. Incidentally, the name of the challenged boat was not a collection of common appellations but the specific names of three prominent

Maryland politicians. Under the later ownership of Harry Ogden, the tender of *Brown, Smith, and Jones* was named *Tom, Dick, and Harry*.

Much publicity and hoopla came forth before the race. It was billed as "the race of the century," and most of the best, most colorful sailors were invited to crew. They included the mischievous pair John "Monk" Foster and Lawrence "Bally" Bailliere; George Whiting, owner of the high-tech *White Cloud;* Sam Thomsen, owner of the bugeye *Applejack;* C. T. Williams, regular ocean-racing crew for Bill McMillan; naval architect Bob Henry; Dick Randall, a prominent 8-meter skipper; Alf Loomis, yachting writer and owner of *Hot Spur;* Herbert Stone, the editor of *Yachting* magazine; Bunny Rigg, Linton's brother and later the editor of the *Skipper* magazine; designer/builder Lowndes Johnson; and other stars. I understand that America's Cup skipper Sherman Hoyt was asked to be a helmsman. There was to be no restriction on sails and Caulk Kemp, a prominent log canoe racer, was asked to be the expert on jackyard topsails. Dad was asked to be the expert on mizzen staysails (he was partial to yawls and called himself a "mizzenthrope"). Many crewmembers brought along sails. They came from 8-meters, log canoes, *Hot Spur,* and even the America's Cup defender *Resolute.*

The race course was a little over fifty miles from Baltimore Light to the Sharps Island buoy off the mouth of the Choptank River and return. After a noisy start amid a number of spectator boats, the two bugeyes raced down the Bay on a broad reach, neck-and-neck before a brisk October nor'wester. All kinds of sail combinations were tried including topsails, staysails, and spinnakers on each mast. On *Bee,* Bally, who once made the remark that there was nothing he'd rather do than break up another person's boat, was equipped with a brace and bit. When he thought a sheet lead could be improved, he simply bored a hole in the rail so a new lead block could be installed.

Both boats were blacked out (illegally) for secrecy after dark. They arrived at the turning mark together and, according to one account, there was a collision. *Brown, Smith, and Jones* had a harpoon extended beyond her bowsprit, and some say that it swept over the stern of *Bee,* forcing the helmsman from his station. Soon afterward, *Bee* (or both boats) struck a spar buoy, possibly the one marking a wreck on submerged Sharps Island, and it became entangled

between the bobstays and bowsprit shrouds. This allowed *Brown, Smith, and Jones* to pull ahead and hold her lead on the long beat home. She finished about twenty minutes ahead of her rival. Needless to say, after the exhausted crews had rested, there was a lively party and an outrageous awards ceremony.

In 1958, *Brown, Smith, and Jones* sank at her mooring in Woods Hole. She was raised by the novel method of spreading abundant manure around the sunken boat. As pumps pulled water out of the boat the manure was sucked into her open seams and clogged them. The method was successful, and that's no bull.

Another early bugeye-rigged yacht acquired a modest degree of fame as a result of being featured in a book called *The Life Worth Living* by Thomas Dixon, Jr., published in 1905. Her name was *Dixie,* and she was designed or at least "planned" by her owner Dixon, who lived in tidewater Virginia. Her sailing abilities were aptly described by Captain Isdell, a "sea dog" who delivered the 80-foot *Dixie* to her owner from her builder's yard at Pocomoke, Maryland, in 1897. When asked how she sailed, Captain Isdell replied with a grin, "She's a jim-dandy! She goes through the water slicker'n a eel. She stands up in a blow and leaves a white streak behind her as far as you can see."

Dixie was a shoal-draft centerboarder used not only for cruising and living aboard for extensive periods but also for waterfowl hunting. She was used even in the dead of winter, and Dixon describes one experience in February when the

The yacht *Dixie* with her bugeye rig. From *The Life Worth Living* by Thomas Dixon, Jr., Doubleday, Page & Co. (1905).

temperature dropped to nine degrees below zero while he was far from home on a hunting expedition. *Dixie* was frozen-in for fifteen days, forcing her crew to tear out shelves and break up decoys for firewood. Dixon made some interesting observations regarding the ecology of the Bay in those days. He said that the crabs and clams in front of his home were so plentiful that they were used to fatten the pigs, and at times there were enough waterfowl to darken the sky like great storm clouds.

Replicas: Mention should be made of the historic replica vessels created by Chesapeake builders and architects. Of course, the original vessels were not plea-

sure craft, but many of the replicas might be considered yachts according to one definition in *The Sailing Dictionary* by Joachim Schult,[7] which states that a vessel can be a yacht when "used for state occasions and representation." The earliest such Chesapeake craft are the reconstructions of the Elizabethan ships—*Discovery, Susan Constant,* and *Godspeed*—that brought settlers to the first permanent English colony at Jamestown, Virginia, in 1607. Replicas were first built in 1957 by the Curtis-Dunn yard at Norfolk for exhibition at the Jamestown Festival Park. Their plans, drawn by naval architect/historian Robert Fee, were partly derived from a well-researched painting

90

of the three vessels done by marine artist Griffith B. Coale. Intended for display, the vessels could sail but rarely did. Beginning in 1982, new replicas of the Jamestown fleet were built to somewhat higher safety and performance requirements. One of these ships, *Godspeed*, based on the earlier reproduction but redesigned by Duncan Stewart and William Boze and built by Virginian Carl Pederson, actually sailed from England to Virginia in 1985, duplicating the course followed on the original voyage.

A similar type of replica is *Maryland Dove*, a facsimile of *Dove*—one of two ships that brought colonists to the first Maryland settlement in 1634. Designed by William A. Baker of Hingham, Massachusetts, she was built by one of the Eastern Shore's master boatbuilders, James Richardson, who usually worked by "rack of eye." *Maryland Dove* is on display at St. Mary's City where the original vessel landed. Although primarily a museum vessel, she is also used in a sail training program.

More modern replicas include the recreation of a nineteenth-century pungy, *Lady Maryland,* designed by Annapolitan Thomas Gillmer, a noted marine historian, designer, and former professor at the U.S. Naval Academy. Although highly authentic down to her pink and green color scheme, she was modified to meet Coast

A detailed pencil study of the *Godspeed*, *Susan Constant*, and *Discovery* for an oil painting by Griffith B. Coale from which the 1957 replica vessels were largely derived. Courtesy The Mariners' Museum, Newport News, Virginia.

Guard requirements for a school vessel. Owned by the Living Classrooms Foundation of Baltimore, she is used as part of a training and education program for youngsters from Baltimore's inner-city and other Chesapeake areas.

Two windjammer cruise boats, sometimes called "dude cruisers," are *Mystic Whaler* and *Mystic Clipper,* the former based on a whaling vessel and the latter a clipper-type privateer. They were designed in Silver Spring, Maryland, by the prolific yacht designer Charles Wittholz, who also designed *Providence,* a reproduction of the first authorized ship of the Continental Navy and first combat command of John Paul Jones.

In 1938 the world-famous Howard Chapelle—sailing-vessel historian, author, and naval architect—designed a handsome topsail schooner based on the eighteenth-century American-built British-owned brig named *Swift.* The schooner was built for his own use by William A. Robinson, skipper of the Alden ketch *Svaap,* said to be the first yacht to circumnavigate the world with a two-man crew. Later *Swift* was owned by actor James Cagney and appeared in several Hollywood movies. Chapelle spent many years on the Chesapeake, first living in Cambridge, Maryland, and then in Washington, D.C., where he was a curator at the Smithsonian Institution. He died in 1975, and his ashes were sprinkled on the Little Choptank River.

By far the most widely known replica vessels are the two facsimiles of Baltimore clippers named *Pride of Baltimore,* designed by Tom Gillmer. They have

been goodwill ambassadors for the port of Baltimore and have graced many a foreign port with their rakish beauty. The original Baltimore clippers were engaged in trades such as privateering and slavery that demanded speed and windward ability, but these abilities were not gained without some sacrifice to other qualities including safety. With their lofty rigs, low freeboard, sharp lines, open hulls (lacking watertight bulkheads), and low stability ranges (compared with conservative yachts), the clipper schooners were somewhat vulnerable to the worst kind of weather at sea, and a number of them came to grief. In the words of Melbourne Smith (builder, artist, and authority on historic vessels) Baltimore clippers were "rather dangerous to sail." Captain Francis Bowker of Mystic Seaport Museum remarked that Baltimore clippers "were designed for speed rather than safety" and added, "I have a feeling that a great many of those ships capsized."[8] Unfortunately, much of the publicity gained by the first *Pride of Baltimore* resulted from her tragic sinking with loss of life not far north of St. Thomas, Virgin Islands, in 1986.

On that unhappy occasion, *Pride* was struck by a microburst, the weather phenomenon formerly called a white squall. At the time, she was on a beam-reach under a double-reefed mainsail and forestaysail. The wind force was estimated at about seventy knots. Her forty-two-year-old captain, Armin Elsaesser, was at the helm, and he tried to bear off in order to turn the schooner's stern to the wind. Why he did this has never been satisfac-

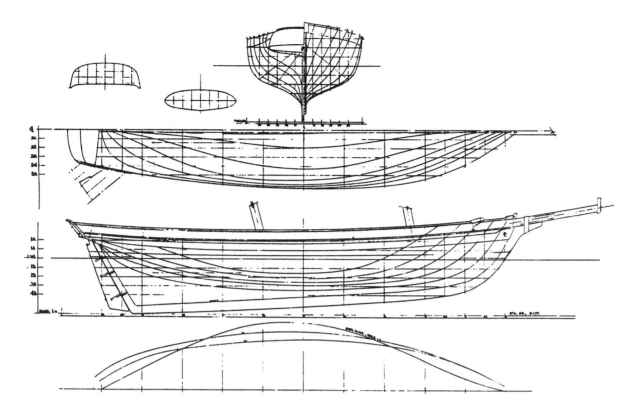

Lines plan of *Pride of Baltimore II*, designed by Thomas C. Gillmer. Courtesy Thomas C. Gillmer.

torily explained despite a thorough Coast Guard investigation. Perhaps he was unable to luff up (the normal action in such a situation) because the staysail sheet was under water and could not be released, and the long main boom was dragging in the water. At any rate, the boat would not answer her helm and could not be headed downwind. In "slow motion" *Pride* lay over until her masts were in the water. She was held down, and as water flowed into the open companionway hatch, she downflooded and sank, drowning the captain and three of the crew. The remaining crewmembers were rescued after spending four and a half miserable days in a life raft. One happy note resulted when two of the

crew—a man and woman—found themselves floating together, and the man said, "Sugar, if we ever get out of this alive, you and I are getting married." They did survive and married soon after their rescue.

At the time there was talk that no vessel could survive such a severe microburst. Had I believed that, I never would have thought about going to sea, because such blows are not uncommon. I am convinced that if *Pride* could have been turned into or away from the wind and her companionway hatch could have been closed, or if she had been fitted with watertight compartments, she would have survived. A former *Pride* captain who doesn't want his name mentioned told me that under the same

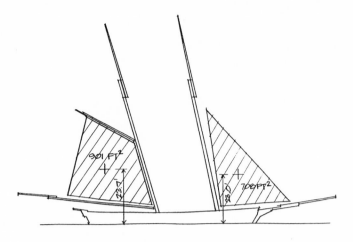

Reduced sails carried by *Pride of Baltimore* at the time of her sinking, drawn by her designer, Tom Gillmer. Courtesy Thomas C. Gillmer.

conditions, he would have used a different sail combination, and in fact he once argued the subject with Captain Elsaesser. The former captain said he would have carried a reefed foresail with the forestaysail rather than the double-reefed

main. With this combination the schooner would have been more maneuverable, and the main boom would not have dragged in the sea. Of course, the strategy is debatable, and Elsaesser was the one who was there. Still, I think it is important not to have a fatalistic attitude, but rather to analyze such accidents and plan ways to avoid them in the future.

Part of the problem with the first *Pride* was that the committee responsible for her existence insisted on almost complete historical correctness, and, although the committee probably didn't fully realize it, some aspects of authenticity came at the expense of certain safety features. As Tom Gillmer wrote, "It was perhaps one element of authenticity in her design—specifically, her open space below deck—that resulted in her rapid flooding and loss."[9]

Pride of Baltimore II sailing in a fresh breeze under mainsail, forestaysail, and inner jib.

CHESAPEAKE SAILS

A year after the accident, a new *Pride* was built, and this vessel was improved from a safety standpoint. Her range of stability was increased from 87.7 degrees to 94 degrees, and more importantly she was given six watertight bulkheads. I presume that her downflood vulnerability was also minimized. She has carried on the tradition of the first *Pride* in visiting many foreign ports and has been an outstanding success, a pride not only of Baltimore but of all Chesapeake residents.

Hotspur: An admirer of the lovely green cutter *Hotspur* once remarked: "Having *Hotspur* is like having a Stradivarius. You don't own her, you just take care of her for a while." For about forty years, her original caretaker was yachting writer Alfred Loomis, who wrote a book or two and a multitude of articles about racing and cruising aboard his beloved cutter. Although *Hotspur* spent most of her life in the waters north of the Chesapeake, I consider her at least partly a native yacht, because she spent almost a decade on the Bay under the ownership of Alf Loomis and another long period after 1971 at Oxford, Maryland, when owned by William Eichbaum. Also, she was designed by a yacht broker/designer who was definitely associated with the Chesapeake, Linton Rigg, former owner of *Brown, Smith, and Jones* and a brother of Bunny Rigg.

An interesting story is connected with the origin of *Hotspur*. Linton Rigg and Alf Loomis were shipmates aboard the Alden schooner *Pinta* during the 1928 transatlantic race to Spain. In a letter to a friend, Rigg, who was the *Pinta*'s

skipper, wrote the following commentary about the race:

> I had selected a good crew, and when Paul Hammond commissioned Starling Burgess to design a boat to win that race, which was *Nina*, built at a cost of $75,000 (Jack Curtis had paid $10,000 for *Pinta*) we realized that our only chance to beat her was to drive like hell in any weather, which we did every minute day and night for 23 days. When we finally made our landfall on Spain *Nina* was way down on the horizon behind us. We had beaten her across the ocean. . . . Then the wind died and came out dead ahead. The best an Alden schooner, gaff rigged, could make on the wind in that light going, was six points, while *Nina* was doing four and a half. It almost broke our hearts to see *Nina* go by us to windward almost within sight of the finish.[10]

Nina won that race, but Alf Loomis, *Pinta*'s navigator, had been planning a boat of his own and was determined not to have his heart broken again. He asked Linton Rigg to design a small oceangoing cutter, and both men agreed that the boat should be close-winded. So *Hotspur* was conceived on *Pinta* and born the following year in the yard of Casey Baldwin at Baddeck, Nova Scotia. Beautifully built with mahogany planking, the finished cutter measured 32 feet, 4 inches overall with a beam of 8 feet, 10 inches and draft of 5 feet, 6 inches. Originally, she had a bowsprit and could carry three headsails, but in 1947 her foretriangle was simplified by Rod Stephens, who removed the bowsprit and gave her a single headsail.

I can attest to the fact that *Hotspur* was close-winded, because the day before the

Cedar Point Race in 1940, Alf asked to have a tune-up brush with our *Kelpie.* Dad agreed and the two boats sailed against each other head-to-head in a moderate southerly breeze. Going to windward with a triple head rig, which seemed to epitomize Dr. Manfred Curry's "slot theory" (then in vogue), the cutter walked away from our yawl, out-footing us and pointing about five degrees higher. The Cedar Point Race turned out to be a reaching affair and *Kelpie* beat *Hotspur,* but there was no question that the Loomis boat was weatherly.

Hotspur was used primarily for cruising, and she did so far and wide, from the Maine coast to the Aegean Sea. But she was also raced extensively, and Alf

Loomis picked up his share of the silver. Although he wrote about his own mistakes when they resulted in groundings or the loss of races, he never had a bad word to say about *Hotspur;* and certainly, she never came close to breaking his heart on a beat to windward.

White Cap II: Preceding chapters of this book have often referred to Lowndes Johnson. To reiterate briefly, he was a Miles River neighbor of my father. With his brother Graham, he won the Star Internationals in 1929; he designed the popular Comet, and was a master boatbuilder of Stars and other small craft. I was a great admirer of Lowndes, and in fact, dedicated one of

Plans of *Hotspur,* designed by Linton Rigg. From *"Hotspur's" Cruise in the Aegean,* published by Jonathan Cape & Harrison Smith, Inc. (1931). Courtesy *Yachting* magazine.

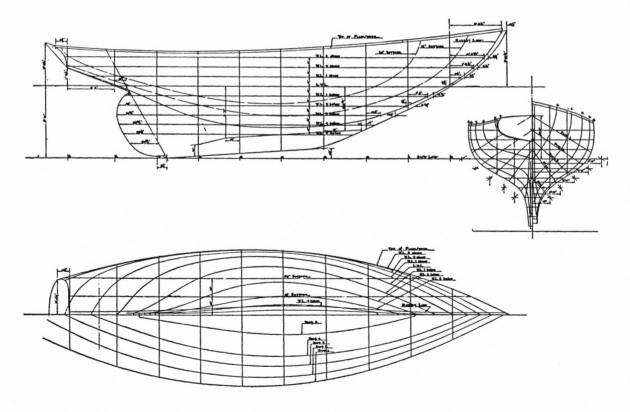

CHESAPEAKE SAILS

my books to him. A quiet, friendly man, almost excessively modest, Lowndes had a subtle sense of humor, and there was usually a twinkle in his eye. I remember his being told by someone who had visited Arnie Gay's yard at Annapolis that "Mr. Gay knows everything there is to know about boats." Lowndes didn't disagree, but he quietly chuckled and said, "Well, he must know a great deal." If ever there was a person who knew all about boats, it was Lowndes himself.

White Cap II was the 26-foot 6-inch ketch that Lowndes designed and built for himself in 1938 and sailed for twenty-three years. He had a tiny boatshop at his home called "the Harbor" on the Miles River, and I think *White Cap II* was the largest boat he ever built. She was a hard-chine, V-bottom type, not unlike a Seabird, but with a more graceful bow, an outboard rudder, and a shallower keel that housed a centerboard. She had a draft of only 2 feet, 7 inches with the board up, which made her ideal for gunkholing the Chesapeake. Her beam was 8 feet, 2 inches. There was space between the cabin trunk and mast for a pram to be stowed athwartships; the pram, named *Decoy,* was also designed and built by Lowndes. The rig was extended longitudinally with a boomkin and a bowsprit that was also useful for catting a fisherman's anchor. The main mast was made the size of a Star's so that Lowndes could use his collection of Star mainsails, some of which were beautifully shaped. Her sail plan was reduced in 1959 for easier sail-handling as Lowndes and his mate Clara grew older.

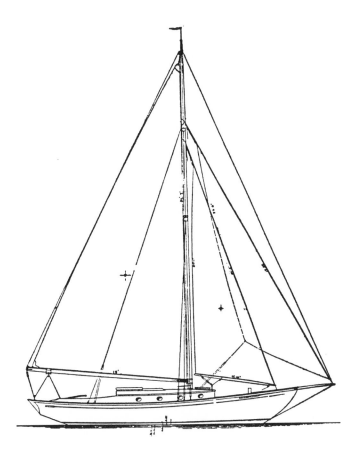

Above : Sail plan of *Hotspur.* Courtesy *Yachting* magazine.

Below: White Cap II at Annapolis Boatworks in 1965. Courtesy Chesapeake Bay Maritime Museum, Ernest Tucker Collection.

It was a privilege cruising in company with *White Cap II* and racing against her in our Cruisken in 1952 during a Gibson Island Cruise Week. With her well-balanced rig and self-tending jib, the ketch was easily handled by Lowndes, often on deck alone while Clara rested below. The two were no spring chickens at that time. I admired their seamanship in the way they handled the boat during a couple of fierce squalls and also how they anchored in shallow water with always enough swinging room even in the most crowded harbor.

In 1974 I received a letter from Robert Brennan from Middle River,[11] who was then the owner of *White Cap II*. He was lavish in his praise of the boat, saying that she would be his last sailboat because he had at last found the right one. Many a time he had been hailed by passing boats with favorable comments and sometimes remarks to the effect that Lowndes Johnson, then deceased, would

Lowndes Johnson sculling out to *White Cap II*. Courtesy Chesapeake Bay Maritime Museum, Ernest Tucker Collection.

be proud to know his creation was still plying the waters he sailed for more than seventy years and loved so well.

Chesapeake Tancookers: It has been suggested that the roots of the shapely double-ender developed in the 1800s at Tancook Island, Nova Scotia, and known as the Tancook whaler may go back as far as the Viking longboats that visited that area long before Columbus "discovered" America. Philip Rhodes called those vessels "gorgeous and technically correct."[12] Two distinctive offshoots of the design were developed on the Chesapeake by two masterful builders: Ralph Wiley on the Eastern Shore of Maryland and Peter Van Dine on the western shore.

Ralph Wiley settled in Oxford in the late 1920s and soon opened his own boatshop. He was an innovative designer as well as an expert builder. A talented sailor, his prowess on the race course as well as his knowledge of boats and avuncular personality earned him the title "sage of Oxford." Mostly, Wiley built sailboats, including his self-designed 16-foot Scrappy Cat that became a particularly popular one-design class in the Tred Avon/Choptank River area. But he became especially well known for his motorsailers that could really sail. At least one, *Quicksilver*, was even raced successfully. She had a lead centerboard trunk, which Ralph rightfully claimed was wormproof, but it also was useful as the kind of ballast that would not affect the boat's rating under the CCA rule extant at the time.

In the early 1930s Ralph became impressed with the Tancook whaler when one of them, sailed by a single man wearing a derby hat and smoking a corncob pipe, easily outran the larger schooner on which Wiley was racing during a New York Yacht Club cruise.[13] Wiley designed his own version of a racing-cruising Tancooker and built her for his own use in 1940. Named *Mocking Bird,* she measured 31 feet, 6 inches overall and 24 feet on the waterline. She had an 8-foot beam and a 4-foot 6-inch draft. Unlike the original whaler, she had outside ballast, greater freeboard, a raised deck cabin, and a deeper keel with no centerboard. She had a number of Wiley innovations including a slide on a track used at the tack end of the staysail boom to adjust the staysail camber, a novel folding boom crutch, an unusual swivel fitting on the rudder head for the attachment of the permanent backstay, and dual companionway ladders with the treads running fore-and-aft rather than athwartships. Cutter-rigged with a self-tending staysail and roller-furling genoa, she carried 400 square feet of sail. There was no standing headroom below, but a large sliding hatch provided "the sky is the limit" headroom. She was a smart sailer that could easily cut through a moderate Chesapeake chop, and she was unusually adept at self-steering.

Wiley built two sisters to *Mocking Bird* and two larger sisters, the most famous of which is *Fox,* the boat he raced extensively and quite successfully on the Chesapeake, winning High Points in Class C in 1953. The 38-foot *Fox* was a striking-looking boat with her shapely double-ended hull, fine ends, pronounced sheer, and ma-

Mocking Bird beating to windward in a fresh wind. Courtesy Chesapeake Bay Maritime Museum, Fred Thomas Collection.

hogany topsides finished bright. In appearance she was a marked contrast to all her competitors. She was outstanding in light air, and part of her success was due to Ralph's sailing ability. In racing against him I learned a valuable lesson about light-air sailing: when you spot a patch of wind on the water, head for it even when it's far from the rhumb line; don't wait for the puff to come to you. I guess I have the unique distinction of twice being protested by Wiley for not

Ralph Wiley's *Fox* becalmed. Courtesy Chesapeake Bay Maritime Museum, Herman Hollerith, Jr., Collection.

observing marks when we were sailing different courses in different classes. At least he knew we were out there.

The western shore Tancookers built by Peter Van Dine came later and their hulls were made of fiberglass. Peter is an Annapolitan who built airplanes, but prior to that, he turned out exquisite boats of his own design based on traditional models. Among the craft he has designed and built are Crotch Island pinkies and Banks-type schooners. He also designed the Classic 31, a conventional racing cruiser with conservative classic lines. I had the pleasure of visiting his boatshop in 1978 in Owings, Maryland, and was impressed with his concept of building tasteful traditional boats using modern fiberglass techniques that were truly high-tech at the time.

The Van Dine Tancooker differs from the Wiley model in having a trunk-type cabin, a schooner rig, less freeboard, and a shallower keel with centerboard. The design was produced in two different sizes: overall length of 25 feet, 6 inches or 35 feet, 4 inches. The smaller model could be made with an open cockpit and small cabin trunk or a self-bailing cockpit well and larger cabin trunk. I prefer the latter arrangement for safety offshore even though there is considerably less room in the cockpit. The small model has a beam of 6 feet, 4 inches, a draft of 2 feet, 10 inches, and carries 301 square feet of sail.

In 1981 I had the opportunity to sail on Roger Taylor's *Nimbus,* a 25-foot open-cockpit Van Dine Tancooker, at Camden, Maine. It was a delightful sail and a thrill to see how the lovely little vessel would slice through the seas with her two gaff-headed sails drawing to perfection while the sharp-ended hull left behind a clean smooth wake. According to

CHESAPEAKE SAILS

Ian Smith's *Ca Va*, a Peter Van Dine 25-foot Tancook schooner. Courtesy Ian Smith.

Peter Van Dine, the centerboard is not needed except when beating in light air, but I noticed we had a slightly slack helm when the board was housed. The schooner rig is usually complicated, and, of course, it is not as close-winded as a single-masted rig, but *Nimbus* had a self-tending jib and the rig was not hard to handle. It offered a variety of sail combinations for all kinds of weather; there was even a club-headed fisherman staysail to have fun with in light air. I'm afraid I disgraced myself when getting underway as I disconnected the jib's downhaul, but Roger made no comment. Now I know the value of a downhaul and often rig it when I'm singlehanding my Cape Dory Typhoon, as it enables me to lower the jib without going forward.

One thing that made me slightly anxious on *Nimbus* was being so close to the water in the open cockpit when the lee rail was almost awash, but because of her generous ballast displacement ratio of 44 percent and the low center of effort of her rig, the boat heels only so far and spills her wind before water floods the cockpit. Nevertheless, it is always pru-

Miller Sherwood's Owens cutter *Rubicon,* four-time Labrot Trophy winner. Courtesy Chesapeake Bay Maritime Museum.

dent to shorten sail in rough seas when wave tops could slosh into the cockpit.

After the centerboard is properly adjusted and the sails trimmed just right, the Van Dine creation shares the self-steering characteristics of the Wiley boats. This is a rare quality in a contemporary yacht, at least in the fin-keel type, and I think most would agree that the modern yacht cannot compare to the Chesapeake Tancookers aesthetically.

The Owens cutter: One of the most famous Chesapeake racing cruiser designs is the Owens cutter, a creation of the Owens Yacht Company of Dundalk in Baltimore, Maryland. The cutter had an overall length of 40 feet, 6 inches and a waterline length of 28 feet. The beam measured 10 feet, 6 inches and draft, 5 feet, 10 inches. From the late 1940s and continuing past the decade of the 1950s, this boat dominated racing not only on the Bay, but also in many other locations throughout the nation. For instance, *Marlin* and *Barb* were "boats of the year" on the Great Lakes, *Dolphia* and *Carousel* were consistent winners in San Diego, California, and *Departure* and *Finn MacCumhaill* were prominent in New England waters. Winning boats on the Chesapeake included *Sashay* and *Fandango,* sailed by the Owens brothers of the Owens Yacht Company; Charles Stein's *Snallygaster,* originally *Rigadoon* (owned by the William Labrots) and then *Babe* (owned by Arnold Gay); Lawrence Dinning's *Teetotaler;* Marion Davis's *Bay Wolf,* Charles Dell's *Trig,* formerly *Fandango;* Miller Sherwood's *Rubicon,* fleet High Point winner four times; and

Morton "Sunny" Gibbons-Neff's *Prim*. The latter was completely redesigned by Sunny himself and is discussed later in this chapter.

Run by three brothers, the Owens Company was noted for its powerboat production, but all the brothers were avid sailors, especially Norman, the director of engineering and a pioneer in the mass production of boats. Norman wrote me that after racing an unusual self-designed Chesapeake 20, an R-boat, and an 8-meter, the brothers acquired their first racing cruiser, a New York 32 that they raced with considerable success during World War II. He described one Poplar Island Race when he and his crew overslept in Gibson Island's harbor and were awakened by the sound of committee-boat guns firing. They hurriedly motored around the island and out to the starting line at Baltimore Light (a distance of nearly five miles), cut off the engine before starting, overtook the racing fleet that had started earlier, and won

the race. The only problem was that they were disqualified for having run the engine after the preparatory gun.

As the war was winding down, the Owens brothers were approached by two Gibson Island Yacht Squadron members to see if they would be interested in producing a stock racing cruiser for the Chesapeake. A Philip Rhodes design had been considered, but eventually an Owens design was chosen because it would lend itself to the company's mass-production methods. It is commonly believed that Ernest Tucker, then an employee at the Owens Company, designed the Owens cutter, but Norman and his brothers have assured me that this is not true, explaining that Tucker's small part in the project was that of a draftsman. I'll let Norman express himself:

. . . . The original hull lines were drawn on my drawing board as were all the powerboats. The next step in the development of the cutter was having the wood shop make a model off my lines. I think

Lines of the Owens cutter. Plans by Norman G. Owens, courtesy Norman G. Owens.

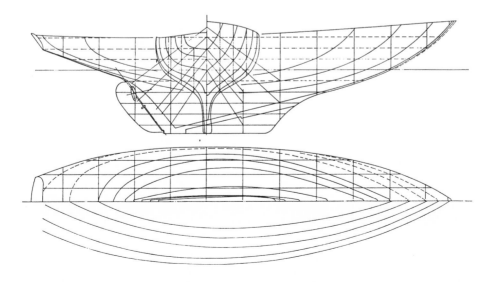

Roy Buckmaster and Bill Campbell laying down the lines of the Owens cutter. Courtesy Chesapeake Bay Maritime Museum, Ernest Tucker Collection.

most designers will claim that the rules develop the boat and I knew the current CCA rule was vulnerable for exploitation. We got a big break having a low B.D. [ballast-displacement] ratio which I took advantage of. I selected displacement that was a little lighter than the average boat because of the success I had sailing the New York 32. I developed a midship section that was quite similar. I was also very impressed with the sailing qualities of the 30 square meter. I extended the rest of the lines very much like the 30 square meter. To get a break on length, I foreshortened the bow and stern to get a longer sailing waterline for a reduced measured length. I reduced the wetted surface of the hull by putting the rudder well under

the hull of the boat. Shortening the length and to get the ballast low necessitated having a bulbous contour on the ballast.

After the hull model was completed, to build the tooling to make the boats, it was necessary to lay the boat out full size. To do this required table offsets. This job of transposing the hull lines from the model was assigned to Ernest Tucker. Any interpretation different from the model, I can assure you, was made by me. Also, all variation from the hull lines to the full size drafting was made by me. The full size work was done by a technician in our employment by the name of Herman Tegler. He made the last modifications, all of which I approved. . .[14]

While tooling for mass production was being made at the Owens loft, offsets were sent to M. M. Davis at Solomons Island, Maryland, to build the first five cutters. These boats were built from the keel up in the conventional manner. After the Owens Company took over the building, it used semiassembly line methods which the company termed "Duraform" construction. Boats were built upside-down from the deck up to the keel using a number of jigs. In Norman's words, "There were about 3500 pieces in the Cutter, each one requiring a pattern and a processing write up for manufacturing that part. After the deck was built, including the cabin house and cockpit, this was turned upside down on a steel jig. Each frame for the boat was constructed on its own individual jig which included the interior parts, floor frame, and anything attached to that particular frame was on it when it was set up on the hull jig. Our keel consisted of a laminated structure and this required a jig."[15]

Despite having freeboard that seemed a bit too generous at the time, the cutter was very handsome with her pleasing sheer and attractive balanced overhangs. The high freeboard allowed a low cabin trunk with small, slim portlights, and of course, it helped to keep the lee rail above the water.

The first Owens cutter, owned by W. M. Deny and named *Den-E-Von,* was taken south in 1946 and attracted attention by winning the St. Petersburg–Havana Race. That same year the Owens plant began their Duraform construction, and the Baltimore operation produced forty-one cutters before the end of the decade, after which the Henry R. Hinckley Company took over building them. Most of the cutters had good racing records, but the Owens-built boats seemed to be exceptionally fast. They were a bit lighter, and according to Norman, had a slightly less bulbous keel. The Hinckley-built boats had almost a thousand pounds more ballast and slightly more sail area. Eventually, the Hinckley Company began producing the boat in fiberglass. Robert Coulson's famous *Finn MacCumhaill* was used as a plug for the mold, and after some modifications to the hull and appendages, the cutter became the Hinckley 41. Other fiberglass versions were the Borsaw 40 and the modified Allied 39.

Occasionally, I raced with Charlie Stein on his Owens cutter *Snallygaster,* originally owned by Bill and Peggy Labrot and later raced by Arnie Gay, who gave her an aluminum mast. One memo-

rable series for me was the 1967 Block Island Race Week, when *Snally* took on a lot of hot boats from New England. Charlie asked me to man the helm in one heavy-weather race, and handling her responsive tiller was a thrill. Later I sailed a Davis-built cutter, and was amazed at the difference in feel and speed between her and *Snally.* Of course, much of the difference was probably due to superior tuning and sails on Charlie's boat. At any rate, we had a successful Block Island week beating all but one of eight Cal 40s in our class. Our most difficult moment came when a boat just ahead of us fouled the windward turning mark and we snagged the anchor line, dragging the mark to our hull. We were protested but exonerated on the grounds that our initial contact was with the underwater rode and the mark had previously been dragged off station.

Not long after the Owens Company merged with the Brunswick Corporation, the Owens brothers retired, but Norman continued to design boats independently. His specialty became 5.5-meter boats, some of which were built and raced in Europe. These sleek craft have been at the leading edge of design in meter-boat racing, and Norman had sufficient confidence in his design ideas to offer them to the New York Yacht Club for a future America's Cup boat. After moving to Texas he built a mahogany 5.5-meter at his home.

Another of Norman's ventures was the design and manufacture of a stock racing cruiser called the Nordstar 25, produced in fiberglass by the Nord

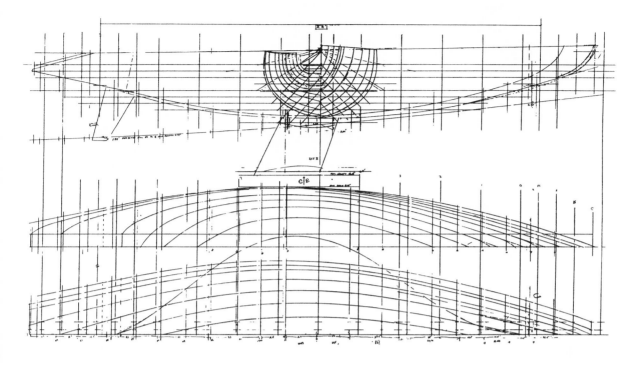

Plans of a 1985 5.5-meter boat by Norman G. Owens. Courtesy Norman G. Owens.

Corporation at Cambridge, Maryland. Although fast and attractive, in many ways anticipating the popular J/24, the Nordstar didn't catch on to any great extent. It couldn't compare in terms of success with the outstanding Owens cutter, which was so prominent on the Chesapeake racing scene and elsewhere for well over two decades.

Robert Henry and the Oxford 400: About the same time that the Owens cutters were introduced, the Oxford 400s came into being. In my opinion, these were the most attractive of the small, lo-

cally created racing cruisers. Designed by Robert G. Henry and soundly built of wood by the Oxford Boat Company, the overall length of the 400 was 28 feet, 10 inches; beam was 8 feet, 4 inches; and draft, 4 feet, 6 inches. Her class name was derived from the fact that she carried 400 square feet of sail. She had a saucy, seagoing look with her bold sheer, jaunty mast rake, and distinctive cabin trunk. Rather than the usual long deck trunk seen on most boats of her size, she had a short, narrow doghouse that allowed generous deck space as well as the extra strength afforded by full length deck beams in way of (near) the mast. A bridge deck at the forward end of the cockpit not only added strength but helped ensure against downflooding. A unique feature for such a small boat was a booby hatch on the

Facing page: Charlie Stein's Owens cutter *Snallygaster* during the 1967 Block Island Race Week with the author at the helm. Photograph by Morris Rosenfeld. © Mystic Seaport, Rosenfeld Collection, Mystic, Connecticut.

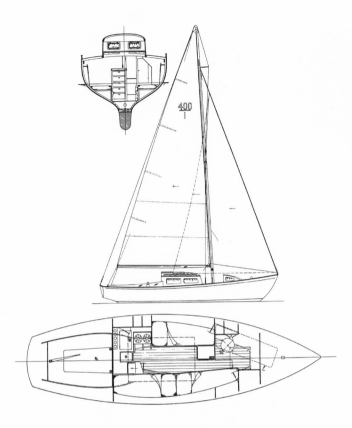

Plans of the Oxford 400, designed by Robert Henry. Courtesy Sally Henry Willis.

foredeck. This was not only distinctive looking, but it also afforded some headroom below, admitted light through its side portlights in rainy weather, and could be reversed to act as a wind scoop when at anchor in fair weather. The first 400 was owned by Henry himself, and he named her *Band Wagon*, hoping, I suppose, that many sailors would jump on it. She was later owned by my good friend George Blome.

A noted design critic as well as naval architect, Bob Henry wrote a most interesting design column for the *Skipper* magazine. He was always friendly and willing to answer my questions, and there was no one I respected more for

knowledge of boat engineering, design, and behavior. Of the few prizes I've been lucky enough to win, one that means the most to me is the "Robert Goldsborough Henry, Jr., Memorial Trophy" awarded by the Chesapeake Station of the CCA, and won with the help of my daughter and her fiancé.

Earning a B.S. degree in Naval Architecture and Marine Engineering from Massachusetts Institute of Technology in 1934, Bob liked to joke about his graduation present. A wealthy classmate was given a yacht, but Bob was presented with a pair of socks. After graduation he went to work for the prestigious yacht design firm of Sparkman and Stephens, where he did pioneering work on aluminum masts and winches and helped design some celebrated sailing yachts. During World War II, he ran the Oxford Boatyard, which earned a number of excellence awards for its defense production, and here is where he produced the Oxford 400 at the end of the war. Later he was head of the Boats and Small Craft section of the Navy Department but found time to design some outstanding racing cruisers such as the International 500s and 600s. One of the latter designs was a yawl named *Premise* that crossed the Atlantic at least four times and, according to Bob, was designed very close to the ideal "base" boat of the CCA Rule.

The Oxford 400 was not only an attractive, seaworthy boat, but was also an exceedingly smart sailer for her day. A

Facing page: A Henry-designed International 500. Courtesy Sally Henry Willis.

NATIVE BOATS MAKE GOOD

An Oxford 400 on a close reach showing her generous deck space. Courtesy Sally Henry Willis.

The first year I sailed a 400 was 1958, when I was invited by new owner Edward Hanrahan to pilot *Linda* from Annapolis to Gibson Island. This boat was well known, for she had been a successful racer and had been owned by the popular local yachting journalist, Charles Lucke. At the time Ed Hanrahan was not overly familiar with the pair of narrows leading from the Chesapeake into Gibson Island's harbor, and he wanted me to show him the way. Well, it so happened that Ed was in the advertising business, and one of his clients was an airline company. When I boarded *Linda,* she was loaded almost to the gunwales with a bevy of gorgeous airline hostesses. We had a delightful sail and when it came time to enter the narrows at the mouth of the Magothy River, an entrance I had successfully negotiated hundreds of times, I ran *Linda* hard aground on "Bally's Lump" (a shoal named after Lawrence Bailliere). Too much concentration on the feminine pulchritude, no doubt. Despite my damaged ego, however, it had been a great day, and the distractions were not sufficient to detract from my appreciation of the Oxford 400.

Tom Gillmer and the Seawind: In addition to being a designer of historic replica vessels, Thomas C. Gillmer of Annapolis, Maryland, has designed a number of attractive traditional yachts. Possessing a rare combination of architectural, engineering, writing, researching, and teaching skills, he also has the eye of an artist and is a talented draftsman. Many of his vessels, even some yachts, are fitted with transom or quarter

glowing write-up in *Yachting* (April 1948) declared that 400s "had been known to outrun *Highland Light* [a 69-foot cutter] in light airs and beat in a breeze with boats twice their size." The article went on to say that Bill Labrot had taken one out in a "prehurricane" blow under jib alone and beat to windward. Not bad for a boat only 22½ feet on the waterline.

CHESAPEAKE SAILS

decorations and carved stemheads or trailboards. I am particularly partial to his mermaid decorations. Whether decorated or not, however, most Gillmer boats of all sizes have a lot of character with their pronounced sheerlines, shapely traditional sterns, and lofty, able-looking bows. Having been a professor of naval architecture at the U.S. Naval Academy for twenty-seven years and Director of the Ship Hydrodynamics Laboratory at the academy, Tom has had great access to the Model Towing Basin there. It is safe to assume that his extensive work in model testing has greatly enhanced his understanding of hull behavior.

One of my favorite Gillmer designs is the Seawind 30 designed in 1960 and produced in fiberglass by the Allied Boat Company. A Seawind ketch named *Apogee* is said to be the first fiberglass boat to sail around the world. Her overall length is 30 feet, 6 inches; beam is 9 feet, 3 inches and draft, 4 feet, 4 inches. *Apogee* left Newport News, Virginia, in 1963 for her five-year circumnavigation, which followed the trade wind route via the Panama Canal and the Cape of Good Hope. She was sailed mostly singlehandedly by Alan Eddy, who had high praise for the boat. Her well-balanced hull with long keel allowed self-steering during the trade wind passages with boomed-out twin jibs. What little heavy weather she encountered she handled very well. Eddy's most frightening experience came when *Apogee* was attacked by a pod of pilot whales in the Indian Ocean. Probably provoked by the boat bumping one of them, the whales repeatedly charged the ketch, ramming her

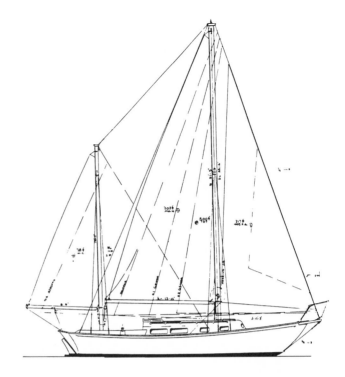

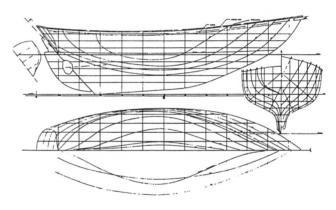

Plans of the Seawind ketch, first fiberglass boat to sail around the world. Courtesy Thomas C. Gillmer.

with enough force, according to one report, to loosen the cabin sole. The sturdy construction that incorporated six longitudinal stringers enabled her to withstand the attack.

At least one owner, Stuart Hopkins, reported a number of faulty construction details on his Seawind and also serious corrosion problems with her stainless steel fittings. I can only say that most stock boats need much modification before going offshore, and in tropic waters, fittings made of 302 or 304 stainless steel must be closely watched and frequently replaced.

Although designed for cruising, the Seawind has a surprising turn of speed. She did very respectably in the SORC in 1963, and *Apogee* once averaged 160 miles per day for eight consecutive days,

The Seawind ketch *Koa* in 1964. Photograph by Fred Thomas, courtesy Katrina Thomas.

truly remarkable speed for a medium-displacement boat under cruising canvas with a waterline length of only 24 feet. After sailing Admiral Sheldon Kinney's *Stardust* in the West Indies, Roger Taylor, the noted boat critic, wrote me: "I was very impressed with her sailing ability. I thought she did wonderfully to windward in a seaway. . ."[16]

At the thoroughly mature age of eighty-five, Tom Gillmer recently had one of his classic early designs built for his own use. Originally the boat was called *Blue Moon,* but the latest version is more appropriately named *New Moon*. Resembling a Falmouth quay punt, this boat is loaded with character. She is built of wood because Tom prefers the traditional material. "It's planked with cedar," he said, "It has a nice smell. Fiberglass is noisy [and] it smells like a medical lab."[17] *New Moon* was built by Allen Cady's Craft Works Marine Woodworking in Annapolis.

The Dickersons: Immediately after the end of World War II, there was a flurry of activity in Chesapeake yacht building and designing, and the Dickerson boats were a notable part of the action. The initial year for Owens cutters, Oxford 400s, and the *Blue Moon* design, 1946 also marked the founding of Dickerson Boatbuilders by William C. Dickerson in his backyard on Church Creek not far from Cambridge, Maryland. Later earning a reputation for excellence in craftsmanship, Dickerson started by building plain and simple hard-chine yachts in the tradition of Chesapeake workboats. His first popular design, having a hull related to a skipjack's and a rig similar to a bugeye's,

CHESAPEAKE SAILS

was appropriately named Simplisma. This was a plain, spartan but sturdy 34-foot cruiser, drawing only two feet with her centerboard raised; she was most suitable for pottering about in the Bay's many meandering rivers and creeks, yet was able enough to withstand the frequent fierce summer squalls. A few of these boats were built with deeper keels instead of centerboards. More than fifty Simplismas were turned out during the 1950s.

After acquiring a reputation for producing practical rugged boats, the Dickerson yard was awarded a contract to build navy patrol boats, and this led to the yard's building trawler yachts and a variety of other craft including some sizable schooners and a series of popular ketches. In the early 1960s Ernest Tucker became involved with design work for Dickerson. He redesigned a popular 35-footer, changing her from a V-bottom to a round-bottom design with an optional centerboard to provide better windward ability. At that time this was one of the few boats offering the option of a center cockpit with aft cabin, but the boat proved a bit small for such an arrangement. A much better size for this accommodation plan was the Dickerson 40, an attractive, strip-planked ketch designed by Tucker.

Dickerson retired in 1967, and the company was bought by Thomas Lucke, son of yachting journalist, Star champ, and Oxford 400 sailor Charles Lucke. Tom moved the Dickerson plant to La Trappe Creek and continued building traditional strip-planked Dickerson boats until 1972, when production was converted to fiberglass. Being a lover of wood construction, Lucke was reluctant to convert but recognized the advantages of fiberglass. As he put it, "I knew I couldn't survive in the marketplace without switching over to the nasty stuff."[18]

The switch to fiberglass was a boon to one Dickerson 41 owner. Near the middle of the 1970s, Neville Lewis, who had owned a Dickerson 35, was seeking a larger, aft-cabin boat for a lengthy family cruise to the South Seas and beyond. To save money, he bought the hull that had been used as the plug for the mold of the fiberglass 41. As Lewis wrote me, "The plug was not really a plug but a regular ship hull that was used as a plug and then finished out. This worked out fine as Dickerson allowed us a big credit toward construction."[19] This boat, named *Southern Cross,* made an east-to-west trade wind circumnavigation via the Panama Canal that lasted for three years and eight months. What little information I could

Preparing to pour the keel of a Dickerson 41. Courtesy Chesapeake Bay Maritime Museum, Ernest Tucker Collection.

obtain from skipper Lewis included the facts that he covered thirty-two thousand miles and put into forty major ports. One of his crew on the leg from Puerto Rico to Tahiti was an offshore sailor named Ted Reed, who became so impressed with the Dickerson 41 that he, his wife, and a third party bought the company from Tom Lucke in 1978.

Thereafter, the Dickerson company underwent considerable modernization, especially after George Hazen was commissioned to create some new designs. The son of Marylanders who had owned two Dickerson 35s, Hazen is an award-winning hydrodynamicist and computer whiz who works with an advanced velocity prediction program (VPP) and he applied state-of-the-art technology to the Dickerson yachts. Bruce Farr has said that Hazen's VPP is a step beyond that of the International Measurement System. Nevertheless, certain traditional features were retained to keep the Dickerson identity. A good example is the Hazen-designed 37-footer which has a modern underbody with separated rudder on a skeg but with traditional stern, overhanging bow, generous sheer, moderate draft, lots of teak trim, and even an optional Sampson post, the trademark of early Dickersons.

Having a similar blend of old and new is the Dickerson 50 designed by Michael Kaufman and his associates in Annapolis. With her tall rig and low wetted surface, this boat was designed to be competitive with the more spartan, less beautiful modern racers under the right conditions. A small cruising racer that departed almost

Neville Lewis's *Southern Cross*, which was used as a plug for the Dickerson 41 and later sailed around the world. Courtesy Chesapeake Bay Maritime Museum, Ernest Tucker Collection.

entirely from the Dickerson look was turned out in the mid-1970s from a design by Robert Seidelman of New Jersey. This was the Seidelman 30, a centerboard sloop measuring slightly less than 30 feet. With a removable skeg and rudder and draft that can be easily altered, one of these boats is now being used by the U.S. Coast Guard to test the drift characteristics of disabled boats in eight different configurations. Another more racing-oriented boat, designed by Bruce Farr soon after he moved to Annapolis in the early 1980s, was the Dickerson-built Farr 37, discussed later in this chapter.

I was privileged to attend a Dickerson Owner's Association rally at Oxford in 1994 after being invited by Jane Goodridge, who owned the 35-foot ketch *Tekonsha*. A longtime member of the group, Elwood Jennings, took me under his wing and introduced me to many prominent Dickerson owners, most of whom owned early wooden boats and kept them in immaculate shape. I was impressed with the friendliness and camaraderie of the group and their devotion to their boats. An annual event, the rally goes back to the late 1960s and consists of a rendezvous, cocktail party, race, and awards dinner. A unique feature of the get-together is that the race winner automatically becomes commodore and must organize the rendezvous and race the following year. At first I wondered how many captains might be trying for second place, but concluded there were none.

A favorite story about Bill Dickerson is the one published by Ferenc Maté in his book *The World's Best Sailboats*,[20] and related by a longtime Dickerson boat-owner Don Griffin. According to Griffin, when Dickerson retired, he built for himself a beautiful wooden sailboat with lots of brightwork—everything was varnished including the transom, cabin-house, spars, and trim. He took her to the Bahamas, and as he told Griffin, "One day I was out there doing the brightwork, sanding her all down getting ready to varnish, and I look up and there were all these guys sitting in their cockpits drinking gin and tonic. Well, I said, the hell with this. I threw down the sandpaper and went out and bought two gallons of white paint and I painted that sonofabitch from the mast to the waterline. Wham! That goddam boat turned white just like she hit a blizzard."

***Delilah*, Plunder, and Gay:** Not much recognition, local or otherwise, has been

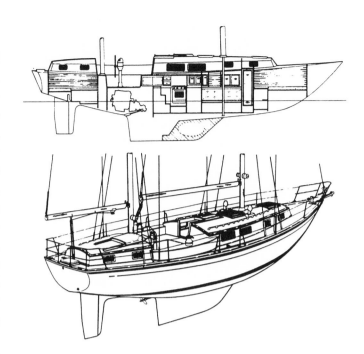

Profile and three-quarter view of center-cockpit Dickerson 37 designed by George Hazen. Courtesy Dickerson Boatbuilders, Alan Willoughby.

given to Franz Plunder, but he was a talented yacht designer from the Annapolis area who ran a small boatyard on Whitehall Creek after World War II. He was a naval architect as well as a skilled boatbuilder. While living in his native Austria in the early 1920s, he designed and built a 46-foot ketch named *Sowitasgoth* (meaning "as far as she will go"). She was shipped from Lake Constance to Hamburg and then sailed to America, where Carl Weagant bought her and changed her name to *Carlsark*. In this boat Weagant embarked on an almost-one-year voyage that included cruising the Mediterranean and circling the Atlantic. For this voyage he was awarded the coveted Blue Water Medal. *Carlsark* was later bought by Charles McComas, a good

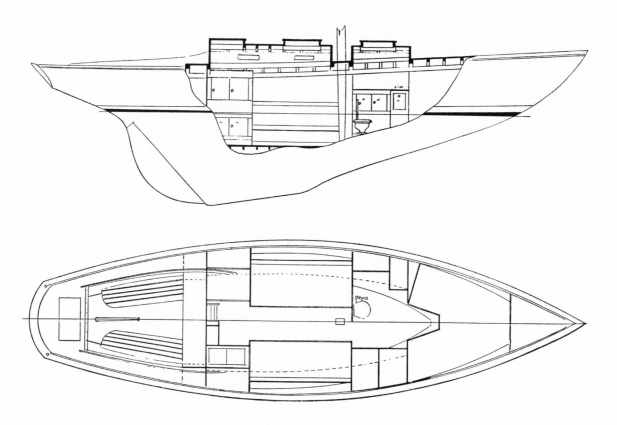

Plans of the Franz Plunder creation *Delilah*, owned by Arnie Gay.

friend of Ernest Tucker, and the Plunder ketch was moved to Annapolis, where she became a familiar sight cruising mostly on the northern Chesapeake.

Soon after moving to Annapolis, Plunder became associated with St. John's College in Annapolis where he taught boatbuilding. According to his friend, designer Ed Burgess, Plunder and his students built several small cruising sloops very similar to the German yachts called "wal boots." After starting the small yard named Cresta on Whitehall Creek, where the Whitehall Yacht Yard is now located, Franz built the Burgess-designed *Persephone,* described in chapter 2, and *Delilah,* a 35-foot cutter

for Arnold Gay. *Delilah* was a Plunder design built at the Cresta yard in 1949 with the help of two students from St. John's. Under the very capable hands of Gay, the cutter had a successful racing record.

Arnie Gay, who ran a well-known service yard and marina in Annapolis, had a strong personality and great self-assurance that was usually, but not always, appreciated. After Arnie won a race in *Delilah* beating his rival Ralph Wiley in *Fox,* Wiley roared at the committee boat after crossing the finish line: "Nobody'll

Facing page: Delilah under spinnaker on a sparkling sea. Photograph by Marion E. Warren.

116

NATIVE BOATS MAKE GOOD

be able to live around Arnie for the next week or so."[21] But Gay had many admirers. CCA historian John Parkinson recalled sailing with him in a Bermuda Race aboard *Windigo* when she sprang a leak, whereupon "Arnie disappeared under the dark waters in her bilge to effect successful repairs." Gay's most notable victory during a long successful racing career was winning the MHS division in the 1978 Bermuda Race sailing a Concordia yawl named *Babe,* but he gained some early national recognition as an ocean-racing skipper with the Plunder cutter after taking her south in 1950 and doing well in the Miami-Nassau Race. Campaigning *Delilah* on the Chesapeake, he won seasonal High Points in Class C three times during the early and middle 1950s. Gay owned many racing cruisers during his career including at least five named *Babe,* but I think he kept *Delilah* longer than any other.

Delilah was a lovely boat with graceful overhanging ends, a pleasing sheerline, swept forefoot, and a low broken cabin trunk with small, tastefully-designed portlights. The break in her cabin trunk allowed full-length deck beams for extra strength in way of the mast. Her strip planking was glued and edge-fastened, and the toerail was placed on the inboard edge of the covering board to allow installation of most deck fittings on the covering board, thereby permitting a clear deck. She was a true cutter with the mast stepped well aft and a double head rig.

Her fame was extended beyond the yachting fraternity when a picture of her, taken by the well-known photographer Marion Warren, graced the cover of the Chesapeake and Potomac telephone book. Warren told me that he expected Gay to be pleased, but initially, that was not the case—Arnie was furious. After mulling it over, however, he decided it was OK, and in fact became proud that his prized possession had become a cover girl.

Cruiskens and Quadrants: Dickerson's Simplismas were not the only economical cruising yachts designed on the Chesapeake. Two other classes were the Cruisken, designed and built at Oxford on the Eastern Shore, and the Quadrant, designed and built at Galesville on the western shore. Both were wood boats designed with hard chines for ease of construction and built of sound but inexpensive materials. They could be bought for under five thousand dollars, a low cost even then. The 30-foot Cruisken first built in 1949 was designed to utilize sheet plywood fastened to longitudinal stringers, while the first $25\frac{1}{2}$-foot Quadrant was built in 1953 in the skipjack fashion with bottom planking laid athwartships in a herringbone pattern.

My wife Sally and I owned a Cruisken in the early 1950s. For some strange reason, after happily sharing the Alden yawl *Kelpie* with my parents, we decided that we wanted a cruising boat of our very own. At the time I was steeped in the lore of light displacement. Boats such as *Myth of Malham* and *Gulvane* were cleaning up in England, while *Flying Scotsman* and *Dirigo,* designed by the Chesapeake's Roger McAleer, were getting attention here. In fact, the latter boat under the ownership of Lawrence Newark had such moments of speed that someone, a competitor, one presumes, actually tied a bucket to her keel. With a displacement of 7,000 pounds, the Cruisken was considered a lightweight in those days, and I envisioned some glory on the race course. Additionally, she had an underbody of very low wetted surface, not unlike a Star's, that bespoke speed in light air. What I didn't take into account, but should have, was that she drew only 3 feet, 9 inches, and her minimal lateral plane definitely detracted from her windward performance. Also, her displacement, marked "very light" on her Delta rating certificate, gave her a rating that was not at all helpful in round-the-buoys racing. Nevertheless, she would fly downwind and had great potential in point-to-point events.

We raced our Cruisken a few times using a borrowed 6-meter genoa. On one Poplar Island Race when the wind was northerly, we planed past most of the cruising fleet, incidentally extracting a protest from Ralph Wiley. But after rounding the Poplar Island buoy and beginning the long beat home, my smile quickly faded. Donald Street once remarked that a certain boat sailed downwind very well on a beat to windward. Well, the Cruisken was much better than that, but I did learn that the Achilles heel of most flat-bilged light-displacement boats is beating against a chop.

Designed by James R. Speer, who, together with Robert Welsh and James Brickell, took over running the Oxford Boatyard in 1948, the Cruisken was considered a larger version of an earlier

The author sailing the Cruisken *Cirrus* with a borrowed 6-meter genoa jib. Photograph by A. W. Sherwood.

Speer design, the Indian Landing 20. There were many differences, however, since the latter was a cabinless open-cockpit daysailer with a centerboard and much less freeboard. Similarities were in the construction, the general hull shape, and the rig. The Indian Landing was one of few, if any, daysailers that carried a masthead genoa.

Our Cruisken *Cirrus* (with a plywood dinghy naturally named *Mare's Tail*), suited us very well in the early 1950s. Aside from being inexpensive, she was easy to handle and practical. She had folding pipe berths that were surprisingly comfortable when properly laced, and they could be folded up with the bedding concealed to serve as backrests for the seats underneath. We could easily remove the forward berth and substitute a playpen for our son Rip, who was exactly one year old when we christened the boat. About the only serious problem we had was the two-cylinder Palmer engine, which constantly failed to start.

In the middle of the 1950s decade, my mother and father were cruising by themselves in *Kelpie,* and we would often rendezvous with them in *Cirrus*. On one cruise *Kelpie* was struck by a twister that lifted her towed dinghy up into the air, snapped the painter, and carried the boat away, never to be found. That experience ended doublehanded cruising for my mother. At the same time, Sally and I had come to the conclusion that it was foolish and wasteful in our circumstance to have two boats in the same family. Somewhat reluctantly, we sold *Cirrus* and took over a half-interest in *Kelpie.*

The other well-known "economy yacht" in the Bay at the time was the Quadrant, first conceived on the bridge of a naval ship during World War II, according to her designer, Laurence Hartge. In an article written for *Chesapeake Bay Magazine,*[22] Hartge wrote that, as a signalman in the navy with plenty of pencils and paper and time to think, he began making sketches of the dream boat he would build after the war. Following the end of hostilities, he spent some time at San Francisco, where he was influenced by some raised-deck designs, most especially the Bird class boats, noted for their heavy-weather sailing ability on San Francisco Bay. In the early 1950s Laurence returned to Galesville, Maryland, where his family had been living and building boats for generations. There he carved a model of a raised-deck sloop and showed it to his uncle, Ernest H. "Captain Dick" Hartge, a well-known builder and designer of the early Chesapeake 16 and 20. Captain Dick helped with refining the lines, lofting, and building.

With her raised-deck cabin, the Quadrant had a remarkable amount of room below for a 25-footer. She had four comfortable berths, an enclosed head, and a galley with sink. One could only fault the side-opening icebox; such a design spills out cold air even when the boat is level and can spill its contents when the boat is heeled. Auxiliary power was supplied by an outboard in a well. A noted psychologist, Dr. John C. Lilly, who had done pioneering research on dolphins and also on the mental aspects of singlehanded sailing, bought the first Quadrant and curiously insisted on having two outboard wells installed. Double motors for singlehanding?

Laurence Hartge decided to name the class Quadrant for two reasons: he

Facing page: Plans of the Quadrant by Laurence and Ernest H. Hartge. Courtesy Laurence Hartge.

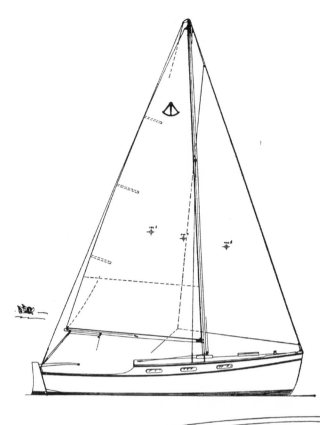

The small cartoon duck directly above the rudder was Ernest Tucker's trademark, indicating he was the draftsman for these plans.

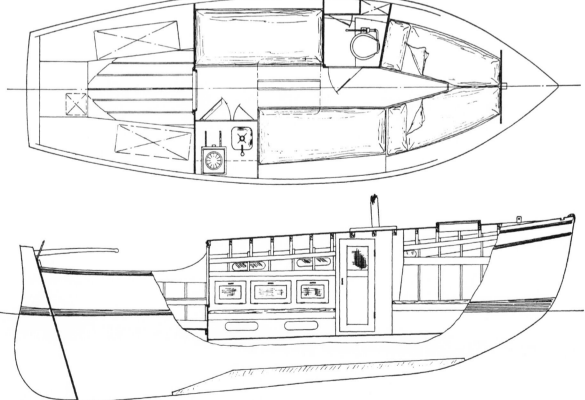

The Hartge Yacht Yard at Galesville, Maryland in 1942. Courtesy Chesapeake Bay Maritime Museum, Ernest Tucker Collection.

was a student of navigation and admired the quadrant instrument, and he envisioned the boat as being suitable for four people. Many of the boats were given names that began with the letter Q such as *Quantum, Quest,* and *Quandry*. They were far from being racers, but after a class organization was formed, Quadrants often raced among themselves. Their extremely long keels and outboard rudders, positioned as far aft as possible, provided a steady helm at the cost of high wetted surface. A modest draft of 3 feet, 10 inches allowed gunkholing, while the 8-foot 6-inch beam with long lead ballast at the bottom of the keel provided adequate stability. Having boomed self-tending jibs, the boats were easy for a small crew to handle. I was told by Robert McLaughlin, who formerly worked for Captain Dick Hartge, that Laurence had owned a Bear Class boat in San Francisco and had kept her sails for use on the Quadrant. So the latter's rig was made to resemble the Bear's.

It was a pleasure spending an afternoon on the water with Laurence Hartge in 1964 when he adjusted the compass on our Ohlson 35 *Kelpie* before we took her up the coast to visit the New York World's Fair. He was an interesting conversationalist and demonstrated his proficiency with compasses and piloting. After years of sailing without winches, electronics, or other gadgets prior to owning our Ohlson 35, I thought our boat was reasonably well equipped, but after Hartge came aboard and looked her over, he said with a grin, "This boat is the ultimate in simplicity." A man who could design the Quadrant could truly appreciate simplicity. I took his remark as a compliment.

Prim and **Proper:** If ever a boat could be described as metamorphic, it is the cutter *Prim* owned by the Gibbons-Neff family based on (or near) the Chester River on Maryland's Eastern Shore. Over a period of many years and through a series of operations performed mostly by the senior owner himself, she was transformed from a stock racing cruiser to an altogether different customized boat. As another mark of distinction, this cutter has had one of the longest continuing racing careers of any yacht. Racing under a number of different handicap rules, *Prim* enjoyed a competitive life that lasted more than four decades.

Beginning life in 1948 as one of the Owens cutters mass-produced in wood by the Owens Company of Baltimore, *Prim* was owned early on by downeaster Robert E. L. Johnson, whom I later knew at Gibson Island. She was originally named *Whirlaway,* but after being sold to Morton "Sunny" Gibbons-Neff in 1952 her name was "properly" changed to *Prim.* Sunny sailed the boat for a number of years without any major changes, but then he decided to rebuild her, initially for structural reasons but later to modernize her looks and improve her speed and rating under the IOR. Having worked for Fred Geiger as a naval architect and having done the survey himself before buying *Prim,* Sunny felt capable of doing most of the redesigning and rebuilding himself, and much of the latter was done with his own hands.

Changes to the boat took place in four stages, but the real metamorphosis occurred during the last two stages. Early structural modifications were prompted by a search for leaks that *Prim* had developed. After tearing her insides apart, Sunny discovered that the major source of leaking was swelling from rust on the bottom of the mast step that was pushing

Details of *Prim*'s bow extension. Courtesy Morton Gibbons-Neff, Jr.

the garboard strakes away from the hull.[23] He also found that leaks under the rail had caused some rot; there was also corrosion in way of the chainplates. Many of the structural problems were solved with the liberal use of fiberglass and resin. Reinforcements were not only glassed in place but also mechanically fastened.

A special barn was built to house *Prim* during her modifications. It was sorely needed, because one of the major alterations took two years to complete. During this period she was given a new stern, a Sparkman and Stephens Swan-type bow (which increased waterline length), and a new keel-attached rudder. Later, with the considerable help of local designer Karl Kirkman, Sunny increased the beam, separated the rudder from the keel, and added ballast to the keel. The beam was increased by using C-Flex—the fiberglass "planks" of closely spaced glass rods held together with roving and cloth.

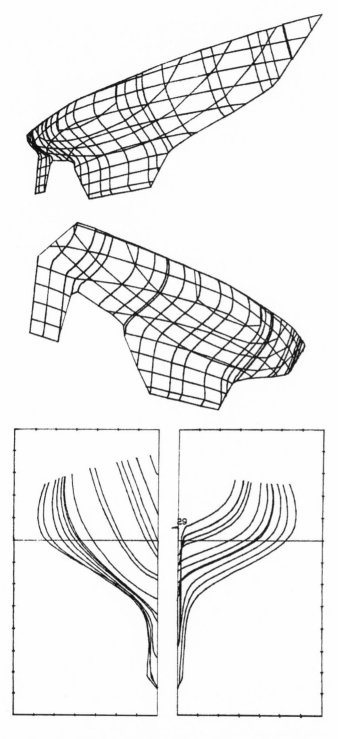

Computer-generated perspectives of *Prim* after fourth modification, plus bow and stern sections. Courtesy Morton Gibbons-Neff, Jr.

One hundred cubic feet of foam filled the voids in the topsides and bow. The reshaped hull was greatly admired by Halsey Herreshoff, who said *Prim* was the best-looking boat he had seen next to some of his own designs. Sunny was also very pleased with her looks but somewhat regretted the appearance of the excessive tumblehome which had been provided for rating advantages under the IOR.

Prim received her first aluminum mast in 1958. It was an elongated Bounty mast obtained with the help of Charles Ill, a nationally prominent yachtsman who also lived on the Chester River. Sunny was fascinated by the tapering process, which required two welders to work simultaneously on opposite sides of the spar in order to prevent distortion. A later aluminum mast for *Prim* had been designed for a Swan 43. It had an unwanted bend caused by a welded-on gooseneck track. However, the mast was straightened by welding two beads on the spar's opposite side, and then grinding them off. The extra-tall rig made *Prim* a bit tender, necessitating the addition of more ballast on the keel. Her displacement went from an original 19,000 pounds to 23,000 pounds.[24]

During her long career *Prim* sailed in thirteen Bermuda Races, competed in seven races between Annapolis and Newport, went to the Caribbean twice, and crossed the Atlantic twice. Racing highlights include the following: a class second in the New London to Annapolis Race in 1955; class win in the Annapolis Yacht Club Fall Series the same year; class third in the 1956 Bermuda Race;

Prim's crew for the 1954 Bermuda Race. *Left to right:* Ross Pilling, Gerellet Gibbons-Neff, Charles Ill, Morton Gibbons-Neff, John Wright, and Henry Chance. Courtesy Morton Gibbons-Neff, Jr.

fleet first in the 1960 Cedar Point Race; fleet and class second in the 1961 Annapolis-Newport Race, class High Point winner in 1961, 1965, and 1985; winner of the Corinthian Yacht Club's Commodore's Trophy in 1962; winner of the William C. Finley trophy in the 1964 and 1966 Bermuda Races; membership of the winning Onion Patch team in 1964; and as late as 1989 a class second in the PHRF division of the Annapolis-Newport Race. Perhaps *Prim*'s most impressive performances were in the stormy Annapolis-Newport Race of 1967 and the 1972 Transatlantic Race. In the former event, in which thirty-four boats withdrew, six were dismasted, and one sank, *Prim* smashed through steep head seas for the entire passage up the coast and won her class despite sustaining a split bulkhead and cabin trunk. In the Transatlantic Race, which ran from Ber-

Prim on a beat after her fourth modification. Spectrum photograph, courtesy Morton Gibbons-Neff, Jr.

muda to Spain via the Azores through the notoriously calm mid-Atlantic high, *Prim* won her class and was second in a fleet of forty-eight competitive yachts.

Returning home via the trade wind route from the Canary Islands to the West Indies, *Prim* averaged a remarkable run of 171 miles per day, completing the passage in eighteen days and nine hours. In late 1972, I saw *Prim* on the ways in

Grenada, and her topsides were entirely painted with antifoulant. Not a bad idea, as I remember that after our cruise to the Azores, *Kelpie* had more than a few gooseneck barnacles well above her waterline in the vicinity of the quarter wave.

In the early 1990s one of Sunny's sons, Henry, became the owner of *Prim*. He actually lived on her for two winters. But *Prim* is still considered a family boat. The last time I heard from Sunny, *Prim* had been entered in a special CCA/New York Yacht Club race, and she would be crewed by three generations of Gibbons-Neffs. Even the third generation has a special affection for the metamorphic *Prim*.

High Wind: Although she is not a particularly famous boat, the 26½-foot sloop *High Wind* is a unique native design that in some respects was years ahead of her time. Built in 1956 by her owner and designer Leavenworth Holden, *High Wind* is thought to be the first sizable boat to be constructed of fiberglass on

High Wind close-hauled in a moderate breeze. Photograph by David Q. Scott, courtesy Leavenworth Holden.

the Chesapeake Bay. A former employee of the Owens Yacht Company, Worth Holden started his own boatbuilding company in Annapolis called Laminated Plastics and became a local pioneer in fiberglass fabrication.

Worth also had some advanced ideas in sailing yacht design. I remember talking to him many years ago about the amount of lateral plane necessary to inhibit leeway, and his thoughts seemed to anticipate some concepts of today. Although *High Wind* draws only 4 feet, the fore-and-aft length of her fin keel above the bulb ballast is amazingly small. Yet her windward performance (with good headway) was sufficient for her to dominate round-the-buoys racing in the Delta class. In fact, she proved so fast that after winning Delta High Points in 1960, she was banned from the class on the grounds that "she could not be rated satisfactorily under the Delta Rule."

Custom-made for Holden's own requirements, *High Wind* has an enormous self-bailing cockpit over 12 feet long. This feature makes the boat ideal for daysailing and keeps the crew amidships for proper hull trim and favorable pitching inertia. Aft, there is a small helmsman's well with a transverse bulkhead at its forward end that strengthens the undecked part of the boat, separates the crew from the helmsman, and allows an almost full-width traveller. The light-displacement hull with minimal wetted surface is somewhat like a dinghy's but better balanced with more symmetrical lines and a finer stern. Then, too, her beam of 7 feet, 11 inches is proportionally

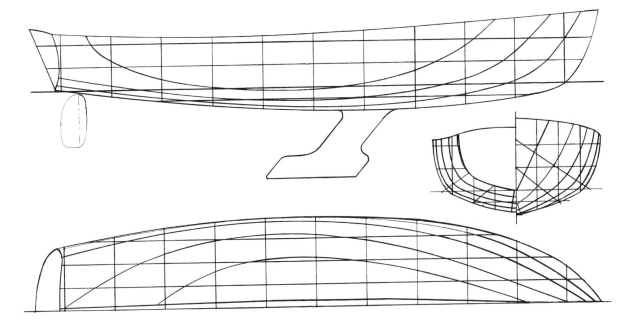

The lines of *High Wind* showing her abbreviated lateral plane. Courtesy Leavenworth Holden.

less than that of the normal dinghy's. *High Wind's* looks are enhanced with a raked transom, moderate sheer, and mahogany trim and cabin sides. The trade-off for the large cockpit with small cabin trunk positioned unusually far forward is the minimal accommodations below, but still there is room for four berths, and the cockpit seats are quite suitable for sleeping.

Worth sold his boat in 1981 but bought her back again many years later. When I last saw him in the mid-1990s, he had just refinished the brightwork on *High Wind* and she was in fine shape. He seemed to be enjoying his creation as much as he had some forty years earlier.

Tom Colvin and *Gazelle:* Thomas E. Colvin, formerly of Miles, Virginia, is a Chesapeake designer/builder/sailmaker/author who is an independent thinker. Not one to blindly follow a modern

trend or copy a stereotypical boat currently in vogue, Colvin has his own ideas, and many of them are based on early, even ancient, concepts. For instance, he stresses simplicity (including the advantages of kerosene over electric lights); he is not in love with electronics, cockpits, or engines; and he favors the Chinese lug rig. One might not agree with all of his ideas, but they should be carefully and respectfully considered, because few boatmen have the broad experience and all-around knowledge of almost every aspect of boating as does Tom Colvin.

Perhaps the most famous Colvin design and one of my favorites is *Gazelle*, a 42-foot hard-chine schooner with a modified junk rig. Built by Tom in 1967, she is a distinctive looking boat with great character. Her initial national fame came from an article called "Cruising: The Good

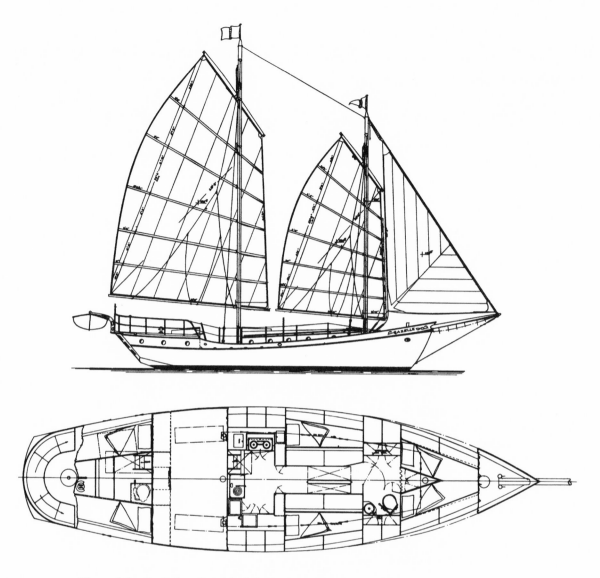

Plans of *Gazelle,* designed and built by Thomas Colvin. Courtesy Thomas E. Colvin.

Life Afloat" that appeared in the June 18, 1973, issue of *Time* magazine. Tom wrote me that over one-thousand photographs of his *Gazelle* were taken for that article, although only four of them were printed. In this letter he added: "At last count, there were over six hundred known Gazelles that have been built and are sailing. They are all over the world.

The last launched was in Australia. Many have circumnavigated, many others have made extended ocean passages . . ."[25]

Gazelle's other measurements are 33-foot waterline length, 11-foot 5-inch beam, and 3-foot 10-inch draft. On first appearance she looks like a heavy plodding seagoer, and indeed she is a seagoer, but her displacement of 18,000 pounds is moderately light, and she is quite fast. A sisterboat named *Migrant,* owned by Richard Johnson, sailed from Hawaii to Seattle, Washington, in only twenty days. During the twenty-one years that Johnson owned *Migrant,* she sailed about a hundred and fifty thousand ocean miles. The shallow keel on the Gazelle (without centerboard) precludes excellence to windward, but as Tom points out, a boat doesn't need to be close-winded for long offshore passages. I might add, however, that reasonable windward ability is required to beat away from a lee shore in heavy weather, and Tom says that the Gazelles have this capability.

The original *Gazelle* was designed and built by Colvin for himself for the purposes of daysailing and cruising on the Chesapeake as well as long-distance passagemaking and short-term liveaboard capabilities for his family of five. She was built of steel because Tom feels this material has many advantages for long cruises in foreign waters, and he is a specialist in steel construction. In fact, he wrote a definitive book on the subject.[26]

Belowdecks *Gazelle* was planned for maximum privacy and convenience with an aft cabin, two heads, galley near the companionway, and pilot berths in the main saloon. But after using the boat for two and a half years and sailing her for about three thousand miles, Tom decided that her accommodations could be improved. In his book *Coastwise and Offshore Cruising Wrinkles,* Colvin describes how he took the drastic action of clearing out the old accommodations (in order to install new ones) with the use of a sledgehammer. "Before the first blow," he wrote, "I could only recall that I had spent a thousand hours putting it in. But with the second blow, I began to think how nice it was going to be when it was rebuilt." The new plan resulted in moving the galley forward away from the companionway, changing the pilot berth arrangement to alcove bunks for privacy, installing a settee and swivelling table, and changing the aft cabin from a single double-berth to a double single-berth arrangement.[27]

Colvin's greatest concession to modernism was the installation of an auxiliary diesel engine, a 20-horsepower Saab that could be started by hand-cranking it. Regarding this engine, Tom wrote me that during a cruise to the Bahamas, "We had started the engine up since there was very little wind. It ran for about 20 minutes and quit. I was busy in the engine room for the next hour troubleshooting the engine and finally came up on deck and told (my wife) Jean that that was the trouble with engines . . . they never worked when you wanted them to. After ranting for about five minutes about what was wrong with engines and why have engines, she asked if there was any fuel in the tank. I said, 'of course, I put five gallons in there six months ago!' Upon checking, and after adding five more gallons of fuel, we never experienced any more trouble with that engine."[28]

In England H. G. Hasler championed the Chinese lug rig, and he used it

Close aboard under the lee quarter of *Gazelle*. Photograph by Gary Miller, courtesy Thomas E. Colvin.

in the first formal transatlantic race for singlehanders in 1960, a race cosponsored by the Chesapeake's Slocum Society. The pioneer of this rig in America was Tom Colvin, but his version is highly modified. Unlike the Hasler rig, it has standing rigging and a jib. Some of the advantages of the Chinese lug sail are that it can be reefed and lowered easily, twist can be precisely controlled with multiple sheets, and being a balanced sail (with luff projecting forward of the mast), the helm is better balanced when running. Also, jibing is a relatively tame

operation. Of course there are trade-offs, but Tom found his rig most satisfactory on *Gazelle*.

After selling *Gazelle* in 1974, Colvin built a larger boat for himself named *K'ung Fu-Tse*. She was constructed of aluminum because Tom had a lot of that material left over from other projects. He wrote, "I built my personal vessels with whatever material I had on hand that was plentiful, and I have often said that if all I had was a big pile of horse manure I would probably give that a try, for the object was to build boats."[29] Tom and his family lived aboard and cruised *K'ung Fu-Tse* for sixteen years, but I have the impression his first love was *Gazelle,* as he wrote, "Of all the designs that I have done, which are close to 300 now, I think I had more fun with *Gazelle.*"

Kirkman Boats: A well-thought-of naval architect from the Chesapeake, highly praised by the likes of Olin Stephens, is Karl L. Kirkman. Although a talented designer of racing yachts, Karl is probably best known for his work with model-testing in the towing tank, especially his important participation with the McCurdy Committee on Safety from Capsizing, jointly sponsored by the United States Yacht Racing Union (USYRU) and the Society of Naval Architects and Marine Engineers (SNAME). This committee was formed to investigate the reason why so many yachts capsized during the disastrous Fastnet Race of 1979 and to make recommendations for the design and construction of safer ocean racers.

A genuine native designer, not a transplant from another area, Karl summered just north of Gibson Island during his youth and learned to sail in Gibson Island's Eagle Cove in a Ralph Wiley designed Scrappy Cat. He became interested in boatbuilding and design after his uncle, a shipyard naval architect, gave him a copy of Sam Rabl's book, *Boatbuilding in Your Own Backyard.* Later he attended the Webb Institute of Naval Architecture and afterwards worked for some prestigious vessel design firms such as Hydronautics and M. Rosenblatt and Son. His independent Chesapeake yacht designs, however, were done as an ama-

teur, as he designed them for friends without charge. Karl tells about these yachts in his own words:

After graduation from Webb Institute of Naval Architecture, I purchased a bare hull of a Luders 24 which I finished in the shed in Bert Jabin's original yard. This boat called *Cobra,* with a redesigned keel reflecting the latest 12-Meter practices and a cloud of sail in a redesigned rig, was very successful locally, winning Race Week and High Point at the time [1969]. Right next to us in Bert's shed while we were building was an old Owens Cutter (another great Bay design, by the way) owned by Pete Geis, and as Pete had recently moved from Racing Division where we were to race *Cobra,* we became acquaintances and eventually good friends.

At about that time I designed a boat for Charlie Stein who was considering replacing his Owens, *Snallygaster,* and I had the good fortune to have the plans appear in *Yachting* magazine although the boat was never built. Pete called me one Sunday at my little apartment in Laurel, and asked to build the boat but I told him I would prefer to create a new version with hull form improvements coming into the CCA yachts from the active 12-Meter campaigns of the time, and we agreed to proceed. I produced a set of plans for this *Anthem* in strip planking, and the boat was eventually raced by Pete with some success. The handicap it carried was that it was a late CCA design, but since he built it himself over a period of some years it was somewhat outdated when finally launched. I did sail with Pete in its first regatta, the AYC Fall Series in which we placed well against a top notch fleet, but it was tough going. In particular, we had added a set of those foam blisters amidships to bump the boat for IOR, but it was still an older CCA design at

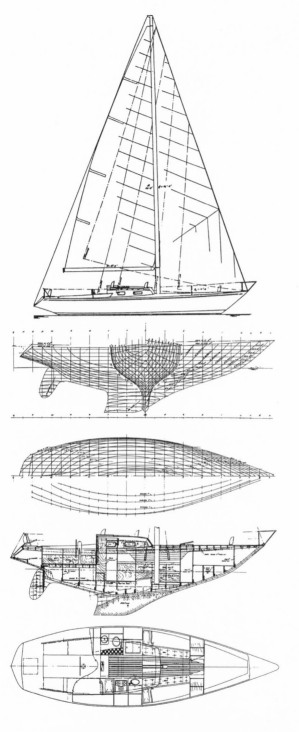

Karl Kirkman's design for Charlie Stein, which led to the building of *Anthem* in modified form. Courtesy Karl L. Kirkman.

heart. Pete did a nice job of building his "home-built" and I visited regularly to supervise construction. That boat had a number of innovations: a loose footed mainsail to allow draft shaping, and a then rare tapered aluminum mast with internal tangs and halyards which I built in the shop at work in the evenings and installed in the mast tube in my driveway before delivering to Pete.

One of the unusual features was airfoil shaped spreaders of spruce about which I will relate an interesting story:

One Sunday in June some years later and during an Annapolis-Newport Race, I received a telephone call from a crabber on the Eastern Shore saying that early that morning he had been passed a message on a boathook from Pete (Geis) to call me and have me make him a new set of spreaders for delivery immediately in Newport. It turned out the wooden spreaders had been penetrated by rain at the roots and had rotted, and one had carried away beating down the lower Eastern Shore during Saturday night. Pete made a splint from a piece of stainless tube and finished the Race, but needed new spreaders immediately for the following week at Block Island. Of course we made the new spreaders of aluminum this time at the shop the next day and shipped them off to Pete with a humorous set of installation instructions. Those same spreaders are still installed on the mast today of the new *Anthem*. By coincidence some years later, beating along the same shore on another design of mine, *Spindrift,* with Captain David Saunders, another close friend, we suddenly heard a tinkling sound and a machine screw slid down the mainsail and landed in the cockpit. We could find no clue to the source until some hours later, when the leeward spreader came adrift, and David's son Craig went up the mast in a bosun's chair and refitted the screw and secured the spreader while beating in moderately rough head seas. To add to the pressure, we were on starboard tack and converging with shallow water and could not tack for fear of losing the mast, until he completed the repair. This was a real feat of seamanship for Craig, as it was lumpy enough that some of the crew were suffering from motion sickness at the time.

To return to the story, Pete sailed this *Anthem* for a number of years including every Annapolis-Newport Race and Bermuda Race of the time. I particularly remember going out early for a CBYRA Race Week (back when it was in July) and seeing *Anthem* beating back up the Bay and into Annapolis harbor at dawn after a rather rough passage home through the Gulf Stream, and this passage figures in her eventual demise as best we can tell. At the time she was about ten years old and she had fallen off of a number of waves on the return passage with no obvious damage. But in the subsequent Cedar Point Race Pete encountered rough conditions and close reaching back from the Point under full No. 1 (while others had to shorten sail; *Anthem* was very stiff) in one of those wild cold front passages we all know well, experienced a massive failure in the strip planking forward and almost lost the vessel. As I recall the story, only good seamanship wrapping a sail around the hull, allowed her to return home, and the damage was sufficient to cause us to pause before proceeding with repairs; and so the new *Anthem* was born. In inspecting her structure forward, we found a cracked plywood ring frame in the bow area where the failure in the planking started, and the crack was sufficiently blackened by water stains to persuade us that she had been carrying this broken frame for some time. Pete and I always believed it occurred during that

rough Bermuda return, but of course we will never know with certainty.

In any event, the economics of repair were such that I proposed to Pete that he pocket the adjustment funds for the damage, scrap *Anthem,* and build a replacement of fibreglass using all of the old components. This decision was not easily taken because Pete had a lot of loving care invested in building and maintaining the boat, but the design was by now even more badly dated. He agreed to proceed, and we made the fateful choice to build the replacement using everything— mast, sails, pulpits, engine, tanks, icebox, etc.—everything, in a new boat to be rated under IMS which was then emerging. This turned out to be a large challenge because the new boat was of greatly different form and proportions, and yet we were determined to salvage everything.

I produced a set of lines, and Pete began construction in his new boatbuilding shed. We chose to adopt Peter Van Dine's insulation foam mold construction technique and so the boat was strip planked foam over plywood stations, glassed, faired on the outside, and then taken outside and rolled over, the molds stripped out, and glassed within for a foam core hull. Pete hated the glass work, but he persevered, and a rather nice-looking, very moderate boat resulted. As I recall he eventually used everything from old *Anthem* in the new boat which was a very competitive racer under IMS and eventually won her class in the Bermuda Race in 1988. By that time her single spreader telephone pole aluminum mast assembled in my driveway over a decade before was certainly a distinguishing feature. Regarding her construction, I served on the Bermuda Race Committee throughout the 1980s and when the CCA adopted a requirement for certification that all

CHESAPEAKE SAILS

entrants met ABS requirements, I felt that it was conflict of interest for me to make such a declaration, and I shipped a set of plans off to Jim McCurdy and asked him to offer an opinion on the adequacy. His answer, vintage Jim McCurdy for those who knew him, was that he considered the only hazard to be posed by the yacht was to the reefs surrounding Bermuda. This *Anthem* was truly heavily built, but competitive at the time in spite of it; I have always believed the "secret" of the boat to be moderate in every way.

Returning to *Spindrift*, she was the fourth boat by this name that Captain Saunders had owned, and I knew him from sailing generally and had helped him with some design modifications on a predecessor. David had been working with Tom Lucke, the owner of Dickerson yachts, on a new project of an IOR One Ton yacht. Together they approached me and asked me to do the plans which I was delighted to undertake and so Dave and I would trundle down to Trappe on the Eastern Shore regularly to oversee progress. Two of these yachts were built to the plans and designated Chesapeake One Ton. They did well; David won CBYRA Race Week and High Point [first in Class Race Week 1975 and second Class B High Points 1975] with his, but they were certainly never particularly outstanding boats, and it was more the excellent sailing than the design which succeeded.[30]

Peter Geis's home-built Kirkman 38 *Anthem*, class victor and winner of the T.F. Day trophy in the 1988 Bermuda Race. Photograph by Tom Leutwiler, Daedelus Photography, courtesy Peter A. Geis.

The preceding write-up by Karl Kirkman entitled "Ramblings for Jud Henderson" and describing his Chesapeake designs is most interesting and greatly appreciated by me. Reading be-

Facing page: Peter Geis building his *Anthem* in his backyard while designer Karl Kirkman looks on with approval. Courtesy Peter A. Geis.

tween the lines I think anyone can appreciate not only Karl's talent but also his modesty and generosity. I might add that another of Karl's Chesapeake designs that received wide acclaim was the radio-controlled (RC) model yacht named *Bone XIII*. Designed and built in the early 1980s, she was very advanced for her time with a tank-tested hull and exotic construction. She was the national champion RC model yacht in the United States and Canada and truly dominated the competition for several years. I recall Karl telling me years ago that in an effort to maximize her effective sailing length, *Bone* was given a large submerged transom. That strategy did not work for Britton Chance on an America's Cup 12-meter sailed by Ted Turner, but it was most successful on the smaller scale for *Bone*.

A few words should be said about the Chesapeake owners of Kirkman yachts. Pete Geis, a longtime resident in the Annapolis area, is not only a skilled amateur boatbuilder, but also a yacht racing administrator and former president of the CBYRA. He is also the owner and publisher of *The Boating Almanac*. Tom Lucke, son of two prominent Chesapeake sailors, Charlie and Barbara Lucke, hails from the Eastern Shore as the name of his boat, *Muskrat,* suggests. He was a former Alberg 30 sailor who won High Points in the class at least once. As mentioned earlier, Tom owned and ran the Dickerson Yard for a number of years.

Annapolitan Dave Saunders, a retired navy captain, is the son of a noted naval architect, Harold Saunders, who designed a famous towing tank (formerly known as the David Taylor Model Basin) and who wrote a classic textbook on naval architecture. Dave Saunders himself is interested in yacht design and has often extensively modified his various boats named *Spindrift*. One of his favorite stories is about Arnie Gay telling him he could never win a thing in his newly-bought Galaxy 32, yet she turned out to be the hottest boat in her class after Dave performed a few modifications. Perhaps his most successful year was 1985 with a Beneteau One Ton named *Airmail* which he co-owned with my friend John Quinn, now the director of offshore sailing at the U.S. Naval Academy. But Dave had great success with all of his *Spindrift*s, including his Chesapeake One Ton designed by Karl Kirkman. Dave was also involved with Karl's radio-controlled model yachts, and he skippered one of them in the U.S. Championship regatta at Port Washington, New York.

Bruce Farr: A New Zealander transplanted to the Chesapeake, Bruce Farr came to Annapolis in 1981. Six years before, when I was in England, the newspapers were full of praise for Farr because his Admiral's Cup boat was cleaning up at Cowes Race Week. At the time none of my sailing friends had ever heard of him, but now, of course, every Chesapeake sailor knows of this legendary designer. He brings this chapter up-to-date, as Farr designs represent the state of the art in high-performance monohull ocean racers.

As an old lobscouser, I don't particularly like some of the modern trends in sailing yacht design such as deep high-aspect bolted-on vulnerable keels and freestanding rudders on offshore yachts. Aside from their unsuitability for shoal waters, a number of these appendages have caused stress resulting in hull damage or have actually broken off. As for the rigs, it is preposterous having to send a person to the masthead of a Whitbread 60 in order to jibe a spinnaker. However, these types of boats are extremely fast, and risks may be acceptable if there is an ample margin of safety in the engineering and construction. Farr boats are well-engineered; his firm normally selects a compatible builder who understands the stresses that will be put on the boat and has the proper know-how in working with modern exotic materials. These are vital requirements.

Some of Farr's outstanding designs and their racing triumphs were discussed briefly in chapter 2. In 1998, a new multistop round-the-world Whitbread Race (now sponsored by Volvo) was completed, and it was not surprising that a Farr boat won it, since eight of the ten contestants were designed by Bruce and his associates. These boats, called Whitbread 60s, are primarily downwind machines designed to run before the prevailing westerlies of the southern hemisphere. They are light-displacement "sleds" with long waterlines, fine bows, and full quarters. Ordinarily, with a minimum of reserve buoyancy forward, such unbalanced hulls tend to bury their bows when heeled, but the broad quarters help prevent heeling, and the Whitbread 60s are kept upright with water ballast (rarely used or allowed on standard racing boats). It has been said that Farr boats are less difficult to steer downwind in heavy weather than many other modern boats with short keels and extremely asymmetric hulls, because the typical Farr hull is more rockered, has less forefoot, and perhaps has more buoyancy forward. Nevertheless, it is not uncommon for any fast-moving Whitbread racer to "stuff" or plow into a trough or back of a

Chessie Racing alongside *Toshiba* immediately after the start of the eighth leg of the 1998 Whitbread Race with the Chesapeake Bay Bridge in the background. Photograph by William Boykin.

wave when its buoyant stern is lifted by a large following sea, with the consequence of its being swept with green water.

Much media hype has been associated with the Whitbread Race. It has been called the Mount Everest of sailing, but it really pales in comparison to some of the nonstop round-the-world races for singlehanders, especially the first one, in which many of the competitors had no electronics and in some cases not even basic sending radios. Incidentally, the winner of that race was a modified sister of *Eric,* a double-ender that spent nearly forty years on the Chesapeake. No one will deny, however, that the Whitbread is *among* the most rugged, endurance-testing races. As a friend of mine said, "it may not be Everest but maybe the K2."

Chesapeake sailors had a special interest in the 1997–1998 Whitbread, since for the first time, a local boat named *Chessie Racing* competed. Created by a syndicate headed and financed by Gibson Islander George Collins, the boat was, of course, designed by Farr and Associates. Collins decided not to sail on the longest legs of the race, but a number of Bay sailors, mostly professionals, were crewing, including Jim Allsopp, who was coskipper on the first long leg. Sailing all legs was Greg Gendell, raised on the Magothy River, who sustained a serious laceration requiring ten surgical staples after he was washed aft from bow to mast when Chessie stuffed and was swept by green water in the Southern Ocean.

The seventh leg ended at Baltimore, Maryland, with *Chessie* finishing a disappointing eighth. Many of the racers used the local knowledge of native sailors and even a Bay pilot to negotiate the tricky waters of the Chesapeake. After more than a week of rest amid much commercial hoopla, the racers started the eighth leg just north of the Chesapeake Bay Bridge, which was packed with spectators along its over-four-mile length. (One of them attempted suicide by jumping off the bridge but succeeded only in making a big splash.) As noted in chapter 2, *Chessie* finished the race with the sixth highest score but had been in contention for third prior to the last leg.

Two stock racing cruisers designed by Farr are closely identified with the Chesapeake since they were designed for local residents and constructed by local builders. They are the Farr 37, designed in 1982 and built by Dickerson, and the Farr 33, designed a couple of years later and built by Annapolis Custom Yachts.

The Dickerson yachts are not all-out racing machines but more versatile boats that can be used for limited cruising as well as racing. Although very fast, they are less extreme than many out-and-out racers and have greater displacements, finer quarters, and nicely finished accommodations. They are optimized for the light air of the Chesapeake with powerful masthead rigs and minimal wetted surface through relatively narrow waterline beam and abbreviated appendages thickened sufficiently to delay stalling. Weight is concentrated amidships to provide responsive motion that minimizes the harmful effects of hobbyhorsing in the notorious Chesapeake chop. A trade-off for having the engine just abaft the mast is a somewhat inefficiently-angled propeller shaft that exits the hull at the after end of the high-aspect-ratio fin keel. Construction is a far cry from that of traditional Dickerson boats. Hulls are made of laminated fiberglass with vacuum-bagged Divinycell cores and extensive use of Kevlar in the bows and sterns.[31]

Two of these boats dominated racing on the Bay in 1983: Bert Jabin's *Ramrod* and Scott Allan and Brad Parker's *Sugar*. It is interesting that *Sugar* beat *Ramrod* in class High Points, yet the latter won the Labrot trophy that year as a result of separate scoring on a fleet basis. *Sugar* also won her class in the 1983 Annapolis-

Facing page: Chessie Racing as seen from the Bay Bridge. Photograph by William M. Shvodian.

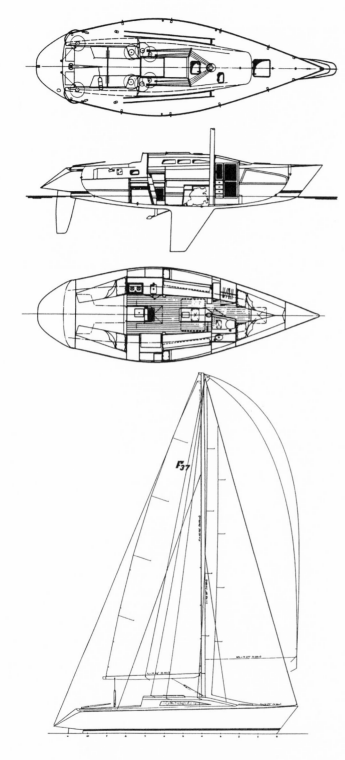

Plans of the Farr 37 built by Dickerson. Courtesy Dickerson Boatbuilders, Alan Willoughby.

Newport Race. A Farr 37, *Crescendo*, owned by Dr. Steve Hiltabidle, has also done well in Bay racing and won her class and was second overall in PHRF in the 1995 Annapolis-Newport Race.

The Farr 33 was built by a relatively new Annapolis boatbuilder with considerable supervision by Farr's head engineer, Russell Bowler. Construction was high-tech using vacuum-bagged foam-core, Kevlar, and special resins. In one sense this boat is a smaller version of the Farr 37, as it was based on a similar concept: a competitive IOR racer with cruising accommodations, fast but not tricky, and optimized for sailing in the Chesapeake.[32]

My friend and former racing rival, Charles "Sunny" Smith, has had two of these boats and has enjoyed great success with them. A veteran racing skipper and former Hampton Class champion, Sunny was recently recognized by the Annapolis Yacht Club as being the first member to race for that club for more than fifty years. His reason for ordering a second Farr 33 is that it was structurally superior to his first. According to Sunny, the 33s perform very well in most conditions, although they are a bit "squirrelly" downwind in a blow. At any rate, he liked his first 33 well enough to order a near duplicate.

Another successful Farr design built by Annapolis Custom Yachts is the Farr 43. One of these boats, *Snake Oil*, won her class in the 1985 SORC, skippered by Geoff Stagg of Farr International and crewed by some Annapolis sailmakers.

In addition to the Concept 80 that was briefly described in chapter 2, another innovative racing cruiser—not built on the Bay but ordered by a well-known Chesapeake client—is the 44-foot *Reindeer* designed for Newbold Smith. Being an avid racer as well as a long-distance cruiser, Blue Water Medalist Smith ordered a compromise boat that gave away little in speed or seaworthiness and comfort. With a laminate of Kevlar, a core of Divinycell, and much interior joinerwork honeycomb-cored, the boat's displacement was kept quite light despite a heavily ballasted keel. An unusual feature, the short but shallow fin keel can be extended with a hydraulic-ram-operated centerboard to increase the span of the keel for windward efficiency. She has a fairly tall sloop rig for speed in light air.[33] This is not the kind of boat that most sailors would like to take to the Arctic, but in 1994 Newbold sailed her to Hudson Bay, one of the bleakest and most remote regions in the world, where he had to cope with pack ice and fierce currents.[34] This boat has also done well racing, winning her class in the 1995 Annapolis-Newport Race. She is indeed a versatile boat. It seems that Farr and his associates found a way for their client to have his cake and eat it too, though a large part of the boat's success is due to her owner's expertise.

Other Chesapeake designers: Sailing yachts designed by some other Chesapeake natives have had somewhat lesser, or at least less conspicuous, roles in Chesapeake yachting history.

As mentioned in chapter 2, John Trumpy moved the Mathis-Trumpy boatbuilding operation to Annapolis in 1947 and continued to build wooden power

Charles "Sunny" Smith's Farr 33 *Uh-Oh* racing off Annapolis. Photograph by Norm Baldwin, courtesy Charles Smith.

yachts of the highest quality. Before Fred Geiger moved to Annapolis, John Trumpy did most of the design work on these power craft, but he was also an enthusiastic sailor who was said to love a beat to windward in a rail-down breeze. Only five sailboats were built by the Trumpy plant at Annapolis, and one of them, John's fifth and last *Sea Call* (a 36-foot sloop) was designed by John himself in 1952 as a sort of celebration of his retirement as president of the company.[35]

A well-liked yacht broker from Annapolis, Walter "Wiki" McNiel, who cruised extensively in the Caribbean and also in the South Seas, was an amateur yacht designer as well. In the mid-1950s he designed for himself a 37-foot shoal-draft sloop named *Tropic Bird,* and later he designed a cutter-rigged motorsailer with the same name.

In addition to being a gifted sailor who won fleet High Points with his

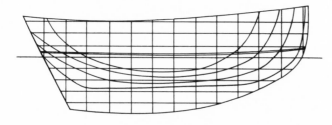

The 20-foot Fred Geiger–designed *Wee One*, sailed to Bermuda and back by Harry Young.

handling little piece of wood I ever got my hands on." She was also very able for her size. Ernest Hemingway's brother sailed a sister boat from Mobile, Alabama, to Cuba.

An even more ambitious voyage for a tabloid cruiser was carried out by Baltimore boatbuilder Harry Young when he sailed the 20-foot cutter *Wee One* from Baltimore to Bermuda and home again in 1938. Built by Ralph Wiley, *Wee One* was designed by Fred Geiger before he moved to Annapolis to work for John Trumpy and Sons. As previously noted, Geiger also designed the handsome Trumpy-built *Sanban* and the Ranger class that did well in handicap racing on the Bay. Harry Young claimed that his best-known boat was *Blue Water*, a 26-foot ketch also designed by Geiger.

Other small Chesapeake cruising designs are only slightly above the tabloid size: *Persephone*, designed by Ed Burgess and described in chapter 2; a 25-foot hard-chine clipper-bow sloop designed by Eric Steinlein; and the Annapolitan, a 23½-foot round-bottom fin-keel sloop by George Meese. I'm not sure if the latter two were ever built, but they are certainly attractive designs. A nautical historian and promoter of safety in yacht design, Steinlein drew a seaworthy and practical sloop that is exceedingly handsome for a boat with hard chines. Some of her safety features are a small cockpit well with bridge deck, small portlights, head above the waterline, and pronounced sheer elevating the bow and stern. High-grade wood construction allowed the economical use of sheet plywood. The

Sparkman and Stephens yawl *Chance* in 1955, James Rider of Annapolis was an occasional designer most noted for the creation of his sloop *Puffin*. Built of aluminum in 1962, she was a handsome and fast 45-footer that carried with pride the insignia "JR 1" on her mainsail.

Sam Rabl, who inspired Karl Kirkman with his book on backyard boatbuilding, attracted some attention in the early 1920s for a tabloid cruiser called *Picaroon* after her plans were published in *Motor Boating* magazine (June 25, 1925). An 18-foot hard-chine cruising sloop, *Picaroon* was designed for Rabl's own use on the Chesapeake. He described her as, "the slickest

CHESAPEAKE SAILS

boat was offered with either a full keel or centerboard housed in a ballasted keel.[36]

George Meese, a most versatile Annapolis naval architect, designed everything from an oceanographic research vessel to a cruising lifeboat. His Annapolitan sloop was a modern fiberglass design with fin keel and skeg-attached rudder, but unlike most contemporary boats with this configuration, the Meese design has a lovely traditional hull with attractive overhangs and aft-raking transom. The designer wisely resisted the temptation to overly elevate the cabin trunk for more headroom and to crowd more than two bunks into the interior.

Also very versatile is veteran naval architect Charles Wittholz, an alumnus of the famous Philip Rhodes design team. Earlier mention was made of the Wittholz historic replicas, but he is also known for his many cruising yacht designs, some of them suitable for home construction in wood or steel. Of this type, one of my favorites is *Departure,* a 35-foot hard-chine cruiser with a rig that seems a cross between a yawl and ketch. The adaptability of her rig together with her reasonably shallow keel make her well suited to Chesapeake cruising.[37]

Still another versatile native designer is Annapolitan Mike Kaufman who at one time teamed with Rob Ladd. He produced a wide range of designs: a magnificent high-performance offshore cruiser, the Skye 72; a British workboat-type gaff-rigger; and modern racing machines such as the 40-foot "Screamer," an ultra-light-displacement design with a PHRF rating of 24 (indicating blazing speed).

The handsome Dickerson 50 ketch designed by Kaufman and Associates was briefly described earlier.

An imaginative designer with tremendous variety in his yachts is Jay Benford, who moved to Maryland from the Pacific Northwest in the early 1980s. Some of his off-the-Bay designs achieved considerable notoriety. I have in mind his 35-foot double-ender *De Zeeuwse Stromen* (gracing the jacket of my book *Singlehanded Sailing*), which once held the record for a nonstop solo circumnavigation, and the miniature offshore cruiser, only 14 feet long, named *Happy* in which a record-breaking circumnavigation was attempted.[38] *Happy* made a remarkable voyage to the South Seas, but not so happily she was lost there on a reef. Her skipper, Howard Smith, survived. An unusual Benford design, a 34-foot junk-rigged dory named *Badger,* has been sailed more than 100,000 miles by Annie and Pete Hill to many of the world's most remote regions. In recent years a number of Chesapeake sailors, including myself, have seen Benford cruising in his distinctive 34-foot pinkie ketch named *Sunrise.* This Benford design is as colorful as a sunrise with her bright-finished hull and "great pyramid rig"[39] of multicolored triangular sails suspended from a yardarm. This unusual rig designed by Benford carries on the mainmast a triangular main course, raffee, and a pair of stuns'ls.

Al Mason is not usually associated with the Chesapeake, but this highly respected designer, noted for his exceptional draftsmanship, did reside in Annapolis for a while. One of his best-known boats spending time on the Bay was the remarkable

Dutch Treat grounded at Cape Hatteras after her abandonment. H.K. Bramhall, Jr., *Salt Water Sportsman*.

45-foot steel motorsailer named *Dutch Treat*, a handsome comfortable shoal-draft "70-30" (indicating she was more sailer than motor yacht). She was surprisingly competitive on the race course. Unfortunately, she received some less-than-desirable publicity in 1960 after being abandoned during a stormy coastal passage off Charleston, South Carolina.[40] Although she was not in any real danger, her seasick and disconcerted crew sent out a distress signal and was rescued by a tanker. *Dutch Treat* drifted as a derelict for eight days before grounding on the sandbanks off Cape Hatteras. Hardly damaged at all and with little water in her bilge, she was recovered by her owner only after a number of costly legal disputes with salvors.

A more unfortunate circumstance befell the gifted Chesapeake designer

144

Roger McAleer when he lost his 36-foot sloop *Vignette* after a dismasting and grounding during the stormy 1967 Annapolis-Newport Race. Several times I raced against *Vignette* and was impressed with her looks and sailing ability. The successor to this boat was another *Vignette*, which was the prototype of the McAleer 35 class. This was a single-head-rigged cutter with a clipper bow. It will be recalled that McAleer also designed the Raven class and the light displacement *Dirigo*. As mentioned earlier, the latter presumably scared a competitor to such an extent that he affixed a bucket to her keel. After sensing that his boat was not performing as well as she should, *Dirigo*'s owner, Larry Newark, had her hauled and discovered a canvas draw bucket securely tied to her rudder post with a bowline.[41]

A worthy successor to Ralph Wiley, Edmund Cutts took over the Wiley yard after the "sage of Oxford" retired. Like Wiley, Cutts is a designer and traditional boatbuilder with innovative ideas. A master craftsman with a love for wood, Cutts once told me that he attended a symposium on fiberglass construction. After a lengthy discussion of fiberglass blistering, he announced to the audience that he had completely solved the problem: he built his boats of wood. And that he does, but often in a high-tech original manner. For example, his Cutts Patent Method reinforces wood planking with Kevlar windings for rigidity, lightness, and longevity. Cutts has been a longtime admirer and disciple of L. Francis Herreshoff, and the influence can be seen in

his designs, a prime example being the exquisite 47-foot ketch *Spellbound* built by Cutts and Case at Oxford for a New York client.

Also from Oxford was sailor/designer/builder James Brickell, who at one time was a part owner of the Oxford Boat Company. Brickell became well known on the Bay for his racing success with the 44-foot cutter *Starlight*, a Sparkman and Stephens design. After selling her in the mid-1960s, Brickell drafted what I think was his first and only cruising design—*Starflame*. She was a 28-foot short-ended sloop built of wood by the Oxford Boat Company. An able boat with comfortable accommodations, she was also fast enough to be competitive in the MORC. Brickell had a special affection for *Starflame*. Sadly, he died of a heart attack in her cabin.

Another Chesapeake "one boat" designer was Raymond M. Brown of Hampton, Virginia. After successfully campaigning his well-known Invicta

The Edmund Cutts method of wood boat building using ribbing of Kevlar cord. Courtesy Edmund Cutts of Cutts and Case Boatyard.

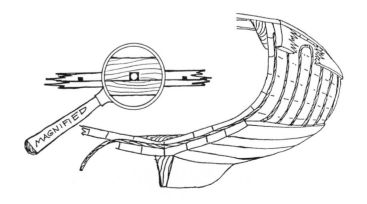

sloop *Fleetwind* for many years, he designed and built, largely with his own hands, a modern 45-foot ocean racer named *Flying Cloud*. More about Ray Brown can be found in chapter 6.

A trio of bugeye-rigged wooden cruisers with hulls based on indigenous workboats are the 37-foot Bay-Mate designed by Edgar Van Dyke of Cambridge, a 30-foot bugeye/sharpie designed by Owen Davis (also of Cambridge), and a 52-foot skipjack named *Lady June* designed by Vernon Behm. The latter was built in Yorktown, Virginia, by John Belvin, whose small yard was almost destroyed by a tornado in 1973, along with four boats being built. Belvin saved himself by jumping overboard and clinging to the riverbank.[42] The yard was resurrected, however, and Belvin completed *Lady June* five years later. Unlike a work-

ing skipjack she is very carefully built and finely finished. All of these craft are hard-chine shoal-draft centerboarders with self-tending rigs. They are well suited to leisurely cruising the Bay, but they are not suitable for extended offshore voyages, primarily because of their low range of stability. The 30-foot bugeye/sharpie, built in 1948, was created by a talented marine artist and illustrator. This craft was an unusual combination of bugeye above the waterline with sharpie flat-bottom form underwater. Drawing only a foot and a half, she was ideal for gunkhole cruising and even "eel rut crawling."

The Chesapeake has had many gifted designers. This book includes most of those who have played a significant part in local yachting history. My apologies to any I have overlooked.

CHAPTER FIVE

TIDEWATER CLASSICS IN RESIDENCE

Except for one or two, the sailing yachts in this chapter and the next are not local designs, but they are closely identified with the Chesapeake as a result of their having spent a lot of time on the Bay. Many of them are well known, even legendary, in yachting circles, and in most cases their owners have lived on or near the Bay.

Australia: One of the oldest, if not *the* oldest, of the vessels used as yachts on the Chesapeake and still in existence is the 64-foot schooner *Australia,* which was owned for many years by Paul Du Pont of Wilmington, Delaware. At one time she belonged to the British; Du Pont was informed by the British Admiralty that *Australia* was probably a supply ship during the War of 1812 and "undoubtedly" was present at the bombardment of Fort McHenry.[1] However, according to the book *Chesapeake Bay Schooners,* by Ann Jensen and Quentin Snediker,[2] *Australia* was built at Petcock, New York, in 1862, and under the name *Alma* was a blockade runner during the Civil War. Du Pont bought her in 1939 from an Eastern Shore waterman who had been using her as a coal carrier, and her conversion to a yacht was done in a way that preserved

Australia as a head boat in 1933 sailing on the Chester River. Courtesy The Mariners' Museum, Newport News, Virginia.

her original appearance and character. During the 1940s, the Du Ponts cruised her on the Bay with only a yawlboat for power and at one time with no yawlboat at all. *Australia* has been partially rebuilt a number of times, and presently she is owned by the Marine Historical Association at Mystic, Connecticut. Hauled out of the water, her hull has been put on display as an educational exhibit.

Replicas of *Spray*: Every sailor knows about Captain Joshua Slocum, the first person to sail around the world alone, and his hefty 37-foot *Spray,* which began life as a working sloop of a type similar to those that oystered in Delaware Bay and Long Island Sound. Although *Spray* had no real connection with the Chesapeake, Howard Chapelle did write that she resembled two working sloops from

CHESAPEAKE SAILS

Cambridge, Maryland. Slocum's record-setting feat, completed in 1898, was all the more remarkable when you consider that his circumnavigation was made in an ancient hulk which the destitute captain completely rebuilt himself; the voyage was made prior to the existence of the Panama Canal, so the course led through many remote and poorly charted regions; *Spray* had no engine, no electricity, no autopilot or self-steering vane, no radio of any kind, obviously no GPS or even a chronometer; and much of Slocum's equipment—turpentine flares, bucket still, and wooden anchor—was homemade. The captain did spend some time on the Bay after completing an earlier voyage from Brazil to Washington, D.C., in a homemade junk-rigged sampan/dory named *Liberdade.*

The well-publicized circumnavigation inspired many a replica of *Spray.* These are well documented in the book *In the Wake of the Spray* by Kenneth E. Slack.[3] Most replicas were not exact copies, but two of the most accurate were built in Oxford, Maryland, in 1929 and 1930 at the Oxford Ship Yard. First established in 1866, this yard built numerous workboats, and a newspaper article stated that in 1877 it built a sailing yacht named *Florence* designed by David Block.[4] The first of the local copies of Slocum's boat was named *Spray,* but she was usually referred to as the Oxford *Spray.* She was built by Captain Robert D. "Pete" Culler for his own use from plans published in Joshua Slocum's book *Sailing Alone Around the World.* The plans were scaled up by Slocum's son Victor. Pete

Culler and his wife lived on this *Spray* for twenty-three years, cruising up and down the U.S. East Coast and spending much time on the Chesapeake. In addition to serving as a home and family cruiser, the Oxford *Spray* was occasionally used for hauling cargo and taking out charter parties. On rare occasions she competed in workboat races. I had the opportunity to go aboard and inspect her at San Juan, Puerto Rico, in late 1970.

The other *Spray* replica, built at Oxford from the same set of plans as Culler's boat, was *Basilisk,* owned by marine biologist/author Gilbert Klingel. She was taken to the West Indies and used as a biological research vessel, but unfortunately she was wrecked on an island in the Bahamas.

Spray imitations were popular at one time, and they had their good points in ample room, natural self-steering ability, high initial stability, and easy motion. However, compared to modern yachts,

Pete Culler's Oxford *Spray* at Annapolis in 1937. Courtesy Chesapeake Bay Maritime Museum, Ernest Tucker Collection.

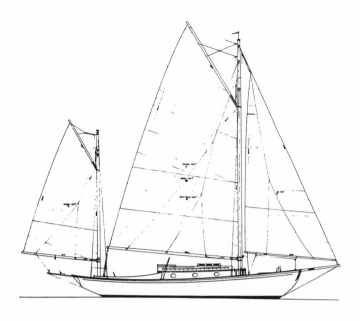

Sail plan of *Seawitch* with her original gaff rig. Courtesy Paul D. Barefoot, executor to the estate of Philip H. Rhodes.

they were clumsy, lacked maneuverability, had less-than-desirable ultimate stability, and were far from close-winded. Many sailors believe that Slocum accomplished his remarkable voyage in spite of *Spray,* not because of her. They must admit, though, that the old boat had real character, and, in the modern vernacular, she got the job done.

Seawitch: One of the first commissioned designs for a racing cruiser from the board of famous naval architect Philip L. Rhodes was the 34-foot yawl *Seawitch.* She was commissioned in 1926 by Donald H. Sherwood, a prominent member of the Gibson Island Club, who claimed that her plans were actually drawn on the Rhodes's dining room table. She was also the first racing cruiser built by the Davis Yard at Solomons, Maryland. Prior to then Clarence Davis

had built workboats almost exclusively and though he was not anxious to undertake a yacht with rigid specifications, Sherwood managed to persuade him, and *Seawitch* was superbly built.

It is worth repeating an amusing story told by Donald in his privately printed memoirs entitled *The Sailing Years.*[5] After *Seawitch* had been sailing successfully for a year, a similar Rhodes yacht named *West Wind* was launched, and while the mastless hull was tied to a dock at the Davis yard, Clarence Davis stepped aboard her. As Sherwood described it, "She gave a nice little roll which so frightened Clarence that he jumped back on the dock in a panic and went to call Phil over long distance. He told him that *West Wind* was so tender he was afraid to step the mast. He thought she would capsize." The distressed Rhodes then called Sherwood to ask if he could borrow some money to buy *West Wind* and scrap her because she was a failure. It turned out that Davis was accustomed to the high initial stability of workboats and didn't fully realize that a deep-keel yacht with external ballast was initially tender but stiffened considerably after a few degrees of heel. Both *West Wind* and *Seawitch* proved to be excellent sail carriers, seldom requiring a reef.

There was a keen rivalry between my father's Alden yawl *Kelpie* and *Seawitch.* The former generally did better in the 92-mile Cedar Point Race, and the latter usually triumphed in the 38-mile Poplar Island Race. There were no restrictions on sails in the first Cedar Point Race held at the end of August 1929. Don Sherwood wrote that one boat set a squaresail

CHESAPEAKE SAILS

and another increased her sail area by hanging her cabin carpet from the main boom. On *Seawitch* one of her crew, the ebullient sailor/yacht broker Gordon Raymond, climbed aloft and lashed a boat hook to the masthead to support a spinnaker borrowed from a Fisher Island boat. That race was won by a Herreshoff light-displacement yawl named *Scarab*, owned by George Pulver of Philadelphia.

In 1936 *Seawitch* was sold to Gibson Islander Albert Ober. This was a period of great activity for International Rule racing. Corrin Strong wrote in his 1936 log that there were thirteen 8-meter boats competing in the Swan Point–Love Point Race.[6] That summer Don Sherwood campaigned the 8-meter *Ariel*, but the following year he bought the 59-foot Herreshoff-designed cutter *Flying Cloud* to serve as both cruiser and summer home. A tragedy occurred during the coastal passage when Sherwood and his Chesapeake crew brought *Flying Cloud* from New Bedford, Massachusetts, to her new home at Gibson Island. On the midnight watch, Albert Ober fell overboard and was never recovered. His *Seawitch* was sold Down East, and she spent the next twenty-five years in Maine. Later she was sold to a charter boat operator in the Virgin Islands. Her owner, Jack Strickland, wrote me in 1984 that after fifty-seven years *Seawitch* was still going strong, and he had raced her successfully (never out of the money) in a number of Classic Yacht Regattas. Unfortunately, she was seriously damaged the following year by an out-of-control cruise ship during a hurricane, but I think she was satisfactorily re-

Seawitch at anchor in the late 1920s. Courtesy Donald H. Sherwood.

paired. Strickland wrote that she was "a fine sailer and still doing her stuff."[7]

My present boat is the 19-foot Cape Dory Typhoon *Sea Witch*, named after the above Rhodes yawl. She was co-owned with me by Donald Sherwood's son Arthur, now deceased, who founded and was an early director of the Chesapeake Bay Foundation, an organization devoted to the conservation and ecological protection of the Bay. Art derived much of his love and concern for the Chesapeake from his early days aboard the original *Seawitch*.

***Caribbee, Narada,* and other Rhodes designs:** Aside from *Seawitch*, many other Phil Rhodes designs have graced the Chesapeake. When I say graced I mean it in the sense of adorning or embellishing, because Rhodes creations are noted for their beauty. Indeed his sheerlines have been called "sensuous." His boats were smart sailers and comfortable as well.

Without a doubt, the most famous Rhodes ocean racer to spend time on the Bay is the 58-foot centerboard yawl *Caribbee*, owned for five years in the late

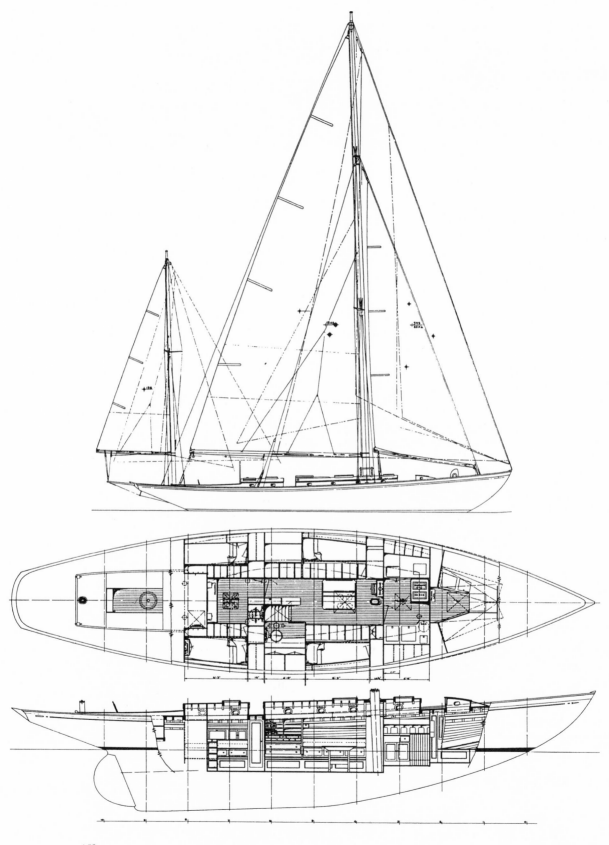

CHESAPEAKE SAILS

1940s and early 1950s by Annapolitan Carleton Mitchell. Just prior to his purchase of *Caribbee*, Mitchell had owned *Carib*, formerly *Malabar XII*, a 47-foot Alden ketch. With her generous draft, *Carib* proved too deep for cruising grounds such as parts of the Chesapeake and the Bahamas, and Mitchell wrote me that he "dragged bottom" quite often.[8] Undoubtedly this contributed to his thinking about centerboarders and influenced his move to *Caribbee* and the even more famous *Finisterre*. Originally named *Alondra, Caribbee* was not only renamed but extensively rerigged by Mitchell following recommendations by Rod Stephens. The hull was even strapped to allow taut rigging.[9] This effective tuning, together with expert handling, produced a champion racing cruiser that compiled a truly outstanding record. Her best years were 1952 and 1953, when she won the SORC both years, took fleet second in the 1952 Transatlantic Race, and won three out of four starts at Cowes Week in England. On the Chesapeake, she won the Labrot Trophy in 1950 and 1953.

A handsome Rhodes cutter that was well known on the Bay prior to World War II was Corrin Strong's *Narada*. Built in 1936 by M. M. Davis at Solomons, Maryland, this 46-footer had more than her share of victories in local racing. An important figure in Chesapeake yachting activities, Corrin Strong was a prominent commodore of the Gibson Island

Yacht Squadron and president of the CBYRA. Under his leadership in 1939, the CBYRA first established High Point rules, scoring, and awards. Far from being a stuffy official, Corrin was a fun-loving sailor; he also established the Timid Skipper's Union described in chapter 3.

Corrin kept detailed personal logs and in one of them he described the launching of *Narada* on a hot day in June. To lubricate the railway, tallow was used, but it kept melting and running off. It became necessary to use several hundred pounds of crushed ice to keep the tallow from melting. Phil Rhodes was present at the christening but refused to mount the viewing platform, stating that "he was worried enough as it was, without taking on anything additional."

In *Narada*, Rhodes created a boat that was fast, comfortable, and beautiful. Her thoroughly tank-tested hull was used as a prototype for a number of future well-known Rhodes designs. Despite her meticulous planning, however, an important detail was overlooked. Her cockpit scuppers were placed aft instead of forward, and every time she reached a certain speed the stern wave would rise up and flood the cockpit.[10] This fault was later corrected.

As noted previously, *Narada* was sunk after a collision off Norfolk, Virginia, while she was serving in the Coast Guard's Offshore Patrol during World War II. Corrin Strong made several attempts to recover her, but she was never found. Her memory has been perpetuated by an annual award, the *Narada* Trophy, presented to the highest scoring

Facing page: Plans of *Caribbee* (ex *Alondra*). Courtesy Paul D. Barefoot, executor to the estate of Philip H. Rhodes.

Gibson Island boat participating in the Gibson Island–sponsored races.

There were several sisters or near-sisters to *Narada* on the Bay. Although the yawl *Cherry Blossom* and the cutter *Elda* have been called sisters and they were very similar, they differed enough to have different numbers in the Rhodes design index. Owned by Gibson Islanders Paul Patterson (first) and Henry Wise (later), *Elda* was lost on a reef off Bermuda in 1958. Approaching the island at night, she was swept into the reef by a current that had been underestimated. She promptly sank, but her crew was saved after spending the night in a life raft made fast to the rigging that extended above the turbulent water.

True sisters, but with slightly modified stem lines, were the cutter *White Squall,* owned by Donald Sherwood (who had previously owned *Seawitch*) and the yawl *Pavana,* the replacement boat for Corrin Strong's *Narada.* Both were built

The author steering *Pavana* with what appears to be an all female crew in 1950. Photograph by Henry Strong.

by the Balco Yacht Company at Baltimore in 1949–1950. The three sons of Corrin—Henry, Peter, and Toby—often raced *Pavana* on the Bay, and on one occasion during a squall, the spinnaker sheets escaped, causing the chute to stream out from the masthead like a flag. The problem of how to retrieve the out-of-reach sheets was solved by Toby, who was an avid fisherman. He went below and got his fishing rod, cast for a sheet, and snagged it. Then the crew was able to haul in the flapping nylon and save the sail.

After Corrin became the ambassador to Norway in 1953, his son Peter sailed *Pavana* across the Atlantic to Norway, covering the thirty-three-hundred-mile course without setting light sails in twenty-four and a half days. A member of the crew was Norris Hoyt, making the first or second of his twenty-three Atlantic crossings on small yachts. My wife Sally and I had the pleasure of cruising on *Pavana* while she was at Oslo in 1954. Not long ago her deteriorating hull was discovered in a Maryland woods, and she is being lovingly restored by Kevin Corrigan.

Former Star sailor and founder of Gibson Island's Junior Fleet, Nathaniel "Cap" Kenney successfully raced a sleek 32-foot sloop named *Nightcap* for several years prior to World War II. Built by the Annapolis Yacht Yard (later bought by Trumpy), *Nightcap* was a Rhodes Lake One-Design, which could have been considered more cruising racer than racing cruiser. She came close to dominating Class C for a while, but in 1940 she was beaten in the Poplar Island Race by a small Stephens-designed cutter named *Babe* that was under charter to William Crouse of Oxford. The *Baltimore Sun* proclaimed "Freakish Craft Takes Annual Gibson Island Yacht Squadron Race—Corrected Time Gives Little Yacht Place Over *Nightcap*." Our Alden yawl *Kelpie* finished third, and my father remarked that the headlines should have read "Two Freakish Craft Beat *Kelpie*."

In 1939 Rhodes designed the first Bounty class, said to be the first inexpensive sizable racing cruiser to be mass-produced. Offered at prices 35 to 40 percent lower than similar boats then being produced, the 39-foot Bounty sloops were built upside down on an assembly line by the Coleman Boat Company in New England. Several of these boats came to the Chesapeake and were successful in local racing. John R. Sherwood's *Gibson Girl* won the Labrot Trophy in 1941. Very occasionally I crewed on *Gibson Girl*, and on one race was almost knocked overboard when we were rammed in a T-bone collision with a navy yawl. John's brother, Miller Sherwood, injured his hand trying to fend off the yawl. Another Bounty I sometimes sailed was *Wyvern*, skippered by Ann Palmer. While getting underway from a mooring one day, my godfather, George Blakiston, was standing on *Wyvern*'s bow facing forward, and Ann, in her soft feminine voice, asked him to cast off the mooring line. No action was taken, so in a stronger voice she ordered him to "cast off." Still no action. Finally she yelled, "Throw the rope in the water." Blakiston turned around indignantly and

Cap Kenney's *Night Cap* before the start of a race off Gibson Island. Photograph by Richard Kenney, courtesy Carter Kenney Williamson.

growled, "I know as many goddamned nautical terms as you do."

Much later came the Bounty II class, the first large stock racing cruiser to be built of fiberglass. It is commonly believed that this boat is simply a molded version of the first Bounty, but the fiberglass boat is actually an entirely different design.[11] It evolved from *Altair*, a boat that was designed for Bradford Smith of Georgetown, Maryland, in 1955. She enjoyed some success racing on the Bay and won her class in the 1957 Annapolis-Newport Race. A centerboard counterpart of this model was also successful; one of them, well known on the Chesapeake, was Henry Chance's *Hirondelle.* The Pearson-produced Bounty II had slightly more freeboard than the original and was called the Pearson 41. Handsome but considered outdated for racing, one of these boats, *Restless,* was sailed to first in her class in the 1996 Bermuda Race by Eric Crawford (son of Blue Water Medalist Jim Crawford) of Easton, Maryland.

Other Rhodes-designed boats I have sailed on or raced against on the Chesapeake are the Vanguard, the Swiftsure, the Chesapeake 32, and the Reliant. These are all stock fiberglass racing cruisers. My favorite, largely for aesthetic reasons, is the 41-foot Reliant, which has particularly graceful lines and a low cabin trunk with small portlights. I had some memorable sails on *Calypso,* the Reliant owned by the late Dr. Roy Scholz.

The Alden schooners: Among the more gorgeous creations of man were the schooners designed by John G. Alden of Boston. One that cruised well beyond the Bay was the 48-foot *Fiddler's Green,* a handsome husky seagoer with clipper bow, bulwarks, a fidded topmast, and a yardarm on her foremast. After being damaged by the New England hurricane in 1938, she was bought, repaired, and brought to the Bay by Dr. Edmund Kelly of Baltimore. *Fiddler's Green* was cruised so extensively by the doctor and his relatives that they became known as "the cruising Kellys." From the Chesa-

peake they made numerous passages up and down the East Coast and as far away as the Galapagos Islands. Their schooner served in the offshore patrol during World War II, and the Kellys resumed cruising after the war. Unfortunately, *Fiddler's Green* was wrecked off the coast of South Carolina in 1953 during a nighttime passage: a photographic light meter had been placed near the compass, causing deviation that resulted in a serious grounding. The schooner was salvaged but ended her days ignominiously as a commercial barge.

There have been a number of Alden ocean-racing schooners on the Chesapeake, especially during the period between the late 1920s and mid-1930s. Some of the better known of these are *Merry Widow, Water Gipsy, Tradition, High Tide, Lelanta,* and *Freedom.*

Both *Tradition* and *High Tide* were ordered from Alden by J. Rulon Miller, called by *Yachting* and *Rudder* magazines "the father of yachting at Gibson Island." My father sailed with Miller on both of these handsome schooners. Not long after the 60-foot *Tradition* was built in 1928, she was entered in the Bermuda Race, and Dad was her navigator. At New London, Connecticut, before the race, one of the contestants dragged her anchor, drifted down on *Tradition,* and poked her bowsprit through *Tradition's* shrouds. Fearing a dismasting, Miller grabbed the ax that was on board for

Facing page: Tradition on a broad reach. The inscription is from Jay Miller to the author's father, who was her navigator in the 1928 Bermuda Race.

To William R. Henderson
The navigator
Bermuda 1928.

TIDEWATER CLASSICS IN RESIDENCE

W. L. Henderson's yawl *Kelpie* sailing past an Alden schooner in the early 1930s with the author on the cabin top. The hatchet inspired by Jay Miller is mounted on the after end of the cabin trunk.

emergencies and began chopping away on the bowsprit. Before it was completely amputated, however, the crews managed to get the boats untangled. Dad was so impressed with that experience that he permanently installed a hatchet on the after end of our *Kelpie*'s cabin trunk. It remained there as an essential part of her safety gear until *Kelpie* was sold thirty years later.

Returning home after the race, *Tradition* encountered a gale in the Gulf Stream. Being a rugged fisherman-type schooner, she lay to with reasonable comfort under jumbo and a deep-reefed foresail. Dad stood deck watch with the paid hand, Captain Haskell, a veteran merchant mariner, who really came alive during the blow and told about many of his adventures at sea. On one occasion his ship had foundered; Haskell and the ship's cook were castaways on a long floating wooden ladder. As Haskell told it, they drifted for three days with nothing to eat, and then the cook pulled out his leather tobacco pouch and began chewing on it. Haskell growled, "That sonofabitch ate the whole pouch and never offered me a bite." Dad loved Captain Haskell's description of his preparing to take an elephant ride in Rangoon, Burma. In Haskell's words, "When they brung 'er [the elephant] alongside, I looked aloft at 'er superstructure and there settin' on the fo'c'sle head was a little Hindu . . . with a boathook."

The Miller family loved *Tradition*, but Jay and his sons were avid Star racers and they wanted a cruising schooner that would be more competitive on the race course. So *Tradition* was sold and eventually went to the West Indies, where she was used as a charter boat for many years. I was informed by Jay's son Robert that in the 1970s, *Tradition* was lost during a storm on a passage to the Panama Canal. There was little question about the seaworthiness of her model, so one might

Facing page. High Tide under her staysail rig showing her beauty and power. Courtesy The Mariners' Museum, Newport News, Virginia.

speculate that the old boat's seams opened and she could not be kept afloat.

By the end of the 1920s, John Alden was generally considered to be the hottest designer, and Jay Miller went to him again for his *Tradition* replacement. This time he ordered a 71-footer, a sleeker schooner with a stays'l rig for better upwind performance. She was built by M. M. Davis at Solomons, Maryland, in 1931 and named *High Tide*. In her first distance race from New London to Cape May, she was the first boat to finish, but the winner on corrected time was Alden's famous *Malabar X*. (In 1927 Miller had finished a close second to another *Malabar* with his schooner *Blue Water* in the Cape May to Gibson Island Race.) Unfortunately Jay Miller died not long after he had acquired *High Tide*, and she was bought by Eugene Du Pont. As mentioned in chapter 1, *High Tide* was first by four hours to finish the 1933 New London–Gibson Island Race, and she fittingly won the J. Rulon Miller Memorial Trophy for best corrected time in the fleet of forty-one ocean racers.

Regular crewmembers under Miller's command were given caps with the name *High Tide* sewn on the front. Dad earned one of these, and he wore it for several years. On one occasion, after he returned from a long, hard, and unsuccessful race, my sister looked at him and commented, "That hat may say *High Tide*, but it should say *mean low water*."

High Tide went on to have a long adventurous career. My wife, Sally, and I saw her in the early 1970s in Grenada when she was a West Indian charter boat

named *Golden Eagle* (nicknamed *Golden Bagel*) commanded by Theodore "Ted Charles" Cohen. She still had some of the original galvanized rigging that had been spliced by Salty Marks at Gibson Island.

The highlight of her career was a four-year circumnavigation under the ownership of Phineas Sprague, completed in 1977. Then named *Mariah*, she had her share of heavy weather and was pooped in the Mediterranean Sea; a sea breaking over the stern threw the helmsman against the wheel, breaking it off. Sprague kept the wheel as a memento.[12]

Under new ownership and in another storm, *Mariah* foundered off the entrance of Delaware Bay in 1980. The almost-fifty-year-old boat opened up, and using pumps and buckets, the crew could not stay ahead of the inflow. The Coast Guard rescued the crew, two of them by helicopter, in hurricane force winds. Details of the sinking can be

The spacious deck of *High Tide*, then named *Golden Eagle*, at Grenada, West Indies, in the early 1970s. Courtesy Robert L. Dwight.

found in the book *A Guide to Small Boat Emergencies* by John M. Waters.

Besides Rulon Miller, the other great Alden fan on the Chesapeake was Baltimorean William McMillan. As a college student McMillan owned the 43-foot Alden Schooner *Jolly Roger,* which burned in 1927 during her first season when a paid hand accidently poured gasoline into a kerosene stove.[13] She was promptly replaced by the 52-foot schooner *Merry Widow,* a sister to John Alden's beautiful *Malabar VI.* As mentioned in chapter 1, *Merry Widow* was third in her class in the 1928 Bermuda Race, and the following year she won her class in the New London–Gibson Island Race. Bill McMillan was mighty proud of his schooner and wanted to take his mother for a sail, but she refused to go aboard because she was embarrassed by the boat's name! How times have changed.

McMillan is best known for establishing the McMillan Cup, sometimes referred to as the "Holy Grail" of collegiate sailing. There is a story that when Bill, as a Princeton sailor, was finally paid by the insurance company for the near total loss of *Jolly Roger,* he was feeling flush and decided to put some of the money into a handsome Tiffany silver trophy for college racing. Since 1949 the McMillan series has been raced in large boats, first Luders yawls and then Navy 44s, at the U.S. Naval Academy. Although the Kennedy Cup is now awarded to the winner of the intercollegiate big-boat nationals, the McMillan Cup Regatta remains the oldest and equally prestigious big-boat event for colleges east of the Rocky Mountains.

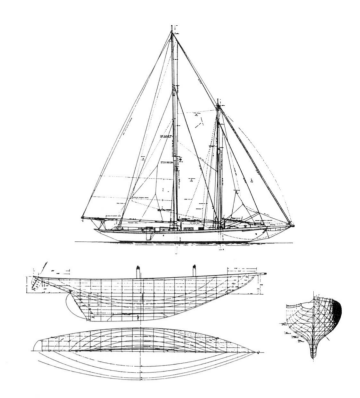

Sail plan and lines of *High Tide.* Courtesy John G. Alden Naval Architects.

After *Merry Widow,* the next Alden schooner owned by Bill McMillan was the lovely 59-foot *Water Gipsy.* I was lucky enough to be taken for a sail on her when I was a young boy, and I still remember her broad flush decks and great power under sail. My father crewed on her in the 1934 Bermuda Race. Although it's doubtful she was built specifically for the 1931 Transatlantic Race (she was intended for cruising as well as ocean racing), she did participate soon after her launching in that famous race from Newport, Rhode Island, to Plymouth, England. This was the contest won by *Dorade* when she finished forty-six hours ahead of the next much-larger boat after sailing a great circle route. Following their return home,

Dorade's skipper and mate, Olin and Rod Stephens, were given a ticker-tape parade in New York by Mayor Jimmie Walker. *Water Gipsy* did not fare well in this race; McMillan and his sailing master Sam Wetherill elected to take the longer, more southerly course to take advantage of the Gulf Stream, but this proved to be the wrong strategy.

In keeping with the times, *Water Gipsy* was given a Marconi mainsail, but she had a gaff foresail because Alden thought this provided more reaching power, and twist could be controlled with a vang leading to the mainmast. The boat was fitted out and provisioned for the Transatlantic Race mostly by certain members of her crew, as Bill had to remain in college almost until the start because he was in the process of obtaining his master's degree.

It is interesting to compare *Water Gipsy*'s provisioning with that of the slightly larger Whitbread 60 of today. Every pound of weight is pared from the latter's stores and the crew must live on a bare minimum of freeze-dried food, but even with three fewer crewmembers, *Water Gipsy* carried over 300 pounds of fresh food such as potatoes and onions, over 500 cans of food, two crates of oranges, and 350 gallons of drinking water. In addition, she carried two heavy fisherman-type dories.[14] Though *Water Gipsy* was obviously not as fast as today's Whitbread racers, there is no doubt that the speed of the older and far more comfortable displacement-type ocean racer was much less affected by heavy loading.

McMillan carried three chronometers during the Atlantic crossing, and this reminds me of a story about General George S. Patton, another admirer of John Alden. The famous hero of World War II owned the Alden schooner *When and If,* which, incidentally, spent some time on the Chesapeake when the general was stationed in Washington. Patton shared a dislike of President Roosevelt with Clifford Swaine of the Alden design firm, and he told Swaine that if he were passed over again by Roosevelt for promotion, he would resign from the army and go voyaging in his schooner. He had a chronometer, but a sailor friend told Patton that he needed another to check the first. He then began to ponder the question of which timepiece to believe if they disagreed. As a result he bought still another chronometer. Of course, Patton got his promotion, so *When and If* never took her lengthy voyage, which had been planned to fulfill the general's ambition of sailing from the U.S. East Coast to the West Coast via Cape Horn.[15]

When *Water Gipsy* arrived in England, she was entered in the Fastnet Race, then referred to as the "Grand National" of ocean races. It turned out to be a heavy-weather affair in which she thrived. Despite some windward work early in the race, she was the first in a sizable competitive fleet to round the Fastnet rock. The return leg to the finish was a rugged close reach against gale force winds, and one crewmember on an English cutter was washed overboard and lost. McMillan's schooner finished second on corrected time, beaten only by the close-winded *Dorade*.[16]

After returning home, *Water Gipsy* continued to demonstrate her speed and seaworthiness. She finished third in class and fleet in the 1932 Bermuda Race and second in class and fleet in the 1934 Bermuda Race.

Although she spent her early years in England, the 66-foot steel Alden schooner *Lelanta* resided on the Chesapeake on two separate occasions, first in 1972 under the ownership of Jonathan McLean, and again in the late 1970s when owned by Dr. Charles Iliff and his son Dr. Nicholas Iliff. This handsome schooner with beautifully matched ends was not often raced, but she had an adventurous career: she cruised in Europe, served as a charter boat in the West Indies, and was used to smuggle drugs in Florida. The Iliffs, who also owned the locally well-known Block Island 40 *Alaris,* acquired *Lelanta* after she was seized by the sheriff in Naples, Florida, for drug smuggling. At the time she was carrying an estimated seven tons of marijuana. The Iliffs bought her at an auction by the sheriff's department; they sailed her up to the Chesapeake in eight days, and then spent about two years reconditioning her. Nick wrote me: "I put about 1,000 hours into her, sandblasting her, priming her with epoxy, and painting her with Imron. We installed an ice maker, a trash compactor, and rebuilt her interior, which had been stripped by the drug runners."[17] The refurbished schooner was cruised quite a lot on the Bay, and in 1981 the Iliffs sailed her to Bermuda. At the end of that year, she was donated to a school in Massachusetts and soon left the Chesapeake.

Perhaps the Alden schooner most familiar to veteran Chesapeake sailors is

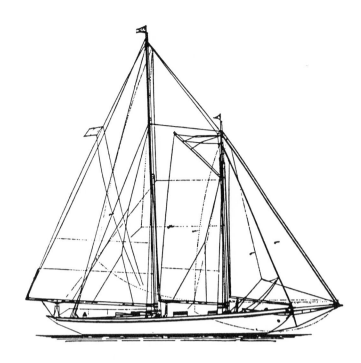

The sail plan of *Water Gipsy.* Courtesy John G. Alden Naval Architects.

the 89-foot *Freedom,* for many years owned by the U.S. Naval Academy. She is discussed in chapter 7, in the section about academy yachts that were used to train the Annapolis midshipmen.

The schooner rig began to lose its popularity in the mid-1930s and subsequently disappeared almost completely from racing. Fortunately, however, the rig has been making a minor comeback in recent years, and limited racing has been revived with the annual 127-mile Great Chesapeake Bay Schooner Race, which began in the early 1990s as a benefit for the Chesapeake Bay Foundation.

Stormy Weather: Next to *Dorade,* the 54-foot yawl *Stormy Weather* was Olin Stephens's most famous early design.

Intended to be an improvement over *Dorade*, *Stormy Weather* was given more beam, not only to benefit her rating but to improve her initial stability and create more room below. Rod Stephens told me that the additional beam also alleviated the tendency to roll when running before following and quartering seas, one of the few faults of *Dorade*.

Bob Henry was a great fan of *Stormy Weather*. He was a designer at Sparkman and Stephens during her heyday, and he'd sailed on her a number of times. Years later, when I asked Bob what kind of boat he'd most like to take offshore, he answered without hesitation, "a boat like *Stormy Weather*."[18] An oft-told story about this famous yawl recounts John Alden's remark when he saw the bottom of a boat in winter storage at City Island, New York. Her top was covered, disguising her identity. Alden stopped abruptly, studied the underbody, and remarked: "In my opinion a better design would be

Bill Labrot, *left*, and Bob Henry with their wives aboard a sizable yacht that is probably the schooner *Seaweed*. Courtesy Leonie Labrot Gately.

impossible to achieve." The boat turned out to be *Stormy Weather*.

Designed for Philip Le Boutillier in 1933, *Stormy Weather* was skippered by Rod Stephens in the 1935 race from Newport to Bergen, Norway. Repeating the strategy used aboard *Dorade* in the previous Transatlantic Race, Rod sailed a great circle course that took him far north of the tracks of his competitors. This took nerve, as the iceberg limit that year was far south of its normal position, and there was above-average fog, but the strategy paid off. *Stormy Weather* finished a mere five hours behind the much larger *Vamarie* and easily won the race on corrected time. She then went on to repeat *Dorade*'s feat of following her transatlantic triumph with a first place in the Fastnet Race.

Cruising from Norway to England, Rod and his crew did some adventurous sailing along the northern shores of Europe. He told me about sailing *Stormy Weather*, then without an engine, through the North Sea Canal in Holland. The wind was dead ahead, and the yawl, carrying a genoa, was tacked an estimated 150 times through the narrow canal. Rod said this performance was witnessed by Cornelius Bruynzeel (later of *Stormvogel* fame), and he was sufficiently impressed to order from Sparkman and Stephens a near sisterboat that

Facing page: Stormy Weather driving to windward in the Gulf Stream. Photograph by Morris Rosenfeld. © Mystic Seaport, Rosenfeld Collection, Mystic, Connecticut. Image acquired in honor of Franz Schneider.

CHESAPEAKE SAILS

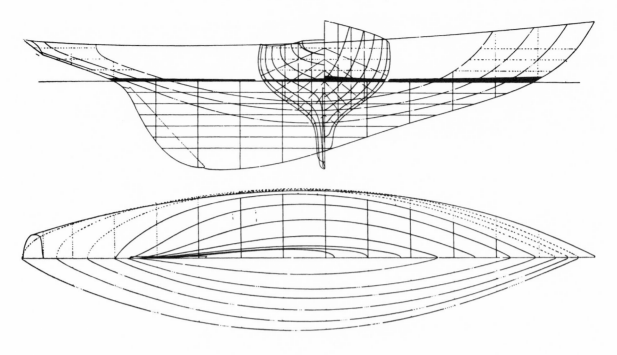

Lines of *Stormy Weather*. Courtesy Sparkman & Stephens, Inc.

would be named *Zeearend*. After their Fastnet victory, Rod and his crew sailed *Stormy* back home against the prevailing westerlies near the peak of the hurricane season in twenty-four and a half days. What a sailor, and what a boat!

Stormy Weather came to the Bay in 1939, when William Labrot bought her especially for the New London–Annapolis Race. With my father a member of the crew, she took a third in her class.

Bill Labrot was one of the most eminent yachtsmen on the Bay. A prominent commodore and prime mover of the Annapolis Yacht Club and a generous philanthropist who donated his land to create Sandy Point State Park, Bill is now memorialized with the Labrot Trophy awarded annually to the skipper of the Bay's top-scoring racing cruiser. His purchase of

Stormy Weather, along with the Naval Academy's acquisition of *Vamarie* and *Highland Light,* brought three of the biggest names in ocean racing to the Chesapeake.

One of the thrills of my youth was being allowed to steer *Stormy* during a day race on the Choptank River in 1940. A teenage Star sailor at the time, I was accustomed to a very sensitive helm and expected *Stormy* to steer like a truck, but to my amazement she had a moderately light helm with quick response and positive feel. Originally she had a tiller, then a wheel, and later a tiller again. I think she had a wheel when I sailed her, but her present owner, Paul Adamthwaite, wrote me that he believes *Stormy* was converted to wheel steering in 1947.[19] If this is true, it is even more amazing that I found the 54-footer so easy to steer with a tiller.

To my way of thinking *Stormy Weather's* underwater configuration is still one of the most efficient and comfortable for blue water sailing. Her keel is moderately long for steady tracking and deep enough for a high range of stability as well as the prevention of leeway; her keel-attached rudder is well protected, resists stalling, and is effective when the boat heels. Although the rudder rake exerts a minor downward force when the boat is level, it exerts almost pure side force when she is heeled. The triangular underwater profile of *Stormy Weather* with deep drag aft and a swept forefoot has proven highly efficient for beating to windward. It not only reduces wetted surface area, but also minimizes the speed-robbing tip vortex at the bottom of the keel. I think there is also a safety benefit to a swept forefoot; it can provide protection against collisions with floating objects, as the boat will ride up on the object and minimize shock loading. Needless to say, an integral keel is far less vulnerable to all types of damaging forces than a deep nearly-vertical bolted-on fin. Furthermore, a flowing rounded hull such as *Stormy's* is more seakindly and less subject to pounding than the hull of a typical modern flat-bottomed ocean-racing sled.

Stormy Weather all but dominated the SORC between 1937 and 1948 under various ownerships. When owned by Labrot, she won the Miami-Nassau Race and was second in the St. Petersburg–Havana Race. Bill Labrot raced her successfully on the Bay until World War II, when she was donated to the Coast Guard for service in the Offshore Patrol. I've been told that *Stormy* was painted gray and gun mounts were bolted to her deck. How many modern ocean racers could survive in the Offshore Patrol? She was sold to Frederick Temple after the war and left the Chesapeake, eventually ending up in the West Indian charter trade. Paul Adamthwaite, a retired British naval officer, found her in deplorable condition at St. Thomas, Virgin Islands, in 1983. Calling himself a "nut case,"[20] Adamthwaite bought the yawl and restored her to her original condition. He wrote me that besides other extensive work on the boat, seventy-six frames were replaced. After her restoration she made numerous Atlantic crossings and continued racing very respectably even against modern boats of fiberglass and aluminum. In 1990 she was still going strong.

Additional Stephens designs: Aside from *Stormy Weather,* a number of notable Sparkman and Stephens racing cruisers resided on the Chesapeake for a period of time. Among these are *Finisterre, Dyna, Running Tide, Reindeer,* and *Loon,* all discussed in chapter 6.

Another well-known ocean racer from the board of Olin Stephens is the 62-foot yawl *Manitou.* Though not a resident yacht in her heyday, she began her life and has spent her twilight years on the Bay. She was built in 1937 by M. M. Davis and Son at Solomons, Maryland, and a painting of her graces the jacket of *The Last Generation* by Geoffrey M. Footner[21] (a book about the Davis yard, its boats, and people). The jacket painting, based on a photograph by Morris

Rosenfeld, is a striking one of a gorgeous boat. *Manitou* deserves to be a cover girl, as she was a source of great pride among the Davis craftsmen. She was superbly built of teak, mahogany, and white oak and paneled below with exotic butternut.

Built for James Lowe of the New York Yacht Club, *Manitou* was taken to New York and then the Great Lakes where she made a name for herself by winning the cruising division of the prestigious 333-mile Chicago-Mackinac Race. She also had an outstanding record in the shorter Port Huron–Mackinac Race, but she became best known later, when owned by the U.S. Coast Guard Academy. At that time she was the favorite sailing yacht of President John F. Kennedy. A former winner of the McMillan Cup and no mean sailor, Kennedy was attracted to beautiful yachts as well as lovely women, and he sailed *Manitou* whenever he had the opportunity.

In 1968 *Manitou* was acquired by the Seafarer's International Union for use by the Harry Lundeberg School at Piney Point, Maryland. That same year she competed in the Skipper Race but her finish was delayed by a lengthy grounding. Six years later, after returning to Solomons for a refit, a low-keyed party was given to celebrate her return home. Seven of the workers who originally built her were present.[22]

When Jacqueline Kennedy and Aristotle Onassis became engaged, Onassis tried to buy *Manitou* as a wedding present for his bride-to-be; however, the Seafarer's Union would not sell the boat to him for any price. It was felt that there should be no dealing with Onassis because his fleet

of oil tankers, sailing under foreign flags of convenience, was contributing to the degradation of the American merchant marine. Onassis sent the union a blank check to be filled out to any amount, but the check was returned to him.

During the early stages of the building of *Manitou,* the 60-foot Sparkman and Stephens cutter *White Cloud* was being completed at the Davis yard for George Whiting of Baltimore. Although not as well known as *Manitou, White Cloud* also won the cruising division of the Chicago-Mackinac. This occurred in 1942 when she was owned by Charles Sorensen of Detroit. Whiting, who had previously owned the beautiful bright-finished 8-meter *Sunny,* ordered *White Cloud* with the 1937 New London–Gibson Island Race very much in mind. She was a state-of-the-art boat with a thoroughly tank-tested hull and sophisticated rigging that was influenced by America's Cup J-boats. Her boom has been called a variation of the Park Avenue boom, but actually it was a bending boom controlled by jack stays on struts. Naval architect Richards Miller has written me that he thinks *White Cloud*'s lofty mast was made by Chesapeake resident George Barr, nephew of the legendary professional skipper Charlie Barr.[23]

Although the cutter was skippered by champion helmsman/designer Sherman Hoyt, she did not fare well in the 1937 coastal race. In his *Memoirs,*[24] Hoyt admitted to being misled by weather reports as well as to having difficulties with the complicated rig. Best known for his America's Cup victories in J-boats (and his insistence that he had sighted the Loch Ness monster from *Dorade* off Scotland in 1933), Sherman Hoyt eventually retired to Maryland's Eastern Shore. At a ripe old age, he often skippered the 8-meter *Hurrying Angel* in races on the Chesapeake.

George Whiting kept *White Cloud* in Gibson Island's harbor until just prior to America's entrance into World War II. He did not race her often, but when he did, she nearly always did well. As with *Stormy Weather,* her hull was so beautifully balanced that despite her size she could be steered easily with a tiller.

An impressive aluminum sloop designed by Sparkman and Stephens in 1962 was the 64-foot *Challenge.* Although her owner George F. Johnson was a member of the Corinthian Yacht Club of Philadelphia, that club is a member of the CBYRA, and *Challenge* occasionally raced on the Bay. She was first to finish in the 1963 Annapolis-Newport Race.

Of the stock Sparkman and Stephens boats inhabiting the Bay, the New York 32 is arguably the most legendary. This is a 45-foot (32 feet on the waterline) sloop designed in 1936 for use as a class racer by the New York Yacht Club. Four of the winningest 32s on the Chesapeake were A. Johnson Grimes's *Folly,* later *Trig* under Charles Dell; Thomas Closs's *Fun* and *Raider;* and Charles Price's *Proton II.* Barry August of the Hampton Yacht Club was still racing his *Legacy* successfully in the nonspinnaker division in the early 1980s. Sometimes the competition among these boats was fierce. During the prestarting maneuvers before a team

race in the 1960s, two of the 32s locked rigging and one was dismasted. A friend of mine was crewing on the dismasted boat and said he had to duck down into the cockpit to avoid being struck by the falling spar.

Those team races, held annually since 1951 by the Sailing Club of the Chesapeake and the Gibson Island Yacht Squadron, pit three boats from one of these clubs against three similar boats from the other. In the first race the SCC put up three Sparkman and Stephens–designed 40-footers (two Mackinac sloops, and the prototype Chesapeake 28) against three Owens cutters from the GIYS. Gibson Island won that contest but in 1998 closely trails in this continuing series with eighteen wins to twenty-three for the SCC. Although these contests are held in fun with much ballyhoo and a free exchange of insults, they are actually taken quite seriously by the participants. At the winning club's annual awards banquet, the victorious team is always presented with the traditional prize, a large broom that symbolizes a clean sweep. Quite often individual members of the winning team receive smaller brooms. Two of these are mounted on the wall of my den, and one day I noticed that one, with a prominent silver plate inscribed with the name *Kelpie,* was facing the wrong way. It turned out that for some time our one-day-a-week maid had been using it for house-cleaning. She thought that we considered the wall a very handy place to store the cleaning broom.

Some other Sparkman and Stephens designs that made names for themselves

A gorgeous lee-side photo of an early New York 32. Photograph by Morris Rosenfeld. © Mystic Seaport, Rosenfeld Collection, Mystic, Connecticut.

on the race courses were Porter Schutt's 49-foot yawl *Egret,* James Rider's 44-foot yawl *Chance,* James Brickell's 44-foot cutter *Starlight* (a forerunner of the New York 32), and Mark Ewing's PJ 43 *Harpoon,* a near sister to *Reindeer,* which is described in chapter 6.

Two Sparkman and Stephens yawls that were famous before moving to the Chesapeake were *White Mist,* formerly owned by Blunt White, and *Figaro,* for-

merly owned by William Snaith. *White Mist* was brought to the Chesapeake by Melville Grosvenor, former Star champion and president of the National Geographic Society. The 46-foot yawl received some publicity when Mel wrote about several of her adventurous cruises in *National Geographic* magazine articles. General Arthur "Tim" Hanson brought the 48-foot *Figaro* to the Bay and renamed her *Foolscap.* It's a good thing the

CHESAPEAKE SAILS

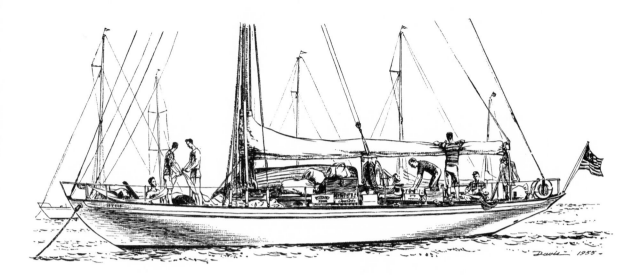

Starlight being prepared for the 1954 Bermuda Race. Drawing by Owen Davis.

general had a sense of humor because after one of his first races, his lovely yawl was listed in the newspaper as *Foolscrap*. She was eventually lost off the African coast by a delivery crew.

Two small stock designs from Sparkman and Stephens have been popular on the Bay: the Rainbow, a 24-foot class racer also used in modified form as a trainer for the Annapolis Sailing School and the U.S. Naval Academy, and the Tartan 27, a cruising one-design. One of the latter class, named *Scot Free*, had an outstanding record in handicap racing during the 1960s under the skillful hand of my colorful friend Richard Jablin. She is now owned by another friend, Richard Schluederberg, a former Ohlson 35 rival who raced a Star named *Blaze* until he was seventy-three years old. His youthful Star competitors were too young to connect the boat's name with Blaze Star, the popular striptease artist from former times.

Another colorful character, Thomas Raby, owned a lovely 40-foot Sparkman and Stephens Mackinac sloop named *Desire*. Tom is locally famous for a remark made while racing in the Annapolis area. When converging with a boat on the port tack that was trying to cross his bow, Tom yelled, "Starboard tack!" The other boat's skipper replied, "Hold your course." Tom answered, "O.K., but which half of your boat do you want to go home on?" The port-tacker promptly came about.

Atom: Unlike the vast majority of yachts in this book, the Tahiti ketch *Atom* was a sluggish sailer, yet she was a legendary offshore cruiser, an able seagoer with remarkable self-steering abilities. Her skipper, the famous singlehander Jean Gau, said there was no need for her to be fast, as he was never in a hurry to get anywhere, and he preferred being at sea.[25] One of his passages across the south Atlantic took 123 days. A French-American, Gau was for many years a New

Plan of the Tahiti ketch. Design by John G. Hanna.

York hotel chef who admitted he didn't like to cook. He practiced his trade between voyages to raise funds for cruising and living at sea. His voyages included two solo circumnavigations of the world and eleven transatlantic crossings, all in *Atom*.

Although her hailing port under Gau's ownership was New York, *Atom* was born on the Chesapeake and spent her first seven or eight years on the Bay, sailing under the name *Lois*. She was built by Marylander Bjorn Egeli, the patriarch of a well-known portrait-painting family, at Shady Side, Maryland, very near the original headquarters of the Slocum Society. It has been reported that the ketch was built in the mid-1940s, but Cedric Egeli, son of the builder, told me she was built in 1936–1937 and sold to Gau during World War II, probably in 1944.[26] Heavily constructed of oak and planked

in cedar (which Gau claimed was impervious to teredo worm), the Marconi-rigged ketch was able to survive the battering of two hurricanes at sea and other stressful events such as being rolled 360 degrees by a rogue wave and being stranded on a lee shore. The latter event was a very literal connection with Maryland, as *Atom* grounded near Ocean City and was left high and dry on a remote beach of Assateague Island. Marylanders were most generous in helping Gau salvage and repair his boat. The major refit was done by John Swain in Cambridge.[27]

In heavy weather Gau usually lay ahull with all sails furled and the helm lashed alee. Indeed this is the way he rode out hurricane Carrie in 1957. This same storm—with over 120-knot winds—sank the 377-foot steel bark *Pamir* with a loss of eighty lives. Aboard *Atom*, Gau went below, battened the hatches, and "slept, ate, read, and drew pictures"[28] while the boat took care of herself (and him). He was also closed up in the cabin while lying ahull when struck by a rogue wave that turned *Atom* upside down in 1966 near the Cape of Good Hope. The wave's approach was graphically described by Gau in the Slocum Society's journal, the *Spray*, in autumn 1966 (translated from *Le Midi Libra*, May 1966):

In the night of February 27 at about 3 A.M., I heard a strange distant sound. It increased in intensity. It appeared to be the roar of a distant waterfall. Second by second it increased. I could not believe it was real. I wondered what would happen. As the roar increased, I instinctively grabbed the edge of my bunk. In a tremendous explosion the huge wave hit the starboard side and tons of water fell on deck. I was thrown against the deck beams and buried under all objects which were on the starboard bunk opposite mine; navigation instruments, charts, etc. The cabin lamp went out.

For a few moments *Atom* remained upside down but was soon rolled upright, although in a shambles with both of her masts broken off and her dinghy missing. In frightful conditions, with the boat rolling her rails under in the gale force winds, Gau managed to cut away the broken rig, repair the drowned engine, and make his way to Mossel Bay, South Africa.

Designed in 1923 by John Hanna—a deaf naval architect and design critic known as the "sage of Dunedin" (Florida)—*Atom* was a 30-foot double-ender with a distinctly salty look reminiscent of the Norwegian sailing lifeboats (redningskoites) designed by Colin Archer. She had a very long keel that gave her great directional stability. Jean Gau said he almost never touched the helm when at sea despite having no self-steering vane or autopilot. He simply lashed the helm, utilizing a spring on the lashing, and *Atom* sailed herself. She was eventually lost off the coast of Africa in 1973.

Atom on the River Orb, Valras, France, circa 1968. Courtesy James Tazelaar, *To Challenge a Distant Sea.*

My familiarity with the Tahiti ketch came from closely observing *Panacea,* kept by the late William Watkins at Gibson Island. Like *Atom,* she had a purposeful blue water look that conjured dreams of the South Seas and oceangoing adventures.

As an interesting aside, when Watkins was almost ninety years old and after more than twenty years of labor, he finished building with his own hands a 25-foot self-designed cutter named *Rose Tree.* His son told me that Watkins had actually planted the tree from which he made the mast!

CHAPTER SIX

LEGENDS OF THE RECENT PAST

To win the fleet award in the CCA-sponsored Bermuda Race is quite an achievement, but for the same boat to win it three times in a row is almost unbelievable. That is exactly what was accomplished by the 38-foot yawl *Finisterre,* a Chesapeake yacht owned and skippered by Carleton Mitchell, in 1956, 1958, and 1960. This was a feat that will probably never by repeated. *Finisterre* also excelled in the prestigious SORC and won the overall prize in 1956.

Finisterre: No racing machine, the Sparkman and Stephens–designed *Finisterre* is a heavy comfortable beamy shoal-draft centerboarder that was intended for extended semiluxurious cruising with guests as well as for racing. Just why she excelled to such an extent on the race course has been a mystery causing considerable head-scratching and speculation by the experts. The late Francis Kinney—a Sparkman and Stephens designer who updated a standard text on naval architecture and wrote *You Are First,* the book about Olin and Rod Stephens—concluded that about 60 percent of *Finisterre*'s victories were due to the skill of her owner and crew and about 40 percent due to good luck.[1]

Superbly built in Connecticut by Seth Persson, *Finisterre* was completed in 1954 and taken to Whitehall Creek near Annapolis where she was moored at Mitchell's waterfront home. Prior to her building, a plywood mockup simulating her cabin interior had been built to ensure maximum comfort and efficiency down below. Equal attention was given to the deck arrangement and rig. Ease of handling was given a high priority. Mitchell once said he wanted no sail to be larger than one that he could carry forward with one hand. I was informed by Carleton that the chief reason for his choosing Sparkman and Stephens as the designer, rather than Phil Rhodes, who had designed his successful centerboarder *Caribbee*, was because of the exceptional rigging expertise of Rod Stephens.[2]

Regarding *Finisterre's* racing success, it is certainly true that the fat little yawl was well sailed. Time and again competitors remarked about Mitchell's strategy and how sails were trimmed and changed to take advantage of the slightest variation in wind direction or velocity. For instance, Charles Iliff, Jr., tells how the 40-foot yawl *Alaris* was well ahead of *Finisterre* in the lighter-going before a storm struck in the 1960 Bermuda Race. Then Mitchell's yawl came alive, and as Iliff put it, "drove all the way through the storm, adding sail whenever the wind moderated slightly, and simply outsailed everyone else in the race."[3]

In *Legendary Yachts,*[4] William Robinson repeated a story told by Stanley Rosenfeld, the famous marine photographer, who was following *Finisterre* close aboard to get

Finisterre in a groove. Note how her fine bow slices the water rather than pushing it.

a good photograph under her lee quarter soon after the start of a Bermuda Race. Having previously taken hundreds of shots from this position, Rosenfeld suddenly realized that something was different. On other occasions the Rosenfeld's photography boat (named *Foto)* needed a lot of steering to stay in position, but this time she could hold a steady course because *Finisterre* was not yawing. With every yaw, obviously, the course would be lengthened and each corrective movement of the rudder would exert a braking force. Here, *Finisterre* was in a groove, sailing the most efficient, relatively steady course as a result of the boat's directional stability and superior helmsmanship.

I have known several of *Finisterre*'s regular crewmembers including Ned Freeman, Bunny Rigg, and Corwith Cramer and can attest to their abilities as all-around corinthian sailors and seamen. Cory Cramer, now deceased, grew up with me in Gibson Island's harbor, and he was the father of my son-in-law Mark Cramer. Cory founded the Sailing Education Association (SEA), which educates students in oceanography and other marine subjects, and a large school vessel was named for him. As the winning navigator aboard *Finisterre* during the 1956 Bermuda Race, Cory won the George Mixter Memorial Trophy. Other crewmembers have included such crack sailors as Richard Bertram, Charles Larkin, Lockwood Pirie, and Bob Henry. Of course, Carleton Mitchell, a Blue Water Medalist, was himself a fine racing helmsman, a skilled navigator, and a thoughtful strategist who knew his boat like few other owners and believed in the most thorough preparations.

In the *Skipper* (September 1958) Bunny Rigg wrote an interesting article called "The Secret Life of *Finisterre*," in which he told of Mitchell's insistence on a clean ship and a well-fed and rested crew. To achieve the latter, he even issued eye masks and earplugs to help ensure uninterrupted sleep for the off-watch crew. In the matter of cleanliness, Mitchell insisted that each crewmember keep his clothes and personal gear stowed in assigned areas and that

the head was to be used sitting down, not standing up. As an example of Mitchell's analytical mind and attention to detail, he ordered a white spinnaker with a dark red top, not for aesthetics but because he reasoned that the sun shining on the dark red color would heat the air within the chute and give the sail some extra lift in light air. Whether this theory is valid or not, *Finisterre* was fast under spinnaker for a heavy boat, and the idea was copied by others.

Regarding Francis Kinney's thought that luck played a large part in the success of *Finisterre*, I like to think that Mitchell made his own luck, but it is certainly true that the yawl did get her share of the breaks. She was not fast in light air, and it so happened that she seldom competed in races that were mostly calm. For instance, in 1955 when High Point scoring placed relatively small emphasis on the number of races sailed, *Finisterre* won High Points in Class C, partly as a result of missing most of the midsummer drifters and cleaning up in the breezy Annapolis Fall Series. I remember a northeast blow during one Swan Point–Love Point Race; that was *Finisterre*'s weather, and she slaughtered her competitors. Being an early summer race, the wind could have been light or heavy, but Mitchell got the condition he wanted. That is what I would call good luck.

Another factor that certainly made some contribution to *Finisterre*'s success was her favorable rating, at least early in

Facing page: Hull plans of *Finisterre*. Courtesy Sparkman & Stephens, Inc.

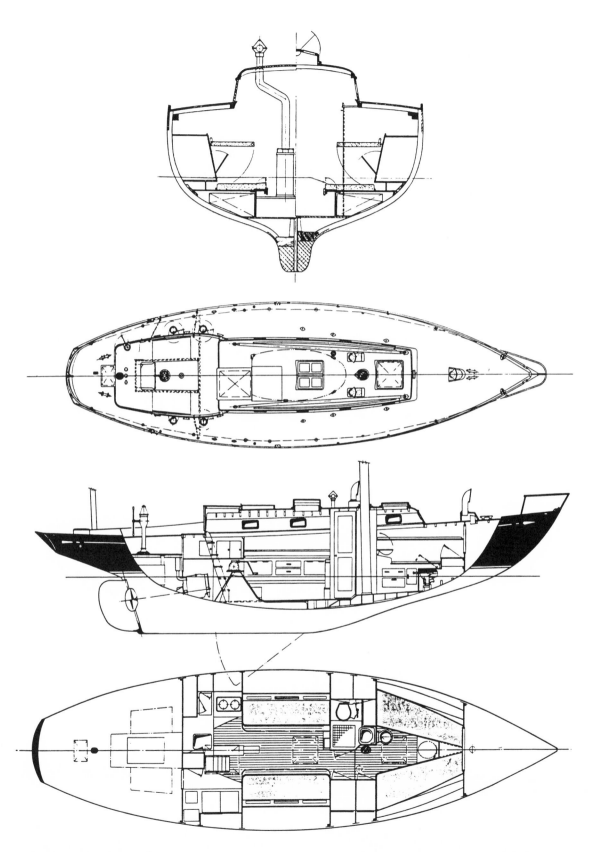

her career, under the CCA rule. In those days initial stability, and thus sail-carrying power, was determined with a ballast-displacement ratio—dividing the weight of the ballast by the weight of the boat and expressing the result as a percentage. The lower the percentage, the better the chance of a good rating. Although *Finisterre* was by no means intended to be a rule beater, she had an exceedingly low ballast-displacement ratio of 26.3 percent. This was achieved without sacrificing initial stability partly by using bronze floors that acted as ballast but did not count as ballast. Carleton Mitchell rightfully claimed the bronze floors had been installed primarily to strengthen the boat's bottom near the centerboard slot and stiffen the hull so that he could carry a very taut headstay, which was helpful when beating in a breeze. The ballast-displacement loophole in the CCA rule was eventually closed with inclining tests to measure stability.

After *Finisterre* attracted so much nationwide interest, there was some speculation among contemporary yachtsmen about who actually drew her lines. Aage Nielsen, then working independently but often with Sparkman and Stephens, has been credited with inspiring *Finisterre*, but her lines were actually drawn by Al Mason. However, I have been reminded by Mitch Gibbons-Neff of the design firm, who was kind enough to supply me with a copy of the Office Plan List, that "a design by Sparkman and Stephens is a team effort and no one design is the creation of any one individual. The final responsibility for this [*Finisterre's*]

design was the Chief Designer, in this case Olin Stephens."[5] As a matter of fact, Carleton Mitchell himself contributed considerable input into the design. I've heard it said that he insisted on a fine slightly-hollowed entrance. *Finisterre's* center of buoyancy was far enough aft to prevent stern squat, and her displacement was heavy enough to provide a comfortable motion and to allow the carrying of ample stores and gear for long passages without excessive harm to her speed.

Was *Finisterre* the perfect boat? Not quite, because there is no such thing; compromises are always necessary in yacht design. I have already mentioned that she did not excel in light air. The greatest weakness of the beamy offshore centerboarder, in my opinion, is its relatively low range of stability. Most boats of the *Finisterre* type have great initial stability and the power to carry sail in a breeze because of their generous beam, but many begin to lose stability somewhere around 110 degrees of heel, and if they should happen to be rolled by a wave to that point they are apt to turn turtle. Once capsized they will not right as easily as a narrow deep-keel boat.

Of course, a capsize in a ballasted boat is very improbable, but it can happen in the worst conditions at sea. One publicized example is the capsize of the keel-centerboarder *Doubloon* when she was caught in a coastal storm. A friend

Facing page: Plan list showing the various designers and draftsmen who worked on the plans for *Finisterre*. Courtesy Sparkman & Stephens, Inc. and Mitchell Gibbons-Neff, Jr.

PLAN LIST   (TROLL)   FINISTERRE

1054   27'-6" W.L. AUX YAWL (CARLETON MITCHELL)

			DWG BY	DATE	DWG NO	
1	1054-A	INBOARD PROFILE & ARRGT	F.J.J	DEC-4-52	1054-A	1
2	1054-B	SAIL PLAN (MAST HEAD RIG)	F.J.J	" 5-52	1054-B	2
3	1054-C	SAIL PLAN	F.J.J	" 7-52	1054-C	3
4						4
5	1054-1×	OFFSET TABLE	A.M		1054-1	5
6	1054-2×	LINES	A.M.		1054-2	6
7	1054-3	CONSTR SECT & FASTENING SCHEDULE	F.J.J	DEC 29-52	1054-3	7
8	(VOID) ×	CABIN CONSTRUCTION PLAN (INSKOR)	F.J.J	MAR-3-53	1054-4	8
9	1054-5	DECK & FRAMING PLAN			1054-5	9
10	1054-6	SAIL PLAN			1054-6	10
11	1054-7×	JOINER SECTIONS (SHEETS I to 5)	F.J.J	MAR-7-53	1054-7	11
12		CABIN CONSTRUCTION PLAN (TRACED) ALT.F 1054-4x41-T	DP.M, F.J.J.	JULY 23,1953	1054-4T	12
13	1054-8	SPAR PLAN	D.P.M		1054-8	13
14	1054-9	MAINMAST FTG. DETAILS	D.P.M	DEC.28,53	1054-9	14
15	1054-10	MIZZEN MAST FTG. DETS.	D.P.M		1054-10	15
16	1054-11	AUTOMATIC PILOT HOOK UP (ARRGT PLAN)	D.P.M.	FEB.4-1954	1054-11	16
17	1054-12	SKETCH OF REVISED TRUNK SHAPE	D.P.M	FEB 5 1954	54-C1-12	17
18	1054-C1-4	CABIN CONSTRUCTION PLAN	FJJ.DPM	JULY 23 1953	1054-C1-4	18
19	1054-C1-7	JOINER SECTIONS (SHEETS VI-VIII)	D.P.M	MARCH.18,54	1054-C1-7	19
20	1054-13	ARRANGEMENT OF MAST WINCHES, CLEATS ETC	D.P.M.	MARCH 18,54	1054-13	20
21	1054-14	INSTRUMENT LOCATION	D.P.M.	MAR. 8,1954	1054-14	21
22	1054-C1-15	REVISED FWD. STATEROOM	D.P.M.	MAY 5, 1954	1054-C1-15	22
23	1054-C1-8	Arrgt of Refrigeration Compressor, Pump, etc	D.P.M	May 7 1954	1054-C1-8	23
24	1054-C1-1	ICE BOX	D PM	MAY 25,1954	1054-C1-1	24
25	1054-C1-2	ROLLER REEFING MAIN BOOM	DPM	MAY 27,1954	1054-C1-2	25
26	1054-7T	Joiner Sect's Sh.4&5 (TRACED)	FJJ,DPM,JKB	JUNE 14,1954	1054-7T SHEETS	26
27	1054-5T	Main Deck & Beam Framing See Des #1068	J.E.L.N.	JUNE 14,1954	1054-5T.	27
28						28
29		FJJ = FRANK J. JERABEK (DESIGN DRAFTSMAN)				29
30		AM = ALVIN MASON "				30
31		DPM = DAVID P. MARTIN "				31
32		JKB = JAMES K. BARDEN "				32
33		ELN = ENEZ L. NARDI (FEMALE TRACER)				33
34						34
35						35
36						3

Crew of *Finisterre* after her third Bermuda Race victory. *Left to right:* Carleton Mitchell, Dick Bertram, Chick Larkin, Bunny Rigg, Bobby Symonette, Cory Cramer, and Mell Gatman. Courtesy Government Information Services, Bermuda.

and former crewmember on *Kelpie* was rolled 360 degrees in the Hinckley-built keel-centerboarder *Irresistible* about 300 miles off Cape Cod in 1986. *Finisterre* may have a slightly higher stability range than the typical boat of her type, and she has fairly high roll inertia and thus good dynamic stability due to her hefty wood mainmast and heavy displacement, but I would worry less about the possibility of a capsize in a narrower deep-keel boat with ample ballast. As Rod Stephens wrote me

years ago, "In spite of a certain amount of propaganda from centerboarder enthusiasts, I certainly feel a reasonable keel with the stability range provided, would be my choice for bad weather offshore."[6] In an April 1998 *Cruising World* article by Steve Callahan entitled "Gentlemen Do Sail

Facing page: Finisterre beating to windward on the Chesapeake under her number one genoa in 1955. Photograph by Fred Thomas, courtesy Katrina Thomas.

To Windward," Olin Stephens is quoted as saying: "Our centerboarders became very popular, largely based on the success of *Finisterre*. They were good boats in every way, except they could be capsized—I never did like that about them."

Another compromise for shoal draft is the necessity of a shallow rudder which rises as a beamy hull "rolls out" or lifts up when the boat heels. This can create a vulnerability to broaching on a heavy-air spinnaker reach, but probably because of good handling, *Finisterre* seldom if ever suffered from this problem. Nevertheless, Bob Henry told me that he sometimes felt that he was on the verge of broaching in *Finisterre;* with slightly more heel the rudder might stall and he would lose control.

Because of her great success, Mitchell's little yawl naturally inspired many imitations. A stock model designed by Sparkman and Stephens is the Nevins 40, and one of these boats, Colin Ratsey's *Golliwogg*, gave *Finisterre* plenty of trouble in the 1958 Bermuda Race. I became familiar with a sisterboat, *Brer Fox,* when William Stone, son of the famous *Yachting* editor Herbert Stone, loaned us his Nevins 40 for a cruise in the Abacos, after I had taken over his *Yachting* column while he was away on a six-month cruise in the West Indies. With her shoal draft, *Brer Fox* was ideal for the Abacos, and I was impressed with her comfort and the way she handled. Other notable designs of this type are the Bermuda 40 and the Block Island 40, originally called the Vitesse class. One of the latter is *Alaris;*

more about her is found later in this chapter.

Carleton Mitchell retired *Finisterre* from racing prior to the 1962 Bermuda Race, and she was soon sold to two well-known Chesapeake yachtsmen, Vaughn Brown and Frank Hardy. She was raced a few times, but seldom did well in the midsummer light air of the Bay, even when skippered by my friend, the outstanding marine artist David Scott, who was a very capable sailor. At one rendezvous, I heard that *Finisterre*'s co-owner Frank Hardy met Thomas Watson, skipper of the visiting sloop *Palawan.* After each had inquired about the other's profession, Watson said, "I'm president of IBM," and the well-to-do Hardy replied, "I'm a pig farmer from the Eastern Shore."

Scott boats: Arguably the best native corinthian racing sailor on the Chesapeake, Charles Scott of Annapolis has been a winner in every class in which he has sailed since he was a small child. I remember Charlie winning a Penguin regatta at Gibson Island in the mid-1960s, beating much older talented sailors, including my son Rip, when he was so young that his head barely showed above the gunwale of his boat. On that occasion I was serving on the committee boat with Charlie's older brother Jimmy, who was a relatively new sailmaker. After admiring the set of Charlie's mainsail, I commented that it was a good-looking sail and

Facing page: Gaither Scott's Herreshoff 23 *Mist,* for many years a hot competitor in the racing division. Courtesy Gaither Scott.

LEGENDS OF THE RECENT PAST   183

asked Jimmy if he had made it. Jimmy replied, "No, Charlie made it himself."

Charlie's father, Gaither Scott, is a longtime Chesapeake sailor and distinguished yachtsman who is noted for his race committee work far beyond the Bay. In 1980 he was chairman of the New York Yacht Club Race Committee and ran the America's Cup Races. A prominent past commodore of the Annapolis Yacht Club, he has had a major role in organizing and running the Annapolis races for many years. Gaither first got attention in 1955 when he bought a beautiful Herreshoff 23, which he named *Mist;* the following year she began to excel in the racing division of CBYRA. From her debut until 1969, *Mist* won three High Point championships. The Scott boys, Jimmy and Charlie, crewed for their father and absorbed racing techniques like the proverbial sponge. Charlie was taken on his first race when he was only two years old. I don't think he contributed much on that occasion, but Gaither told me that he soon recognized Charlie's talent and began letting him steer when he was not much older than a toddler. Before long he was skippering on big boats and dominating junior sailing on the Bay.

The racing record of Charlie Scott is truly remarkable. He has won twenty Bay championships in eleven different classes. Some of his most impressive wins are the Midget Middle Atlantic Championship in 1966, the Sears Cup North American Junior Championship in 1971, the highly competitive J/24 North American Championships in 1978 and 1979, the MORC International Championship

in 1984, the One Ton North American Championship the same year, Block Island Race Week (overall honors) in 1987, the Lloyd Phoenix North American Offshore Championship, and the J/30 North American Championship in 1992.

Perhaps his most publicized victory occurred in 1985 when he took fleet first in the SORC, beating some of the world's best sailors on the most technically advanced ocean racers. Racing a stock J/41 named *Smiles,* which was not then considered the latest or hottest design, and with a crew of Chesapeake sailors (including my friend Fred Potts, the spar maker), Charlie was an underdog, but he sailed a remarkably consistent series and creamed some of the best America's Cup sailors and Olympic medalists including Buddy Melges, Lowell North, John Kolius, Dennis Conner, Paul Cayard, Bill Buchan, and others. Competitor John Buchan, brother of Star gold-medalist Bill, had this to say about Charlie Scott: "We never see him, but he's always there. I know he's not doing it with mirrors. He must be one hell of a sailor."[7] Contributing to Charlie's success was an unusual degree of preparation. The rig and deck plan of *Smiles* were highly modified, Charlie and many of his crew had more than two thousand miles of racing experience in this boat prior to the SORC,[8] and according to a report in *Yacht Racing/Cruising* magazine (April 1985), he spent an estimated 350 hours in fairing the stock J/41 keel.

Some say that Charlie is a professional because he has been a dealer for the Rodney Johnstone–designed J Boats and he runs his own yacht yard, but he sails his own boats and his yard offers the same service and tuning for clients that Charlie provides for himself. In an article for *Yachting* magazine (April 1985), Guy Gurney wrote, "Scott is almost the antithesis of the rock star type: He owns his boats, and does things his own way."

After Gaither sold his Herreshoff 23 at the end of the 1960s, he purchased another boat that he named *Mist,* a Britton Chance designed PT-30, and Charlie was the usual skipper. Initially *Mist* was handicapped with a high CCA rating that put her into Class B with much larger boats, but she excelled when the IOR was introduced and won the Labrot Trophy in 1972. Ronald Ward, who sometimes crewed on *Mist,* told me that the boat could be very difficult for most people to steer, but not for Charlie. During a Cedar Point Race when the crew was struggling with her helm, Charlie took over and easily steered with his foot.

In the late 1970s Charlie became the Annapolis dealer for J Boats and had phenomenal success in the J/24, J/27, and J/30 classes as well as with the J/41 One Ton racer. Eventually, however, Charlie parted company with the Johnstones and became a dealer for the California-built Schock 35s, and he vowed that J Boats would no longer dominate the Chesapeake racing scene. With a Schock boat named *Justice* (with the first letter of the name somewhat reminiscent of the J Boat insignia), he did indeed hold back the Johnstone boats. *Justice,* under the ownership of a syndicate, won the Labrot Trophy in 1989.

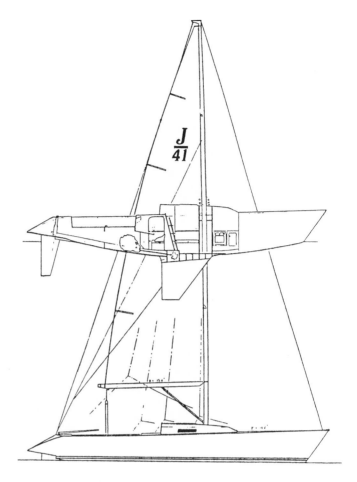

Plans of the J/41. Courtesy J Boats.

Incidentally, Charlie's older brother Jimmy, a prominent sailmaker, is also a gifted skipper, winning nine Bay Championships in four different classes. Gaither told me that Jimmy's son Andrew is beginning to carry on the family tradition and has already won two Bay Championships. So with the help of the Scott family, we can safely say that Chesapeake sailors can compete with the world's best, especially the modern bonny Prince Charlie of Scott land.

Alaris: Next to *Prim* and the Q-boat *Eleanor,* the Block Island 40 *Alaris* has

CHESAPEAKE SAILS

had the longest successful racing career of any Chesapeake boat. Also, she had almost as many modifications as *Prim,* although they were far less drastic. Another similarity is that *Alaris* has been owned by one family through two generations during her lengthy life on the Bay. Just as *Prim* was part of the Gibbons-Neff family from 1952 until the present, *Alaris* was brought to the Bay by Dr. Charles Iliff of Annapolis in 1959, and she is still owned and cared for by his progeny.

The Block Island 40 (originally the Vitesse 40) was one of the earliest stock fiberglass racing cruisers. In fact, I know of only one earlier stock fiberglass design of that size, the Philip Rhodes–designed Bounty II, created in 1956. The Block Island 40, a *Finisterre*-type 41-foot centerboarder, was designed by the late William H. Tripp, Jr., in 1957. *Alaris,* originally named *Saroya* and raced successfully on the Great Lakes, was hull number 6. Her new name, meaning wing-like or pertaining to a wing, came from Charlie Iliff's predecessor boat, a Sparkman and Stephens 35-foot Weekender. Sharing Sunny Gibbons-Neff's penchant for tinkering and modifying, Charlie Iliff installed on his Weekender an unusual masthead rig that supported a jib with two tacks. The upper one, along with the headstay, was attached to a reinforced bow pulpit.

The second *Alaris,* the Block Island 40, arrived on the Bay with a *Fleetwood*

yawl rig (named after a famous yawl on the Great Lakes), having an extra-large mizzen with stainless steel boomkin. Under that rig *Alaris* won High Points in her class in 1959 and finished fourth in a large class in the Annapolis-Newport Race. The class winner, incidentally, was another Chesapeake Block Island 40, *Southern Star II,* owned by Dr. James Mullen of Richmond, Virginia.

The following year *Alaris* entered the Bermuda Race and came close to winning. She was leading three-time winner *Finisterre* when a violent front came through, causing a number of spectacular knockdowns and producing gale force winds after the front passed. A heavy-weather boat even under her *Fleetwood* rig, *Alaris* possibly could have been driven to a victory, but Charles Iliff, Jr., wrote that the crew drastically reduced sail to slow down, primarily because of the alarming pounding the hull was taking in the steep Gulf Stream seas. In those days no one knew how much punishment a fiberglass hull could take, and Iliff's apprehension was not at all helped when crewmember Hal Hallock, owner of the wooden Pilot 35 *Quandry,* poked his head through the hatch and hollered: "Do you know how they make these things? They make one side in a mold over here, and the other side in a mold over there, and then they glue the damn things together with mucilage. This boat is going to split apart like a watermelon."[9] Many of the crew might have agreed with Mark Twain when he remarked: "Bermuda is Paradise, but one has to go through Hell to get there."

Facing page: SORC champion *Smiles* surfing off under spinnaker and blooper. Courtesy Gaither Scott.

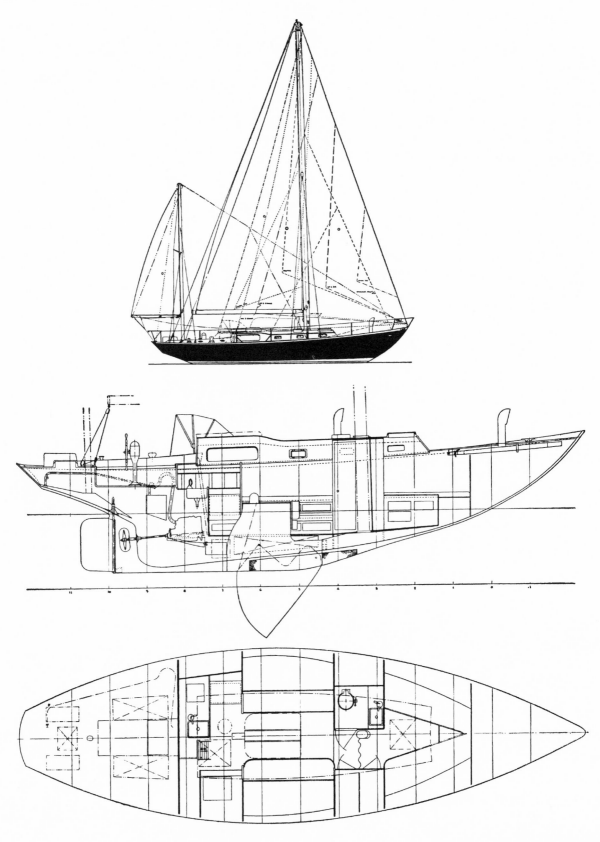

188

Nevertheless, *Alaris* held together, and even with her restrained handling, she finished eighth in a fleet of 136 boats.

Racing on the Bay in predominantly light air, *Alaris* had trouble with some other boats in her class, especially the Ohlson 35s (including our *Kelpie*), so it was time for the Iliffs to modify. Before long *Alaris* had a three-foot-longer mainmast and a bowsprit. Also, she was fitted with a series of experimental centerboards. We are told that the most successful was a high-aspect-ratio board that could not be completely housed.[10] With the board down she drew 11 feet, and this really enhanced her ability to climb to windward.

I remember one Cedar Point Race when, on a dark night, *Alaris* tried to pass us to windward while I was at the helm of our Ohlson 38, a notably close-winded sloop. We had the lee bow position on a fresh air beat, and *Alaris* kept climbing to windward. I saw her bobbing green light, then red and green lights, and then single green again. She came almost close enough to touch, and her bow wave alternately whispered and roared like the heavy breathing of a giant as she cut through the chop. I could not believe that a yawl could run over us to windward. Finally, the effect of our backwind held her back, and she bore away, romping off into the black night under our lee.

After a long successful racing career, Charlie Iliff decided to ease off and do

Alaris under her tall sloop rig with huge genoa in 1986. Courtesy Nicholas T. Iliff.

more leisurely cruising. In the words of Charles Iliff, Jr., "Charlie bought a Whitby 42, *Indian Summer,* in 1976, [and] he sold *Alaris* to his son Nick. He also cheerfully proposed that to celebrate *Alaris's* twentieth year, Nick should sail her in the 1978 Bermuda Race. After about a year of hard preparation, including installing a new rig, Nick did so, with

Facing page: Plans of the Tripp-designed Block Island 40. Courtesy Eric K. Woods, President, Migrator Yachts, Inc.

An Alberg 35 carrying full main and working jib in a fresh breeze. Photograph by Bill-Bert Schill.

three of his brothers as crew and with Charlie as cook. That race was an easy one with good weather all the time. *Alaris* won her class under MHS (later IMS) rule."[11]

Like his father, Nick has a propensity for experimentation, so *Alaris* was due for further modifications. In 1984 he added seven feet and another set of spreaders to the mainmast, put in more ballast, installed a new centerboard, and converted *Alaris* from a low-aspect-ratio yawl to a high-aspect sloop. This change

put new life into her, and she began to shine again on the race course. That year she earned a second place High Point award in her class. After winning her class in the competitive IOR Division of the 1986 Virginia Cruise Cup Race, yachting reporter Dan Winters wrote: "*Alaris* had stomped the beans out of dozens of 'hot' boats . . . and others, boat-for-boat!"[12]

Charlie Iliff was a highly-regarded eye surgeon/ophthalmologist, and two sons followed in his footsteps. Ronald Ward, who often crewed for the Iliffs, tells about the time when he sustained a laceration on board *Alaris* and the sailing doctors sewed it closed. Later, when the cut was examined by Ron's own physician, he asked, "Where did you get those neat little eyeball stitches?" On another occasion, Charlie Iliff noticed that Ron had a minor skin cancer on his eyelid and advised that it be removed. After the operation, performed by Charlie, his two doctor sons walked in to inspect the job. The first had a look and exclaimed, "Oh Christ!" (or words to that effect) and then walked out of the room. The second examined the wound and said, "My God, the old man has fouled up again." Of course they were kidding, as Charlie was as good a surgeon as he was a sailor.

The Albergs: Carl Alberg has long been one of my favorite designers, as his boats are nearly always wholesome, conservative, and aesthetically appealing. Although far from being speedy when compared with modern skimmers, they are able, sure, steady on the helm, and lively performers in most conditions. As

190

A pair of Alberg 30s racing on the Chesapeake. Photograph by Bill-Bert Schill.

mentioned earlier, I now own a little Alberg-designed Cape Dory Typhoon and she serves me well. I once heard that the reason for this boat's class name is that it takes a typhoon to move her, but to the contrary, I have found that she ghosts along splendidly in a near calm, and I almost never use her outboard motor.

Since the introduction of fiberglass to boatbuilding in the late 1950s, there have been a host of Alberg racing cruisers on the Chesapeake. Their proliferation began after the introduction of the Triton and steadily grew during the mid-1960s with the coming of the Alberg 30 class. Then came a number of Alberg 35s and Alberg 37s. One of the former—*Molly Brown*—got considerable publicity after she made a circumnavigation under the ownership of Richard Zantzinger, who

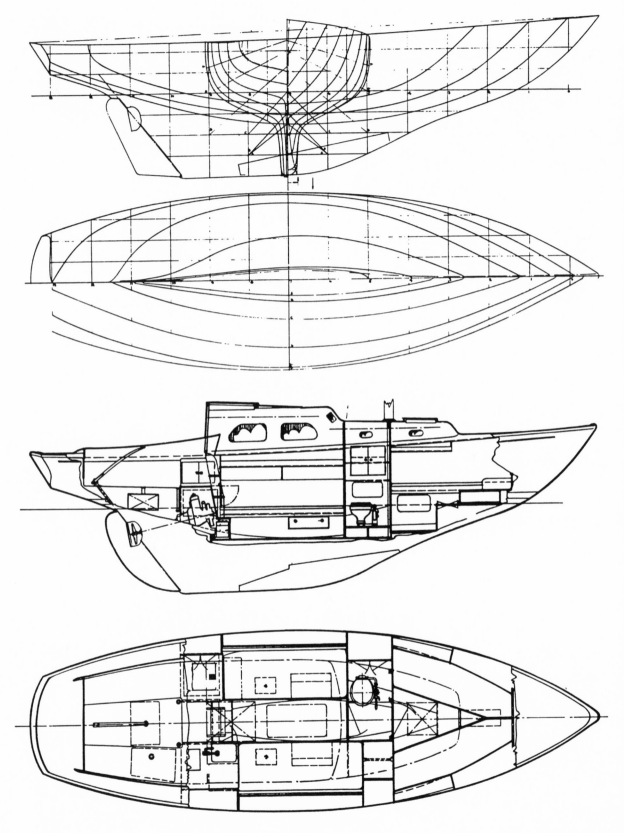

wrote a colorful book about the voyage called *The Log of the "Molly Brown."*[13] This boat had previously resided at Gibson Island under the name *Sonceri,* and we often raced against her. In his book *The Circumnavigators,* Donald Holm describes Zantzinger as "a middle-aged swinger, with an ex-wife, a girl friend, a pad on Spa Creek in Tidewater, Maryland, a bankrupt contracting business, and a $20,000 commitment to the Internal Revenue Service for back taxes."[14] Despite these problems and a lack of experience in offshore sailing, Zantzinger acquired *Molly Brown* and successfully completed his voyage around the world. At least a small part of his success was due to having a good boat. Carl Alberg wrote me about an Alberg 35 that was caught in a gale off Ireland in 1979. Her crew "stripped down to bare pole and sat it out without any damage, and on arrival [in port] were told about the disaster to the Fastnet fleet in the same storm."[15]

Introduced at the New York Boat Show in 1959, the 28-foot Alberg-designed Triton was an immediate sensation producing sixteen orders placed at the show. Some of the earliest boats, built in fiberglass by Pearson Yachts, came to the Chesapeake. Two of the best known were Ridgely Melvin's *Gem* and William Myers's *White Shadow III,* both with outstanding race records, especially the Myers boat. A former Star champion from the Tred Avon Yacht Club, Bill Myers was a skillful light-air sailor, and

Facing page: Lines of the *Mark II* Triton drawn for the author by Carl Alberg.

The Triton *Ojigwan* in 1962 with the author at the helm. Photograph by Fred Thomas, courtesy Katrina Thomas.

he often had some tricks up his sleeve. I remember the start of one race when the becalmed fleet was anchored close to the starting line to await a breeze. Myers had set his anchor some distance to windward, then payed out rode to achieve maximum scope and position his boat in a very good spot on the line. After the starting gun, he gave a strong steady pull on the anchor rode and shot *White*

Shadow III into clear air, getting the jump on everyone.

Myers usually raced with an all-female crew—family-members who were outstanding sailors. His wife Bunny won the Chesapeake Women's Championship, and his two daughters were top contenders in the junior and midget championships.

In my book *Choice Yacht Designs*[16] I included a write-up on the Triton. I had wanted to show her lines, but William Shaw of Pearson Yachts would not give me permission. This irked Alberg, so free of charge he drew me a new set of lines with two minor modifications: a slightly straighter stem line and a *Constellation*-type rudder. We agreed to label this the Triton, Mark II.

The Alberg 30 was a slightly larger version of the Triton with a lower doghouse. It caught on to such an extent on the Bay that a class organization was formed for joint cruising and keen one-design racing among its many members. The Chesapeake Alberg 30 fleet became the largest in the country and continues today.

Having sailed both the Triton and the Alberg 30, I feel the former is stiffer in a breeze. Alberg was not overjoyed when the builder, Whitby Boat Works, Ltd., insisted that the 30 use iron ballast instead of lead. After hull number 27 was produced, the ballast was increased, and the earlier boats were allowed to carry 460 pounds of inside ballast. But the early boats were still slightly disadvantaged because of the higher center of gravity of the inside ballast. In those

times, before the almost universal use of jiffy-reefing, it was common practice to preserve stability by luffing the main on short upwind legs during a race. The boats performed surprisingly well with a shaking mainsail.

The most tenacious and loyal owner of an Alberg 30 is my friend Ronald Ward, a senior U.S. Sailing judge, former commodore of the Annapolis Yacht Club, and a four-time member of the America's Cup Race Committee. He has owned his Alberg 30 *Encore* for about three decades. Leading High Point winners in the class have been Richard Born, Peter Scheidt, and the late Theodore Osius. The Sailing Club of the Chesapeake now sponsors an annual Ted Osius Memorial Regatta.

There have been a number of CBYRA Cruising One-Design (COD) classes on the Bay including Gladiator (now inactive), Triton, Cal 25, Tartan 27 (now inactive), Catalina 27, Pearson 30, Tartan 30 (now inactive), J/24, J/30, Olson 30 (now inactive), J/35, and J/105. In addition, many clubs are giving starts to the relatively new sport-boat types such as the Farr-designed Mumm 30, the Melges 24, and the ID 35. But the classic Alberg 30, going back to 1966, is the earliest class sanctioned by the CBYRA as a COD, and it is still thriving.

Columbia (31) rules the waves: After Billy Myers sold his Triton he ordered a Columbia 31, a trim centerboard sloop designed by Charles Morgan. It was

Facing page: A Columbia 31 racing on the Bay. Photograph by Fred Thomas, courtesy Katrina Thomas.

essentially a smaller version of Morgan's famous SORC winner *Paper Tiger*. Myers decided to switch boats not only because of the Columbia's racing potential but also because of her superior accommodations below. But he told me that he was totally shocked when he bought a mainsail for his new boat and saw how much smaller it was than the main on his Triton. Nevertheless, the 31 had a large masthead foretriangle and could carry a relatively large spinnaker. Myers's new boat, *White Shadow IV*, did exceedingly well in Chesapeake races, winning fleet High Points (the Labrot Trophy) two consecutive years.

Another well-known Chesapeake sailor, John F. Zanks of the Hampton Yacht Club, became interested in the Columbia 31, especially after the Columbia Yacht Corporation of California set up a manufacturing plant in Norfolk, Virginia. Like Myers, Zanks was concerned about the height of the mast on the 31, so when

he ordered his boat (which he named *Surfrider)*, he increased her mast length by four feet. Jack Zanks wrote me that he knew most of the people involved in building boats at the Norfolk Columbia plant, and they made a special effort to give him a "better" boat.[17] This made possible a number of unique modifications: addition of a "pie plate"—a horizontal plate to inhibit hobbyhorsing and act as a cavitation (ventilation) plate; utilization of the centerboard well to minimize the number of through-hull fittings; and installation of a fiberglass centerboard with an NACA (National Advisory Commission for Aeronautics) 0009 sectional shape. Despite the extra care, however, Zanks wrote that his first job after taking delivery was to remove the toerails and rebed them to rectify severe leaking at the hull-deck joint.[18] Dr. Bill Peach, the modern big-boat champ of the southern Bay, has described Zanks as "Ray (Brown's) toughest competition, a NASA engineer,

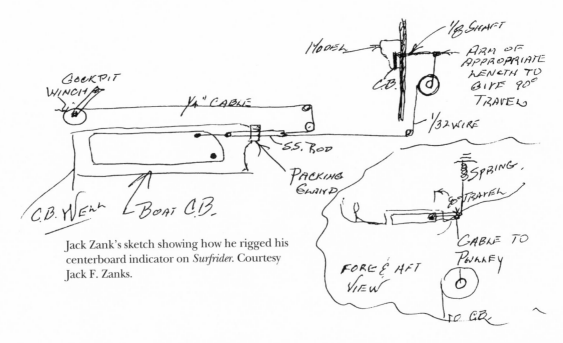

Jack Zank's sketch showing how he rigged his centerboard indicator on *Surfrider*. Courtesy Jack F. Zanks.

who taught all of us the importance of keeping our yachts light and getting weight out of the ends."

The most ingenious and innovative feature on *Surfrider* was her centerboard position indicator. On a cabin bulkhead that was visible from the helm, Zanks put a half model of *Surfrider,* and the centerboard on the model was connected with the vessel's centerboard in such a way that whenever the board was raised or lowered, its exact position would be shown on the model. Jack was kind enough to send me a sketch of its operation, and it is reproduced here. Rube Goldberg would have been impressed, and so am I.

As expected, *Surfrider* did exceedingly well racing on the southern Bay, winning a number of High Point awards. After Zanks sold *Surfrider,* she came into the possession of Buzz White and later was owned by James White of Gibson Island. I had the pleasure of sailing on this boat during a Wednesday evening race on the Magothy River when she was owned by Buzz.

A hankerin' for Cals: A great rival and worthy opponent of Billy Myers was Douglas Hanks of Oxford. In the mid-1960s he bought a William Lapworth–designed Cal 28 which he named *Rumpus,* and he proceeded to dominate most of the local races. He won the coveted Viking Trophy awarded for fleet first in the popular Annapolis Yacht Club Fall Series in 1965 and then duplicated the feat the following year, beating Myers in his Columbia 31 by a narrow margin. The next year he got further attention by install-

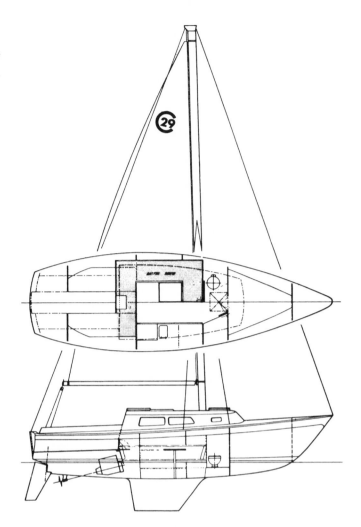

Plans of the Lapworth-designed Cal 29. Courtesy C. William Lapworth.

ing a propeller on his engineless boat in order to gain a handicap rating advantage. At the time this was perfectly legal, but the action did indeed cause a rumpus. The rules were soon changed to require that an engine accompany a prop. An inboard auxiliary was installed on *Rumpus,* but it didn't hurt her speed. I recall one Cedar Point Race when the little 28-footer was skippered by Hanks's son, Doug, Jr., and the boat finished so far ahead of other boats in her class that a number of rival skippers thought that she had (unintentionally) rounded the wrong mark.

It was written in the *Skipper* magazine that the "Only reason there's a big fuss about *Rumpus* is that Hanks is a winner and everyone hates a winner."[19] Perhaps Hanks was more than a little annoyed by the controversy over *Rumpus,* for he named his next boat *Outrage.* She too was a Cal, one foot longer than *Rumpus* and with a trunk-type cabinhouse. The Cal 28 had a raised-deck cabin that, in the opinion of some, detracted from the boat's appearance. Doug once told me that he never looked back admiringly when leaving *Rumpus* because he didn't like the looks of her hunting (raised-deck) cabin. Both boats had underwater configurations related to the famous Cal 40 with the trapezoidal fin keel and spade rudder, but the keel of the Cal 29 was shorter with a more vertical trailing edge, and there was the hint of a skeg ahead of her spade rudder. Despite keen competition from two sisterboats sailed by Charles "Sunny" Smith and Marshall Steele, *Outrage* had an exceptional racing record and topped the fleet, winning the Labrot Trophy in 1971 and 1973.

I'll never forget racing against Hanks sailing his Cal 28 and Myers sailing his Columbia 31 during a spring series at Oxford in the late 1960s. I was crewing for my cousins, Ed Henderson and his older brother Charlie (known as "Hotshot" Henderson when he flew a navy torpedo plane during World War II). We were sailing their Triton *Ojigwan,*

named after my uncle's P-class sloop mentioned in chapter 1. Charlie was also a hotshot in sailboats, and he was determined to beat Myers and Hanks. In preparation for the series, he stripped the boat of all excess weight, bought the almost perfectly-shaped genoa jib that had been used on *White Shadow III,* ordered a new oversized mainsail that could be flattened with a lacing at its foot, and mixed his own bottom paint which, for a week or so, made *Ojigwan* slicker than a greased eel. He did indeed win the series after a real battle with both *Rumpus* and *White Shadow IV.*

On one race when Hotshot was away, I was asked to skipper the boat. After a hairy start and a short beat out to Choptank River Light off Benoni Point, the first mark of the course, we led *Rumpus* by a couple of boat lengths. The light was surrounded by a riprap of rocks, and just before we rounded it, Hanks called out a warning for me to watch out for the submerged rocks. Being overly cautious, I gave the mark a wide berth, and this allowed Hanks to cut inside of us and take the lead. We followed him around the course but were able to stay close enough to save our time. Hanks had done nothing unethical—there really were dangerous submerged rocks—but I later kidded him about his Eastern Shore gamesmanship.

Incidentally, Hank's son Doug, Jr., is also a fine sailor who gained some local fame as an author. He wrote an entertaining novelette called *Muskrat,*[20] an amusing, colorful, and highly fictionalized account of how a group of Oxford watermen went to Australia and won the

America's Cup using entirely Eastern Shore talent for boat creation, sails, and crew. The watermen succeeded with the help of some secret weapons that included "longnecks" (a certain brand of beer), winch-grinding muscles developed from tonging oysters, and jibing centerboards that could be angled to the water flow to increase lift when beating to windward. Jibing centerboards have actually been used on Chesapeake workboats since the earliest of times.

Doug Hanks, Sr., finally sold *Outrage* and went full bore into log canoe racing, in which he was also outstanding, but he retained a special affection for his Cal 29. I was told that when he died a few years ago, he was buried with a bottle of his favorite sipping whiskey and the tiller of *Outrage.*

Boats of Raymond Brown: Following the success of the Triton, Pearson Yachts produced the larger fiberglass Invicta designed by William Tripp. A keel-centerboard racing cruiser, this boat differed from the Tripp-designed Block Island 40 in that she had a deeper keel which increased her stability range (for a given ballast-displacement ratio) and enabled her to sail upwind moderately well with the board housed. One of these boats, *Burgoo,* was fleet first in the 1964 Bermuda Race, becoming the smallest yacht, at 37 feet, 8 inches overall, to win this prestigious event.

One of the Bay's great sailors, Raymond M. Brown from Hampton, Virginia, became interested in the Invicta around 1959 and ordered a bare hull to be individually finished with his own

hands. Being an engineer and an amateur carpenter, Ray felt capable of finishing the hull as well as making some variations that differed from the standard model. The greatest modification was to change the rig from yawl to sloop. Bill Tripp did not approve of this, as he had designed the boat to be a yawl and was afraid the change would disrupt her balance. Nevertheless, Ray insisted on the sloop rig, and eventually, after it proved successful, Tripp offered the sloop as an option.

Although *Burgoo,* the yawl-rigged Invicta, often excelled in long-distance races, Ray's sloop nearly always beat her when the two boats went head-to-head. At the windward start of the 1967 Annapolis-Newport Race, Brown started to leeward of *Burgoo* and soon worked up across her bow. Ray won his class in that rough contest. This was his second class win with his Invicta in the Annapolis-Newport Race. He named the boat *Fleetwind,* but she should have been named *Fleet Win,* because she won the Labrot Trophy four times, duplicating Miller Sherwood's feat with the Owens cutter *Rubicon.* It was written in the *Skipper* magazine at the end of 1965 that *Fleetwind* had "never been out of the money in any major race."[21]

Ray was brought up at Hampton, and his first small boat was a dinghy named *Bail and Sail.* I'm not sure if she was built by Ray, but apparently she had some problems with leaks. He soon graduated to the Penguin Class and did well with this popular Rhodes design. His first cruising boat was a Sound Interclub named *Argo* to which Ray added a cabin. Then came *Celerity,* a 39-foot yawl custom-designed for a previous owner by Bennett Fisher and Bill Luders. Being an inveterate experimenter, Ray made a number of modifications to *Celerity* including a rig change and the addition of outside ballast at her forefoot. He did well racing her, taking a class second in the 1958 Bermuda Race.

After the arrival of *Fleetwind,* Ray became concerned about Bill Tripp's lack of enthusiasm for the conversion of his Invicta to a sloop. The boat's underwater configuration placed her center of lateral resistance quite far aft, and Ray worried about her developing a lee helm. To counteract this possibility and to enhance windward performance, he boldly added an innovative appendage at the forefoot. This was a bow rudder or articulated "canard" in the words of Ray's friend and tactician, naval architect Howard Fawcett. It could be controlled with a short tiller positioned between the V-berths in the forward cabin. The tiller could be set a few degrees from center on ten different notched settings, and of course, it had to be reset after each tack. Howard wrote me that the device added little if any improvement to windward performance and added drag downwind.[22] Of course, it was also vulnerable and apt to become fouled with seaweed, so it was removed the following season. With or without a canard, Brown knew how to coax his boats to windward. In the words of southern Bay champion Dr. William Peach, "What I learned from him [Ray Brown] was how to best sail a boat to weather. He had an instinct as to how to maximize the VMG [velocity made good] to weather long before we had the newer instruments and velocity prediction programs were available."[23]

Brown's foredeck boss Tom Hunnicutt is a colorful sailor and was at one time a curator at the Mariners' Museum in Newport News, Virginia. He described Ray as a very cool skipper who raised his voice only once, when *Celerity* was nearly run down by a freighter in the fog. After hearing the increasingly loud "thump, thump" of the ship's screw, Ray sent a man to the bow with an air horn, but after one tiny "peep," the crewman's finger slipped off the trigger and the horn fell overboard. *Celerity* was fended off the ship by its bow wave.

Tom was very possessive of his territory on the foredeck and kept it marked off with tape. I was told that he sometimes wore a helmet after being beaned by the spinnaker pole when one of the after guard accidentally (?) released the pole lift. A spirit of fun often accompanied the efficient crew work, as exemplified by the time the crew packed Tom's spinnaker bag with ladies panties and bras.

Hunnicutt's most exciting experience occurred when *Fleetwind* was about to cross the finish line during an Annapolis Fall Series race. She was fouled by a Navy Shields sloop on the port tack near the committee boat, which was a Navy YP. *Fleetwind* was forced to make a

Facing page: Fleetwind close-hauled with her crew hiking out. Photograph by Fred Thomas, courtesy Katrina Thomas.

sudden luff and Tom was thrown overboard. To avoid being crushed between *Fleetwind* and the YP, Tom had to dive under the water quickly. He swam under his boat's keel and surfaced on her opposite side. Understandably, it took a while for the crew to locate Tom, but they managed to get him back aboard unharmed.[24]

With the advent of the IOR, Ray Brown realized that *Fleetwind* would be less competitive. (Incidentally, I served on the Cruising Committee chaired by Brown that dealt with the CBYRA's acceptance of the IOR). He began thinking about a more IOR-friendly replacement boat for *Fleetwind*. The new boat was designed by Ray himself with the help of Howard Fawcett. It was also built by Ray with his own hands. Named *Flying Cloud,* the new boat was a 45-foot sloop, drawing only 3½ feet, with a drop keel extending her draft to 9 feet for weatherliness and increased ultimate stability. Living on a canal in Hampton, Ray had a ship's cargo boom installed at his dock that could lift his boats. He actually made radio-controlled models of *Fleetwind* and *Flying Cloud* and compared their performance.

It took a while to build the full-size *Flying Cloud,* and Ray came to the realization that she would be somewhat outdated by the time she was finished. Nevertheless, she did well in early races, winning Southern Bay High Points in 1979 and placing second in her class in the Annapolis-Newport Race the same year. We competed against *Flying Cloud* in a Cruising Club of America race one fall. The race was called off after the

wind dropped, and I was disappointed because *Kelpie* (the Ohlson 38) was the second boat in the fleet, but *Flying Cloud* was almost hull down ahead of us.

As the IOR was repeatedly modified, *Flying Cloud* became severely handicapped, and Ray turned to flying airplanes. He built his own ultralight and unfortunately was killed when it crashed. Making a sharp turn to avoid a fog bank, he stalled out and the plane dropped to the ground.[25] Thus the Bay lost one of its greatest and most innovative sailors.

Loki* and *Loon: Rod Stephens told me that he greatly admired Gifford Pinchot for the seamanship displayed during extensive cruising when handling his 38-foot Sparkman and Stephens yawl *Loki* (which lacked an auxiliary engine) in all kinds of situations. Gifford and his wife even sailed this boat through New York's East River and Hellgate. Pinchot and Stephens saw eye-to-eye in their passion for simplicity. As said earlier, Rod took the engine out of *Stormy Weather,* and for a while refused to carry a transmitting radio—he went cruising to get away from the telephone. Gifford too believed in developing the ability to handle a boat without electronic aids, engine, or any gadgets that can break down.

The son of a famous governor of Pennsylvania, Gifford Pinchot was a medical doctor, a scientist, and at one time a professor of biology at Johns Hopkins University in Baltimore. He brought

Facing page: A bow view photo of *Flying Cloud* taken by Ray Brown's son. Photograph by Skip Brown, courtesy Pat Brown Fitzgerald.

LEGENDS OF THE RECENT PAST

Loki to Gibson Island's yachtyard in the early 1950s and praised the Lusbys for their excellent work and inexpensive rates. Later he became a member of the Gibson Island Yacht Squadron. *Loki* became well known for a class win in the 1950 Bermuda Race and three years later, a transatlantic passage to Bergen, Norway. That same year she came close to winning the Fastnet Race. The doctor wrote me: "Rounding the rock [Fastnet Rock] we were well up with the bigger boats and almost all the way back to Plymouth in that position we were an easy winner of the race, but we got in very calm weather for the last day and dropped down to third in our class and fourth in the fleet."[26]

By the end of the 1950s decade, *Loki* had become less competitive, and despite her strong wood construction, she had developed some leaks at the garboard strakes during her Atlantic crossing. So Dr. Pinchot ordered a new slightly-larger aluminum yawl from Sparkman and Stephens, which he named *Loon*. The aluminum construction helped ensure against leakage; it also decreased displacement for a speed gain and allowed more ballast for greater stability, but Gifford didn't anticipate the problem he was to have with electrolysis. Using a voltmeter in the bilge, he detected contact between the lead ballast and the aluminum hull. The lead was slightly too large for the keel cavity and had cut through the insulation, requiring that the ballast be removed and cut down in size.

Compared with *Loki*, *Loon* had proportionally more sail area with a higher sail-area-to-displacement ratio and less wetted surface without undue sacrifice to directional stability. She proved to be fast, and in her first two years, she had a great racing record that included class firsts in the 1962 and 1963 Block Island Races, class second in the 1962 Bermuda Race, and winner of the Northern Ocean Racing Trophy in 1963.

The following year Gifford and his wife Sally, also a fine sailor who had crewed for Rod Stephens, took their *Loon* to the South Seas by way of the Panama Canal and the Galapagos Islands. From Pitcairn Island to Tahiti *Loon* made excellent time. She made a three-thousand-mile run in slightly more than seventeen days, averaging seven and a quarter knots, a very good speed for a displacement hull only 30 feet, 4 inches long on the waterline. At Bora Bora the Pinchots met Jean Gau in *Atom* (written about earlier), who was on his first circumnavigation.

Being a biologist with a scientific mind, Dr. Pinchot was greatly interested in the Pacific sea life and concerned about problems associated with El Niño. In recent years, everyone has heard about this phenomenon involving the movement of warm water and its effect on weather, climate, and sea life. In the early 1960s, however, most of us were not aware of its significance. Pinchot theorized that island coral rings could be utilized as basins to hold phytoplankton to

Facing page: The engineless *Loki* in Hamilton Harbor with Sally Pinchot at the helm after a class win in the 1950 Bermuda Race. Courtesy Government Information Services, Bermuda.

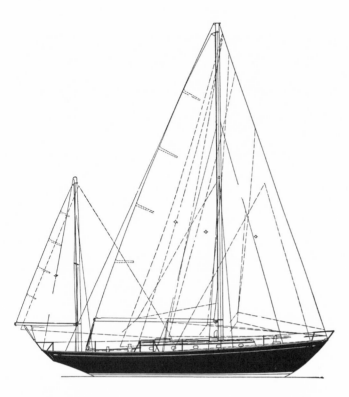

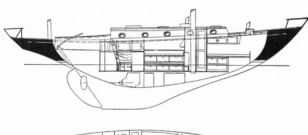

Plans of Gifford Pinchot's *Loon.* Courtesy Sparkman & Stephens, Inc.

feed fish, birds, and sea animals. All of this is described in his book *Loki and Loon.*[27]

Loon was shipped back to the Caribbean. At a boatyard in Tahiti where her shipping cradle was being built, the Pin-

chots met the crew of *Easterling,* a Giles-designed sloop that was attacked by a whale in the mid-Pacific. She was stove in, but the crew kept her afloat by closing the hole with rags, pillows, canvas, and sheet metal patches. After cruising the West Indies, the Pinchots sailed *Loon* home to Gibson Island, where she was based for a number of years. She was often cruised on the Chesapeake and, like most Bay boats, was occasionally caught in squalls. A favorite tactic of Gifford was to ride out a squall with only the mizzen hoisted. This worked well until one day when a chainplate broke and the mizzen mast went over the side. In 1984, twenty years after her cruise to the South Seas, *Loon* made an Atlantic crossing from Maine to the Azores and then sailed on to the British Isles, the European low countries, and Scandinavia.

In *Loki and Loon,* Pinchot expressed his opinion on the changing state of yacht racing and its influence on yacht design. He wrote: "In 1950 the ocean racing group was relatively small. We all knew each other and were old friends. This was before the days of 'factory teams' supplied to crew boats, making it very hard for nonprofessionals to win. . . . Owners skippered their boats almost universally, instead of going along as passengers, as some do nowadays. All in all, it was a lower-keyed sport, much more amateur but still highly competitive, and, in my opinion at least, more fun than the modern high-pressure situation." About the light-displacement stripped-out lightly-rigged boats being produced in the mid-1980s, he wrote: "Today's 'disposable' ocean racers, which cost enormous amounts, are competitive for only a season or two and then aren't much use for anything else."[28] I hope the rule-makers and powers at large in yacht racing will heed this criticism from one of the greatest all-around sailors whose cruising range extended far beyond the Chesapeake.

Dyna: In the early 1960s, a distinguished yachtsman from the Great Lakes, Clayton Ewing, moved to Maryland's Eastern Shore and brought with him his famous 57-foot aluminum yawl named *Dyna*. Designed by Sparkman and Stephens, *Dyna* was a centerboarder drawing 5½ feet with the board up. Soon after her launching in 1957, she took overall honors in the Port Huron–Mackinac Race and won her class in the Chicago-Mackinac, then repeated her performance the following year. Two years later she was a class winner in the Bermuda Race. After her move to the Chesapeake, she immediately began to excel in major East Coast events, winning her class in the 1961 Annapolis-Newport Race and the following year taking her class and a fleet second in the Annapolis Fall Series. She accomplished the remarkable feat of winning fleet firsts in the next two Annapolis-Newport Races.

Her greatest fame came while sailing in the Transatlantic Race of 1963 when she lost her rudder in midocean. During a boisterous spinnaker run with confused following seas, the lower gudgeon broke, the rudder stock sheared off where it penetrated the hull, and the entire rudder disappeared into the depths. Her ingenious crew, which included some Eastern

A Fred Thomas photo of *Dyna* on the Bay in 1965. Courtesy Chesapeake Bay Maritime Museum.

Shore sailors, used a number of jury rigs to steer her, including a stern sweep and various combinations of sails, and they continued sailing her nearly one thousand miles to the finish line off the Eddystone Light in England. In smooth seas the boat balanced well under a poled-out headsail with reefed mainsail. *Dyna* sailed 184 miles during one twenty-four-hour

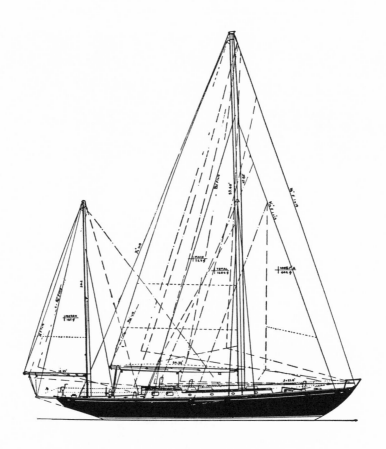

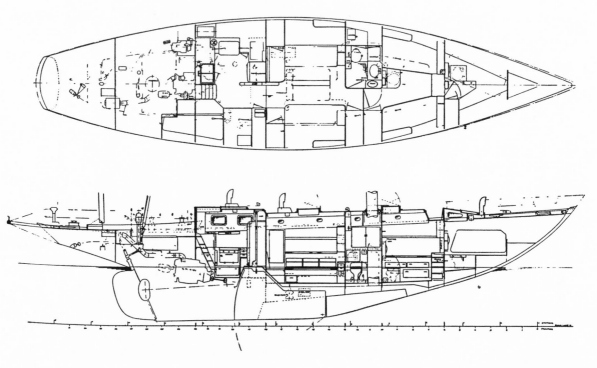

CHESAPEAKE SAILS

period, which is almost incredible when you consider that she had no rudder. She actually took a fourth place in the race, beating ten competent competitors. A special prize for outstanding seamanship was awarded to Ewing and his crew. According to Francis Kinney of Sparkman and Stephens, the rudder loss was due to corrosion that resulted because the builder had not adhered to specifications.[29]

One of the crewmembers and a splendid sailor was Clayton's son Mark Ewing of Trappe, Maryland. Skippering his PJ 43 *Harpoon,* Mark won his class in the 1970 Bermuda Race, took second two years later, and twice won his class in the Annapolis-Newport Race.

Apart from his ability as a seaman and racing sailor, Clayton was a capable administrator and leader in the yachting world. He was a commodore of the New York Yacht Club and a member of the club's America's Cup Selection Committee; a commodore of the Cruising Club of America; a member of the Pratt Committee that developed the IMS Rule; a member of the Fales Committee, which advises the navy on its sailing program; an organizer of the USYRU Safety Committee; and a major promoter of the Chesapeake Bay Maritime Museum.[30]

Despite his important and sometimes solemn duties, Clayton was anything but stuffy. During one formal CCA banquet when he was commodore, he pretended that he had received a tele-

gram from Princess Grace of Monaco. He pulled out a piece of paper that looked like a telegram and in a rather serious voice, read to the gathering of ladies and gentlemen Grace's expression of respect for the CCA, explaining how she loved boats whether they were large or small. After a brief pause, he continued reading. The Princess complained that she had been accused of marrying Prince Rainier for his yacht, but she wanted to make perfectly clear that she was really interested only in his dinghy. Ewing's performance nearly brought down the house.

Clayton Ewing owned a total of four boats named *Dyna,* all successful racers, but the first, the 57-foot yawl, had the best record and was the one he owned for the longest period of time. After Clayton died in 1981, then-commodore of the CCA Richard McCurdy wrote, "When you went aboard a boat called *Dyna,* you not only knew that she was a vessel to be proud of but also that she would be operated in a style with a level of seamanship and sportsmanship rarely equaled and never surpassed."[31]

Angantyr: One of the most interesting boats belonging to owners who have lived on the Chesapeake is the 61-foot cutter *Angantyr* designed by MacLear and Harris for James Crawford of Florida's west coast and Easton, Maryland. Unlike many of the boats in this book, *Angantyr* was not designed with even the slightest thought of a rating rule in mind. Although she is far from slow and has been raced occasionally, she was intended for family living onboard and

Facing page: Plans of Clayton Ewing's most famous *Dyna.* Courtesy Sparkman & Stephens, Inc.

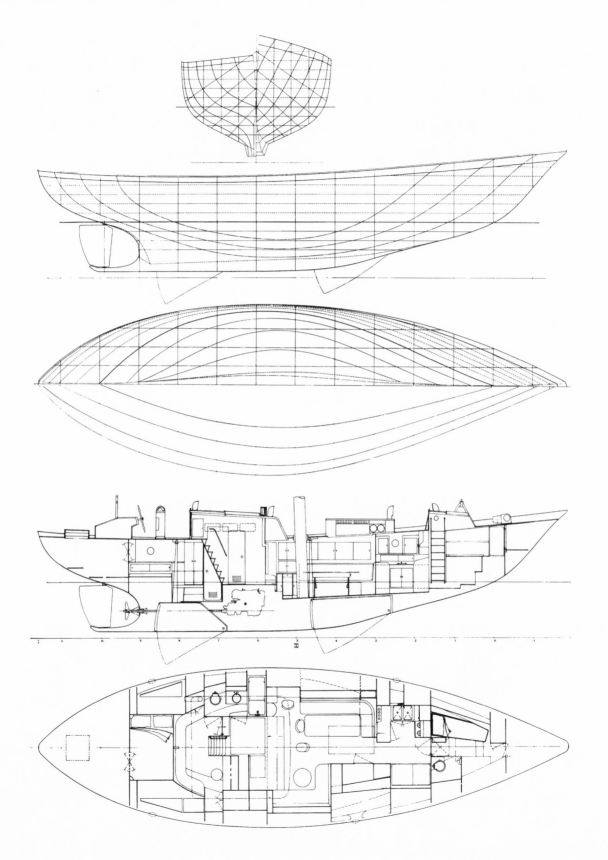

CHESAPEAKE SAILS

distance cruising. A handsome boat with canoe stern and the hint of a clipper bow, *Angantyr* has a somewhat unusual underbody with a moderately long shallow keel housing tandem centerboards and a spade-related balanced rudder, which, unlike the normal spade, is supported at its heel with an after extension of the keel's bottom. This configuration, forming a lovely semi-S-shaped curve from the stern to rudder heel, provides the advantages of a spade (with its far aft location and balance for easy steering) while reducing the vulnerability of a free-standing spade.

Her rig is that of an extreme cutter with a huge foretriangle. In fact, her mast is stepped so far aft (slightly abaft amidships) that Crawford called her a single-masted schooner. Some advantages of this rig are the ease of handling due to a smaller mainsail, a large self-tending staysail, and more space around the mast; concentration of weight amidships, which enables the boat to better respond to the waves and gain speed; and good balance with reasonable power under stays'l alone. As a matter of fact, balance can be fine-tuned with almost any sail combination by changing the center of lateral resistance with the tandem centerboards.

Heavily built of steel in Germany, *Angantyr* proved ideal for Crawford's purposes. After her shakedown cruise across the North Sea in 1964, her owner wrote:

Facing page: Lines and hull plans of *Angantyr* designed by MacLear and Harris. Courtesy MacLear and Harris, Inc.

Sail plan of *Angantyr.* Courtesy MacLear and Harris, Inc.

"How wonderfully the ship behaved! Kindly motion, easy to handle, and surprisingly fast, considering she is surely the strongest vessel of her size afloat. She balanced like a dream—the twin centerboards giving the hoped-for control of lateral plane. Close-reaching at nine knots, we could stroll away from the wheel for 20 minutes at a time. The balanced rudder gave her one spoke control."[32] She was marvelously comfortable with such features as diesel-oil heating, bathtub, washing machine, ample tankage, and three water catchment systems. Her spacious flush deck allowed ample room for two nested dories. Prior to owning

Angantyr under sail showing her unique mast-amidships rig. According to the boat's designer, Frank MacLear, this jib is the size Crawford preferred even when racing in moderately light weather. Photograph from *Count the Cats in Zanzibar* by Jim Crawford.

Angantyr, Crawford had experienced four severe knockdowns, sometimes submerging the masts; he wisely insisted that all hatches be located on the cutter's centerline to lessen the risk of downflooding.

As noted in chapter 2, Jim Crawford is an experienced offshore sailor who in the late 1950s sailed around the world in his Alden schooner *Dirigo II*. A veteran of numerous ocean races as well as long-distance passages, he made a total of ten transatlantic crossings and in 1974 was awarded the most highly respected CCA Blue Water Medal "for extraordinary accomplishment in worldwide cruising." Seven of his transatlantics were made in *Angantyr,* four of them with his son Eric, who lives in Easton, Maryland.

Having great admiration for the oceangoing singlehanders, Crawford had a hankering to sail across the Atlantic alone. He did so aboard *Angantyr* in 1970 during a nineteen-day passage from the Canary Islands to Antigua in the West Indies. Many years before he had sought advice on singlehanding from two-time solo circumnavigator Harry Pidgeon. When asked how he managed alone, Pidgeon replied: "You can sail one day by yourself, can't you, Jim? That's all it is—one day after another."[33] That's just how Jim did it—one day at a time.

I had the great pleasure of witnessing Jim Crawford solo-sail his hefty cutter through a somewhat crowded harbor at Oxford, Maryland. As he tacked between anchored boats, the slide for the staysail sheet's lead block failed to slide all the way to leeward on its traveler. Jim left the wheel, strolled forward (to amidships), kicked the slide to leeward, and calmly walked back to the helm. I was impressed with both man and boat.

His friend and frequent crewmember, Sennett Duttenhofer, had this to say about Jim Crawford: "He is really one of those men born in the wrong century. Would have made a great sea rover for Queen Bess."[34]

Reindeer: Except for the preference for martinis that are stirred, not shaken, and the overdeveloped libido, Newbold Smith has much in common with Ian Fleming's fictional character James Bond. Like Bond, he is a man of broad interests and expertise—a remarkable athlete, an incurable adventurer, a man of exceptional courage, and, I've been told, even a connoisseur of wines. I doubt if Bond's expertise as a sailor could compare with that of Newbold Smith's, however, because the real-life character is not only a racing sailor of great distinction but also a long-distance cruiser who has sailed his own yachts to the High Arctic no less than three times and has been awarded the Blue Water Medal. Although he resides in Pennsylvania, his boats have been kept on the upper Chesapeake.

A star athlete at the U.S. Naval Academy, Newbold won ten varsity letters in football, wrestling, and track. He won the Eastern intercollegiate heavyweight wrestling championship in 1948 and was undefeated in dual-meet competition. Also, he was selected by United Press International to be on their all-American football team. His Navy team defeated Notre Dame once and tied them once in a snowstorm at Cleveland Stadium.[35] A decade or more after his graduation, he was stopped by a policeman for making a U-turn in his car, and an argument ensued. The officer made the mistake of striking Newbold, who made a bigger mistake and returned the blow. This resulted in a brief prison stay and the case being appealed to the Supreme Court.

While in jail, Newbold was the star of a mostly black football team.

At the Naval Academy, Smith got plenty of exposure to big-boat sailing, and he took to it like the proverbial duck to water. His first ocean racer was the fourth-hand English cutter *Galliard.* Then came a procession of boats named *Reindeer,* the first being the previously mentioned Block Island 40 that had a great racing record including fleet first in the 1961 Annapolis-Newport Race and first in the Northern Ocean Racing Circuit. A recent *Reindeer* is the Farr 44 described in chapter 4. In 1994 Newbold and his crew sailed her up into Hudson Bay, which he said is much bleaker than any part of the High Arctic. The third *Reindeer,* which also cruised far north, was designed by C & C (Cuthbertson and Cassian) and presently resides at Gibson Island. She is now named *Dancer.*

In response to my question about how he selected the name *Reindeer,* which seems appropriate for his voyages to the far north, I was told by Newbold that he and his wife wanted a reindeer name such as Donner, Blitzen, or the others, but after consulting Lloyds Register, they found all those names had been taken. He wrote: "My wife suddenly said, 'What's wrong with *Reindeer*' and it clicked. No one had that name, and, yes, it did make a hit in Norway and Greenland, where it's a popular animal."[36]

My favorite of the Smith *Reindeer*s is the second one, a Swan 43, that Newbold sailed to the Arctic on a voyage that earned him the Blue Water Medal. Superbly built in 1969 by Nautor in Finland,

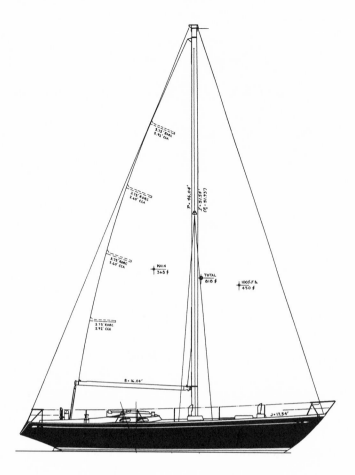

Plans of the Sparkman and Stephens–designed Swan 43. Courtesy Sparkman & Stephens, Inc.

Reindeer II's construction and rigging was supervised by Rod Stephens, who Newbold said "comes pretty close to the ultimate authority."[37] Even so, the boat had her share of bugs that needed ironing out. I'm sure that Newbold was more than happy to have his rigging inspected by such an expert as Rod, for in 1960 he had his fittings x-rayed before the Bermuda Race and found four defective castings. *Reindeer II*'s hull was beefed-up somewhat, but this did not add enough weight to seriously affect her speed on the race course. No part of the hull was greater than

$\frac{5}{8}$-inch thick, which is amazing when you consider the ice-filled waters she was to explore.

The accompanying perspective drawing done for me by master designer/ draftsman Al Mason (formerly with Sparkman and Stephens) reveals a fairly balanced hull with minimal wetted surface. The latter characteristic gives her the speed in light air that is desirable in the Chesapeake without the need for a large rig to complicate handling and overpower the boat in strong winds. The balanced hull with rather narrow V-sections aft trades off some downwind speed, stability, and perhaps resistance to pitching for superior windward performance, resistance to rooting (burying the bow), and the reduction of weatherhelm when heeled. The short keel compromises some directional stability to reduce wetted surface. Unlike most modern fins that are bolted on, the keel of the Swan 43 is integral with the hull, and it has a sloped leading edge which reduces shock-loading in the event of collision with flotsam.

The boat was amply equipped with electronics, but it is interesting that Newbold, even after four years of electrical engineering at Annapolis, claims that electrical problems are the greatest source of worry for the small-boat voyager. And incidentally, Frank Casper, another Blue Water Medalist, came to the same conclusion. Though his profession was electrical engineering, he told me that his first act after acquiring his famous ocean cruiser *Elsie* was to permanently remove almost everything electrical.

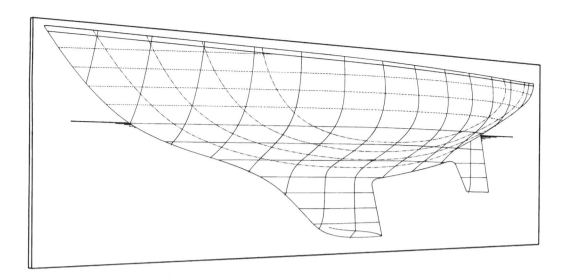

Lines perspective of the Sparkman and Stephens–designed Swan 43, drawn for the author by Al Mason. Courtesy Sparkman & Stephens, Inc.

In 1972 Newbold suffered a horseback riding accident that made him an instant—though temporary—quadriplegic. Before being discovered, he could only lie on the ground unable to move; he even worried that some nearby crows might pluck out his eyes. Fortunately, he was soon found and taken to a hospital. An operation restored his ability to move, but he remained partially paralyzed on one side. Despite a fairly good recovery, Newbold recognized that he would have to forego many of his sporting activities, and he elected to concentrate on sailing, where he could still be competitive.

Two years later, he entered the Bermuda Race in *Reindeer II* and got a second in class behind Chesapeake sailor Don Tate. After the race he took the boat to Labrador, and this helped whet his appetite for cruising in the far north. The following year he decided to take *Reindeer* to the Arctic, and he began serious preparations that included a trip to Norway to get information about harbors, ice conditions, and so forth.

The voyage is described in detail in Newbold's book *Down Denmark Strait*.[38] *Reindeer* left from Georgetown, Maryland, in May 1976 bound for Spitsbergen (a group of islands that are the world's northernmost inhabited land area) via Newport, Newfoundland, Iceland, the Faeroe Islands, and Norway. Eventually she reached Moffen Island off the northern coast of Spitsbergen, a point closer to the North Pole than any other American yacht had ventured. The return passage was through the notoriously stormy Denmark Strait to the often ice-packed anchorages of south Greenland. Newbold and his crew were exposed to such experiences as visiting a Soviet research vessel at Newfoundland; going through four gales on the way to Iceland; passing the Arctic Circle and seeing twenty-four hours of daylight on June 21;

Newbold Smith's *Reindeer II* after finishing a Bermuda Race. Courtesy Government Information Services, Bermuda.

fouling a fisherman's net in the Norwegian Sea (necessitating a dive overboard by crewmember Phil Parish); undergoing magnetic anomalies (necessitating navigation by dead reckoning and using a local apparent midnight sun sight!); visiting a Russian settlement in Spitsbergen; beating with only a number four jib to mountainous Jan Mayen Land (north of Iceland) in "foehn" winds (similar to williwaws) with gusts that pinned the anemometer at sixty knots;

nearly becoming trapped in a cul-de-sac of pack ice on the east coast of Greenland (requiring a 180-degree turn and a man on the bow fending off "bergy bits"); undergoing a grounding and inadvertent careening to a heeling angle of 60 degrees in Prins Christians Sund, Greenland; and landing at the Grenfeld Mission near the northern tip of Newfoundland.

Reindeer arrived at New York three and a half months after leaving the Chesapeake. She had sailed to a place less than 600 miles from the North Pole. Being a very modest fellow, Newbold gave much credit to his crew, especially Phil Parish of Georgetown, Maryland, and he praised the accomplishments of his forerunners, British Arctic yachtsmen Lord Dufferin and Major H. W. Tilman. In 1979 Smith sold his second *Reindeer* primarily because she was becoming increasingly disadvantaged for racing under the IOR. His next boats of that name were increasingly more racing-oriented, but that didn't stop him from voyaging to the far north in them.

Modern boats of the ultralight-displacement semi-planing type are often called "sleds." I don't think that Newbold plans to compete with Santa Claus for having the most reindeer, and let's hope he doesn't follow Santa's example of taking a sled to the North Pole.

Running Tide: My personal favorite of the larger boats with home ports on the Chesapeake is the lovely 61-foot sloop *Running Tide*, designed by Sparkman and Stephens. In my opinion, her underwater configuration, evolved from *Palawan III* (which Olin Stephens once

216   CHESAPEAKE SAILS

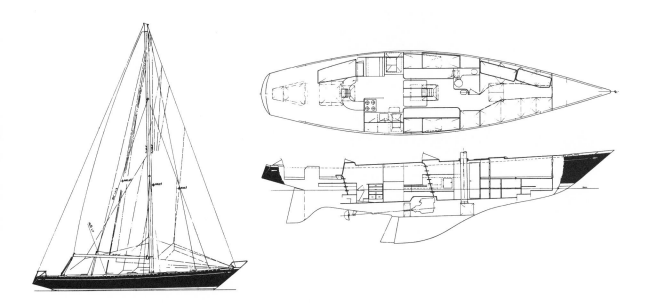

Plans of the Sparkman and Stephens–designed *Running Tide*. Courtesy Sparkman & Stephens, Inc.

said was "possibly the nicest boat to steer I have ever designed"[39]), is still the best compromise for the combination of speed, ease of handling, and seaworthiness. Her underbody consists of a sloped forefoot and leading edge of keel (to inhibit rooting, minimize the tip vortex, and afford impact resistance); a short but fairly deep integral keel (for the combination of strength, resistance to leeway without excessive draft, range of stability, and low wetted surface); and a skeg-mounted rudder far aft (for the combination of directional stability, extension of the steering arm, rudder protection, and the inhibition of rudder stalling). Having owned an Ohlson 38 with this kind of configuration for twenty years, I can attest to its merits. *Running Tide* is a bit more extreme than the Ohlson and has a trim tab, which is controversial in its ability to enhance keel lift without excessive drag but which can be

useful for emergency steering if the main rudder is damaged.

Designed for shipping magnate Jakob Isbrandtsen in 1969, *Running Tide* was an immediate success on the race course, winning her class in the 1970 Bermuda Race and the overall award in SORC the following year. She came to the Chesapeake in 1973 after being purchased by Virginia real estate developer Al Van Metre and continued her winning ways for almost a decade. Under Van Metre and his son Beau (who, I understand, did much of the starting and steering), *Running Tide* won her class three times in the SORC and was first overall in the 1976 Bermuda Race. On the Bay she won the Annapolis Fall Series three times and Class A High Points the same number of times. As late as 1983 she topped her class in the Annapolis-Newport Race, repeating her class win of two years earlier.

Al and Beau Van Metre began their big-boat racing in the Cal 40 *Allison* and developed teamwork that led to later success with a Sparkman and Stephens 52-footer named *Bandit,* which they owned just prior to their acquisition of *Running Tide.*

Having sailed with my father for a number of years, I am interested in father-son teams. A few of the notable big-boat teams have been Gaither Scott and his sons Jim and Charlie; Sunny Gibbons-Neff with sons Mitch, Henry, and two brothers; Buzz White and son John; Tom and Tommy Closs; Bates McKee and a family crew that included grandsons (occasionally Olympic gold-medalist Jonathan McKee); Doug Hanks and his son Doug; Charlie Iliff with Nick and three other sons; Clayton Ewing and son Mark; Jim Crawford and son Eric; Sunny Smith and his son Charlie; Marshall Steele and his sons Ron and Olympic medalist Scott; Charlie Ill and his sons Peter and Charlie; and Bill Wallop and his sons Doug and Bill. I'm sure there are many more.

A legendary watch captain of *Running Tide* when she was owned by Isbrandtsen was Victor Romagna, who lived on the Chesapeake's South River for more than a dozen years.[40] Romagna was the noted crew chief who ran the foredeck on the 12-meter boats *Columbia, Weatherly,* and *Intrepid* during the America's Cup Races of the 1960s. Of *Running Tide* Victor said, "She gets up speed in a hurry and holds it . . . [she is] so forgiving and easy to sail. Beautiful upwind and holds her own downwind too."[41]

On the Chesapeake, an important member of the crew was Frederick Hecklinger, one of the best marine surveyors in the Annapolis area. For many years he served on *Running Tide* as professional captain and "later as part of the regular crew."[42] Fred had this to say about the boat's performance: "Although she [*Running Tide*] would not surf off like the boats that are fashionable on the West Coast, she did not lose steering control under any condition. . . . I was never terrified when sailing in *Running Tide* and I assure you that I have been in some other vessels. . . . She would go to windward in any conditions better than anything around."[43]

Another well-known Annapolis sailor who was a regular member of *Running Tide*'s crew during her Chesapeake years was Dr. Raymond N. Brown, not to be confused with Raymond M. Brown of Hampton, Virginia. Dr. Brown was the perfect complement for the after guard. Aside from being a close personal friend of Al Van Metre, Brown was a seagoing medical doctor who often lectured at safety seminars, and he fulfilled the owner's desire to have a doctor on board. In addition, Ray was a gifted sailor who had won numerous High Point awards in the Rainbow class, and he was a skilled navigator. (He navigated *Running Tide* to a number of victories, but Richard Stimson was the navigator during her fleet first in the 1976 Bermuda Race). Tragically, Dr. Brown was lost at sea in 1989

Facing page: A Morris Rosenfeld photo of *Running Tide* in 1974. © Mystic Seaport, Rosenfeld Collection, Mystic, Connecticut.

after being knocked overboard during an accidental jibe while sailing his new Alden sloop to Annapolis.[44]

During her racing years, *Running Tide* was considered by some to border on spartan below. In his previous boat *Good News*, Isbrandtsen had stripped out the accommodations to lighten the boat and improve efficiency for racing, and this thinking was reflected in *Running Tide*. As Fred Hecklinger put it, Isbrandtsen was "not concerned with how you would entertain during a NYYC cruise." Fred added, "At least he [Isbrandtsen] permitted a nice head area which was enclosed with nice plywood bulkheads. Many boats were then developed with the toilet sort of in the middle of things and maybe enclosed with a plastic shower curtain. I'm glad I missed that phase." In writing of her aluminum construction by Huisman Jactwerf in Holland, Fred wrote, "The hull was plated up in a wonderfully fair manner and originally I do not believe that any fairing compound was used on the hull exterior."[45] However, he did note that once there was a serious problem with galvanic corrosion in way of the through-hull fittings. Pipes at the through-hulls were replaced by Trumpy, and there were no further difficulties.

Running Tide is a beautiful boat and has many admirers. It was quite a sight to watch her in an Annapolis Fall Series doing battle with the likes of Ted Turner's *Tenacious* and Don Tate's *Cayenne*. *Running Tide*'s name, of course, was taken from John Masefield's immortal poem *Sea Fever*. In a rather amusing manifestation of the boat's recognition by

Bay sailors, a racing skipper named his boat *Running Toad*.

***Mooneshine* and *Third Turtle*:** Although different as night and day, the two yachts presented here have at least two things in common. Both have sailed the waters of the Chesapeake for extended periods of time, and both have competed in the most challenging long-distance ocean races for singlehanders. One is the featherweight 31-foot trimaran *Third Turtle* mentioned in chapter 2, manned by Bill Homewood when she resided on the Bay; the other is a relatively heavy 39-foot monohull cutter named *Mooneshine*, singlehanded by Francis Stokes. As said in chapter 2, Stokes is not a native of the Chesapeake, but for a number of years he had a yacht brokerage business in Annapolis—Cobb and Stokes—and was the agent for the Fast Passage 39, a stock production class of which *Mooneshine* was one. In recent years *Mooneshine* has resided on the Bay under the ownership of Annapolitan Ronald Trossbach, an advisor/coach in the sailing program at the U.S. Naval Academy and chairman of the CCA's Safety at Sea Committee.

My first contact with Francis Stokes was in 1970 when he challenged me to a singlehanded race across the Atlantic in Cal 2-30s. I seriously considered it—for about five whole seconds. Unaccompanied by any other boat, Francis did sail across alone in his 2-30 *Crazy Jane*, and that started him on a career of solo racing in such events as the Bermuda One-Two and the much longer OSTAR, prestigious transatlantic races for singlehanders held every four years. After two OSTARs in a Valiant 40 named *Mooneshine,* Stokes decided to tackle one of the world's toughest sailing competitions, the BOC Challenge. As in the Whitbread Race, the BOC boats circle the globe in the often boisterous prevailing westerlies of the southern hemisphere, but the latter race is even more demanding because there are only three stopovers and each boat is manned by only one person. For this event Francis chose a new *Mooneshine,* the Fast Passage 39.

Designed by William Garden from the Pacific Northwest, the second *Mooneshine* appears to have a somewhat traditional seagoing hull with pronounced sheer and a Baltic stern. Underwater, however, the hull is more modern with a moderately short keel and rudder attached to a deep skeg as far aft as possible, and the lines show that she is quite fine forward and full in the quarters for a double-ender. Her draft of only $5\frac{1}{2}$ feet is fairly shallow for a boat that is $33\frac{1}{2}$ feet on the waterline, and it trades off some windward ability for suitability in shoal waters. Furthermore, Stokes claimed that the moderate draft inhibits tripping in quartering or beam seas.[46] The tall cutter rig provides good power in light air. Although the companionway is off-center, an arrangement frowned-on by some seagoers such as Jim Crawford, it does allow a private stateroom aft. It would be prudent to heave-to on the starboard tack in exceptionally heavy weather. *Mooneshine* proved able and also fast enough for Stokes to take second place in his class in the 1982 BOC

Francis Stokes at the helm of the Fast Passage 39 *Mooneshine.* Courtesy Herb McCormick.

Challenge. He received a lot of publicity during the leg across the southern Indian Ocean when a competitor, Tony Lush, diagonally pitchpoled in *Lady Pepperell* and was rescued by Stokes. After the disaster, which resulted in broken floors and a loose keel that was threatening to become detached, the two skippers made radio contact and managed to rendezvous. A difficult transfer was

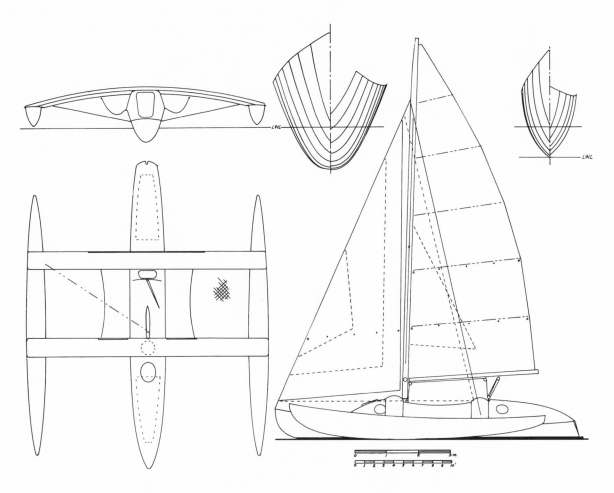

Plans of the Val 31 designed by Dick Newick. Courtesy Richard C. Newick.

carried out in heavy seas: Lush tied a line from *Mooneshine* around his body, jumped overboard, and was hauled to the rescuing vessel by Stokes. Prior to this, Lush had managed to throw a sail bag aboard *Mooneshine* containing a few of his prized possessions, including three copies of Slocum's classic book *Sailing Alone Around the World* and a bottle of Scotch whiskey.[47]

Under the ownership of Ronald Trossbach, *Mooneshine* has continued blue water sailing. He has taken her in a CCA Bermuda Race and crossed the Atlantic at least three times, once with Francis Stokes on board.[48]

Bill Homewood's *Third Turtle* represents an entirely different approach to offshore racing, trading some comfort and ultimate stability for high performance. Multihull sailors often tout their craft as being safe at sea because they are generally considered unsinkable, but the fact remains that without a ballasted keel they can capsize more easily than a monohull and will tend to remain upside down. It takes careful judgment and attentiveness as well as courage to race a small multihull across the Atlantic singlehandedly. Homewood did this twice with *Third Turtle*, in the 1980 and 1984 OSTARs.

Formerly owned by Canadian singlehander Michael Birch, *Third Turtle* is a Val 31 trimaran designed by Dick Newick. Through a mutual friend, I have become acquainted with Dick and have the greatest respect for him as an offshore sailor and designer of high-performance multihulls. I believe his trimarans are safer and more manageable offshore than many other racing multihulls. Nevertheless, Bill Homewood came close to capsizing in *Third Turtle* during a heavy gale in the 1980 OSTAR. He lay to a sea anchor on that occasion, but he told me many years later that, faced with the same conditions, he now favors the storm strategy of continuing to sail at moderate speed under a triple-reefed mainsail. On the other hand, tests that were performed on trimaran models by Donald Jordan and the U.S. Coast Guard indicate the preferred tactic in heavy weather is to stream a series drogue from a bridle at the stern.[49]

An Englishman by birth and education, Bill Homewood emigrated to the United States in 1959 and became a naturalized citizen ten years later. He was a friendly rival of Francis Stokes in the 1980 OSTAR, and the two had a dinner bet on who would finish before the other. Surprisingly, Bill had to buy the meal, which must have been painful as he had said at the start in England that his greatest desire was to beat "that bloody old fart Francis Stokes."[50]

Third Turtle, under the temporary name *British Airways* (in honor of Bill's sponsor), did much better in the 1984 OSTAR. In fact, she finished second in her class, first in her multihull division, and set a new transatlantic record for a 31-foot boat with a time of twenty-one days and slightly more than five and a half hours.

Back home, sailing mostly in the northern Chesapeake, *Third Turtle* racked up three seasonal High Point wins in the CBYRA multihull division, and set a course record for the "the Great Ocean Race," which makes a near circle around Delmarva. Homewood is a colorful character who would lecture at the drop of a sou'wester and gave such seagoing advice as "Always leave your fly undone. They tend to rust shut."[51]

Second Chance: One of the most popular sailors on the Chesapeake (and incidentally one of my very best friends) was Harold R. "Buzz" White of Pasadena, Maryland, and later Gibson Island. As noted in chapter 2, we were friendly rivals in Class C, racing Ohlson 35s. I admired not only the way he sailed but also the way he rebuilt *Temerity*'s interior, installing with his own hands a finely crafted dinette. When the Lusby brothers decided to retire from running the Gibson Island Yacht Yard in the early 1960s, I happened to inform Buzz about the Lusbys' pending departure and half-seriously suggested his filling their

Second Chance racing as a 33-footer in 1976. Photo by Richard C. Kenney, courtesy Carter Kenney Williamson.

shoes. He expressed interest immediately, and it was not long before he took over the yard, joined the yacht squadron, and moved his home to the island. With his vast knowledge of boats, an engineering background, and his likable personality, Buzz was the perfect man for the job. I must add that he was one of the most helpful and unselfish individuals I've ever known. When Buzz's firstborn son John was old enough to do so, he began working at the yard and learning the business. Father and son gradually formed a team not only in servicing boats but in racing them as well.

Around 1976, Buzz bought an Offshore One, a sleek 33-foot IOR racer designed by Britton Chance, which he named *Second Chance*. She arrived at Gibson Island as a bare hull, and the Whites spent quite a period of time finishing the boat and customizing her for their brand of racing. When she first started racing in the Magothy River on Wednesday evenings, our Ohlson 38 *Kelpie*, longer overall but shorter on the waterline, was able to stay with her. Buzz told me that this irked John, who felt that they should be overwhelming a "cruising boat." It wasn't long before I noticed that *Kelpie* was having an increasingly difficult time keeping up with the Whites. They were gradually improving their boat's speed with added ballast, a folding propeller, and better tuning. By 1979, *Second Chance* had sufficient speed and was sailed well enough to compile the best High Point score in the IOR division. With sixty-seven-year-old Buzz steering and John controlling things forward of a sign (placed at the helm by John) that read "No one over age 65 may go beyond this point," *Second Chance* won the highly prized Labrot Trophy.

Following this long-sought-after triumph, Buzz decided to retire from racing, and *Second Chance* was sold to George Wilson of the Tred Avon Yacht Club, who won class High Points in 1982. John White continued racing in a variety of boats in a number of different classes, becoming one of the Bay's top racing skippers, eventually winning numerous High Point awards and triumphing in such impressive events as Key West Race Week, U.S. Sailing's National Offshore Championship, and the J/30 Nationals. In 1986 John was involved in a serious automobile accident that nearly killed him, and surgeons replaced crushed bones with metal or plastic substitutes. But that didn't stop him from racing. Less than three months after the accident, with a full-length cast on his leg, he entered the popular Swan Point–Love Point Race and took fleet first. Newspaper headlines proclaimed "John White Has a Fine Supporting Cast."[52]

It was a most sorrowful occasion when Buzz died in 1985 from Lou Gehrig's disease. *Second Chance* was bought back three years later by John, not just for sentimental reasons, but also because he thought the boat still had the potential to win races. He made extensive alterations that included installing a new deep-draft Tripp 37 keel and a deeper free-standing spade rudder in lieu of the existing rudder attached to a vertical skeg. With her new appendages, the boat competed very successfully in IMS. In 1990, fourteen years after her launching, she captured another Labrot Trophy, in effect signifying that she was the Chesapeake boat of the year.

If this brief chronicle of *Second Chance* were to end here, it would be well worth relating, but the story goes on. The boat was sold again, reacquired again by John in early 1995, and modified even more extensively, this time with a chain saw. John had in mind to enter *Second Chance* in the MORC Internationals to be held in Annapolis that year.

A close-up view of *Second Chance*'s stern after amputation. Photograph by Sarah Cramer.

Since that class was limited to boats under 30 feet, John's solution to the problem of his boat's ineligibility was to saw three feet off her stern. The amputation was almost vertical and brought the bottom of her transom slightly below the load waterline. The immersion was even deeper after John added enough ballast to help lower *Second Chance*'s rating to the point where she would rate at the top of Division B. I was a bit concerned about the extra drag caused by the partly submerged transom, but the boat's performance did not seem to suffer significantly. A submerged outboard rudder was added and also a Sail Drive (modified outdrive) engine plus a pipe frame aft for an outboard motor. With her tall rig, deep keel, and heavy displacement, *Second Chance* was a fascinating contrast to her competitors. Referring to her weight of 13,000 pounds, which was about four times greater than a typical MORC ultralight, John called his boat a "mastodon."

Even for John, it was a great question wondering how *Second Chance* would fare in the competitive MORC Internationals. To the surprise of many, she proved a real contender straight off. She was superior on legs that were dead to leeward and on upwind beats that didn't require a lot of tacking. Her great sail area (on a mast said to be eight feet taller than that of any competitor in the division) overcame any displacement disadvantage in light air. *Second Chance* easily won her division and took fleet first in the regatta. Crabtown's

paper, the *Capital*, reported that John had stunned the international field.[53] He continued racing in MORC that year and at the end of the season was the class High Point winner.

I'm sure Buzz would have been proud of his boat's double comeback under the skillful hands of his son. He was fond of the advice "Never make the same mistake once." With respect to her competitiveness, few if any mistakes were made in the selection and numerous modifications of *Second Chance*.

CHAPTER SEVEN

THE NAVY MAKES SAIL

Many of the most famous Chesapeake resident yachts were owned by the navy and based at the U.S. Naval Academy in Annapolis. A great number of racing-cruising types have been donated by well-known yachtsmen from various parts of the United States.

Starting six years after the academy's founding in 1845, midshipmen were given nautical training on practice vessels—large square-rigged vessels that carried batteries of guns in early times. The historic frigates *Constitution* and *Constellation* (the latter built in Baltimore) were used for such training. A detailed account of the early practice ships and the later history of the academy sailing program is eloquently told by retired Rear Admiral Robert W. McNitt, in his book *Sailing at the U.S. Naval Academy.*[1]

Early yachts: The first practice vessel originally designed as a yacht was the famous fore-and-aft-rigged schooner *America* that beat the British yachts around the Isle of Wight in 1851 and started the ongoing series of international races for the America's Cup. After her celebrated racing victory, *America* was sold in England. She remained there under several owners until the outbreak of the Civil War, when she was bought by the Confederate Navy for use as a blockade runner. Later she was scuttled, then salvaged for service in the Union Navy.

During the Civil War, the Naval Academy was temporarily moved to Newport, Rhode Island, and in 1863 *America* was sent there to serve as a practice vessel.

After the academy was relocated in Annapolis, *America* was not often used, but in 1869 she was reconditioned to participate in the first defense of the America's Cup. Skippered by Commander Richard Meade, head of the Department of Seamanship at the academy, and crewed by navy personnel and midshipmen,[2] *America* made a fine showing in this important event that included the cream of American yachts and the British challenger *Cambria*. With a suit of less than perfect sails, she finished fourth out of fifteen boats, six places ahead of the

R. J. Schaeffer's replica of the schooner yacht *America*. Courtesy Chesapeake Bay Maritime Museum, Ernest Tucker Collection.

CHESAPEAKE SAILS

challenger. That was her last great moment of racing glory.

Although she left the navy a few years later, *America* was given back to the Naval Academy in 1921. She was then put on semipermanent display in the Dewey Basin, where she sat almost continuously for nearly two decades. An attempt to put her into racing condition again, spearheaded by William Halsey, bogged down. But shortly before the United States entered World War II, at the request of President Roosevelt, Congress approved an appropriation for a major overhaul. The old schooner, then with serious rot, was stored in a shed at the Annapolis Yacht Yard to await her refit, but the reconditioning plan was delayed when the Japanese attacked Pearl Harbor. *America's* demise was finalized after the snow-laden shed roof collapsed on her early in 1942.

The Naval Academy was not *America's* only connection with the Chesapeake. Her hull form, designed by George Steers, was influenced by the early sharp-built schooners of the Bay, such as the Norfolk pilot boats and Baltimore clippers. There is also a theory, not universally accepted but believed by L. Francis Herreshoff[8] and others, that *America's* design was influenced by Scott Russell's wave line theory (a vessel's lines should conform to the outline of a wave). In any event, the schooner was exceedingly fine forward, with a form that was a distinct departure from the prevalent (in England) "cod's head–mackerel's tail" theory first proposed by Leonardo Da Vinci. George Steers remarked (with tongue in cheek, one supposes) that his inspiration

for *America* came from the shape of an ivory paperknife. An obvious disadvantage of a hollow entrance is lack of buoyancy forward. In the 1970s, R.J. Schaefer's replica of *America* was sailing on the Chesapeake when she nosed into the wake from a ship. When the bow failed to lift, the wave broke aboard with such force that it washed a prominent Bay sailor overboard. He was promptly recovered.

Another replica of *America* was launched in 1995, this time with her home port on the Chesapeake. She is owned by restaurateur Raymond Giovannoni of Alexandria, Virginia, who charters the schooner in various parts of the world and eventually plans to donate her to the Naval Academy.

Other early sailing yachts donated to the Naval Academy were the 60-foot cutter *Medusa*, later named *Robert Center*, and the 57-foot yawl *Argo*. There is a photo of the former in the Barrie Brothers' book about cruising the Chesapeake. In *Sailing at the U.S. Naval Academy*, Bob McNitt tells us that plebes were expected to reply to the question, "Why did Argo?" with the answer, "Because Robert Center."

With the decline of large square-rigged practice ships, sail training at the academy suffered a serious lapse between 1910 and the mid-1930s, when a popular Midshipmen Boat Club was formed. Early in the decade much of the small-boat sailing was done in gaff-rigged centerboarders called half-raters. Norman Owens of the Owens Yacht Company wrote me that his father Charles

THE NAVY MAKES SAIL

229

CHESAPEAKE SAILS

started a boatbuilding company in Annapolis during the late 1920s and designed a 26-foot sloop for his own use. On many occasions he would encounter the navy half-raters on the Severn River and would "sail circles" around them. Eventually personnel from the academy contacted Owens and asked him to build six boats similar to his lively design.[4] These boats turned out to be the Naval Academy knockabouts, eventually numbering twenty, that were used as basic trainers at the academy for nearly four decades before the fiberglass Rainbow knockabouts were acquired as replacements.

Vamarie: A great stimulant to big-boat sailing at the academy was the acquisition of the famous 72-foot ketch *Vamarie* donated by Vadim Makaroff, son of a Russian admiral. Under Makaroff and expert sailing master Alexander Troonin, *Vamarie* achieved an outstanding racing record as the first boat to finish in all major ocean races, often winning on corrected time. A gorgeous yacht with mahogany topsides that were finished bright, *Vamarie* was designed in 1933 by Jasper Morgan of the New York design firm Cox and Stevens. The most distinguishing feature of the boat was her wishbone rig with main trysail boomed aft with a wishbone gaff above a permanent mizzen staysail.

Facing page: Early knockabouts racing. The set of sails indicates the woeful state of sail training at the Naval Academy in the early 1930s. Courtesy U.S. Naval Institute Archives.

I'm not sure if this rig got its name from the British ketch *Wishbone* that was designed by Uffa Fox in 1934 or whether that ketch was named after the rig. Credit for the rig's creation is usually given to Frederick (Fritz) Fenger, but Uffa Fox wrote that Nathanael Herreshoff conceived of the idea before Fenger. At any rate, the wishbone gaff has two curved arms to prevent the spar from digging into the sail regardless of which tack the boat is on. Some of the disadvantages of a main trysail such as *Vamarie's* are a very high center of effort, too much weight aloft, the possibility of chafe, and difficulty in handling with control points aloft. Indeed, *Wishbone* was dismasted after gear failure aloft. *Vamarie* also had occasional problems. Bob McNitt, who crewed on *Vamarie* in the 1938 Bermuda Race after spearheading the effort to allow her entry, tells how the main trysail's outhaul jammed in a block at the outboard end of the wishbone gaff. The sail could not be properly trimmed or lowered during the race, resulting in severe knockdowns during several squalls and a less-than-desirable finish. Incredibly, *Vamarie* had no means of reefing. It was theorized that shortening down could be accomplished by removal of one or more of her many sails. She must have been considered a bit slack-headed, as her rig was augmented early in her career with a tiny jigger mast on the stern. On a later occasion she took a severe knockdown resulting in some downflooding, and could not be luffed-up until the forestaysail sheet parted.[5]

CHESAPEAKE SAILS

Incidentally, the academy came close to acquiring another famous wishbone ketch, the Alden-designed *Svaap*, which William A. Robinson sailed around the world as a conventional ketch in the late 1920s. During a second attempt to circumnavigate—this time under wishbone rig—Robinson suffered a ruptured appendix and had to abandon *Svaap* in the Galapagos Islands. He donated the boat to the U.S. Naval Academy, but before she could be moved, she was plundered and destroyed by pirates.

Vamarie's entry in the 1938 Bermuda Race was the first participation of a Naval Academy vessel in a major ocean race, and it started a tradition that continues today. Since then there has been a navy boat in every Bermuda Race. The 1938 affair was a learning experience for the midshipmen crew. According to Bob McNitt, *Vamarie*'s skipper was a capable naval officer, generally well liked by his crew but lacking in certain sailing skills and yacht racing know-how. He was also a strict teetotaler who would not allow even a drop of beer on board.

Vadim Makaroff was a drinking man who had excellent scotch and bourbon bottled with either his own name or *Vamarie*'s on the labels. He was in Bermuda when the boat he once owned arrived, and in a gesture of generosity he decided to present a case of scotch to the crew of *Vamarie*. After coming alongside in a small boat, he hefted the case to what

Facing page: Vamarie most often seen as a two-master with her wishbone ketch rig. Courtesy United States Naval Academy Archives.

he expected would be eagerly waiting hands, but *Vamarie*'s skipper, with the pomposity of a Gilbert and Sullivan admiral, firmly declined the gift. As the story was told to me by a witness, Makaroff was stunned and obviously felt he had been spurned. He backed off, telling the skipper that he was rude and in his noticeable Russian accent adding, "And furthermore, Captain, your fly is unbuttoned."

The following year *Vamarie* was quite active racing on the Chesapeake. She did well considering she often had to contend with *Stormy Weather*. Because of her generous draft of 10½ feet, her various navigators had to be on the ball. I remember her grounding on a couple of lumps, one near Sandy Point (unmarked on the chart) and the other near Bloody Point Lighthouse. One year when working the shore to escape a foul current, she attempted to pass to windward of Ralph Wiley who was not at all willing to be blanketed. Wiley ordered a

Vamarie charging through the lee of *Pavana*. Courtesy Gibson Island Historical Society.

crewmember to take soundings with the lead line and call out in a loud voice, "one fathom." *Vamarie* promptly tacked.

During the Oxford Race of 1939, a midshipman fell from the mizzenmast of *Vamarie*. I was on a boat not far away and heard him hit the deck. It was an awful sound. The victim broke his pelvis and was in great pain, but fortunately he survived. Corrin Strong in *Narada* went alongside and transported the injured man to Oxford where he was taken to a hospital. *Vamarie* had no auxiliary power at that time.

Luders yawls: That same year the Naval Academy acquired the first three of what would become a small fleet of 44-foot yawls designed by A. E. "Bill" Luders, Jr., and built in Connecticut by the Luders Marine Construction Company. These were beautiful racing cruisers that were ubiquitous on the northern Bay for nearly fifty years. The first dozen yawls were built of wood, and after more than two decades of exceptionally hard service, they were gradually replaced by fiberglass sisters slightly modified by Robert Henry. Bill Luders once wrote me that his famous L-27 *Storm,* which almost dominated handicap racing on Long Island Sound in the late 1950s and early 1960s, was "a scaled down navy yawl in the proportion of a 9 to 10." He added that "the only original difference was that we moved the rudderpost a little further aft for more lateral plane."[6] The fact that *Storm* was basically a smaller navy yawl certainly shows that her lines produced speed as well as beauty and seaworthiness.

Indeed, the yawls often did exceedingly well in local races and even in some ocean races when sailed by capable crew and skillful skippers such as Lieutenant Wallace E. Tobin. A former America's Cup sailor, Tobin skippered the navy yawl *Fearless* to a remarkable performance in the prestigious Buenos Aires to Rio Race of 1965 with a seasoned crew mostly made up of naval officers, including Charles "Butch" Ulmer, later a well-known sailmaker, and Bartlett Dunbar, who later collaborated with me on a seamanship manual for the Naval Academy. On the sixth day at sea, *Fearless* was up with the leading bigger boats and undoubtedly would have won overall honors but for a costly tactical gamble at the end of the race when she tacked inshore and encountered less favorable wind. She finished third in her class. As further evidence of a Luders yawl's ability to excel in offshore racing, *Lively, Swift,* and *Daisy* have been class winners in the races between Annapolis and Newport.

When Bill Luders decided to move *Storm's* rudder a bit further aft, it probably improved her steering control because the navy yawls had a reputation for broaching when driven hard downwind. Although I had not experienced this, I never sailed one in a hard blow with the spinnaker set. The midshipmen and college sailors competing in the McMillan and Kennedy Cup Races often set spinnakers in very strong winds. There were

Facing page: Intrepid, the first Luders yawl. Photograph by Marion E. Warren, courtesy U.S. Naval Institute Archives.

CHESAPEAKE SAILS

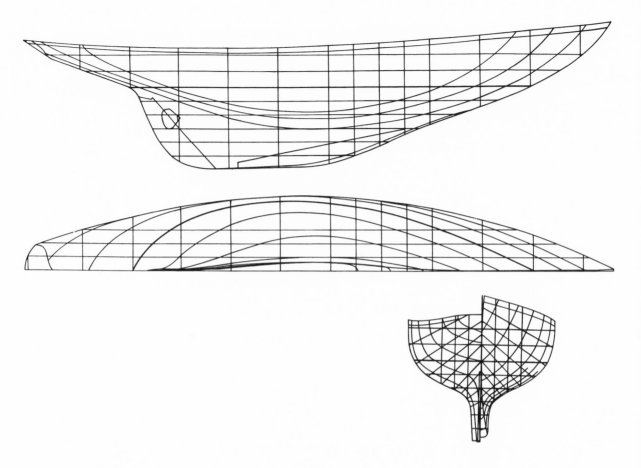

Lines of the U.S. Naval Academy yawls, designed by A. E. Luders, Jr. Courtesy Mrs. A. E. Luders, Jr.

some dramatic photographs taken of sensational broaches in these races and also some well-publicized shots taken at the breezy start of the 1958 Bermuda Race. These photos didn't exactly give the yawls a reputation for being stiff and steady.

When construction of the yawls switched to fiberglass, the rudder design was changed to a *Constellation* shape, named after the innovative rudder on the America's Cup 12-meter of that name. This was done partly to counteract the loss of efficiency due to having a propeller aperture (the wood yawls had no

engine and hence no rudder apertures). At any rate, the *Constellation* rudders, with sharp heel and greater area at the bottom, improved downwind control.

Built by United Boat Builders in Bellingham, Washington, the fiberglass yawls were exceedingly rugged and able to withstand almost constant use and occasional abuse by green midshipmen. Whereas a 1956 collision of two wooden yawls resulted in the sinking (but subsequent recovery) of one, a major coming-together of two fiberglass yawls about a decade later produced very little serious damage. I was told by a (pop-eyed) wit-

Luders yawls racing in a fresh breeze. Courtesy U.S. Naval Institute Archives.

ness that the latter collision was caused when a yacht with a topless female passenger passed close to the yawls.

Highland Light: After *Vamarie* the next famous ocean racer donated to the academy was the 69-foot cutter *Highland Light.* She was a bequest from the estate of Dudley Wolfe, who perished while climbing the Himalayan mountain K2. Designed by Frank C. Paine of Paine, Belknap and Skene (with some input by Arthur Schuman, I understand), she was built by George Lawley and Son in 1931.

The following year, under charter to her designer, she set a course record in the Bermuda Race that was unbroken for twenty-four years. A familiar sight on the Bay from 1940 until the mid-1960s, she excelled in local racing during her first several years at the academy, winning overall seasonal High Points (the Labrot Trophy) twice during the early war years. I still have a vivid memory of starting a race just ahead of the *Light* and watching her charge past like a freight train a short distance to windward. Well-heeled

The mighty *Highland Light,* which held the Bermuda Race elapsed time record for twenty-four years. Courtesy United States Naval Academy Archives.

in a fresh breeze with her great sail area, sturdy ends, heavy displacement, and carrying a sizable "bone in her teeth," she presented a picture of awesome power. Some of her reaching ability came from a long main boom that originally extended far beyond the transom. In his history of the Cruising Club of America entitled *Nowhere Is Too Far,* John Parkinson tells how Frank Paine installed an exceedingly long, well-steeved boomkin in order to have a permanent backstay. It was a strange looking struc-

ture, and some competing yachtsmen called it a "permanent erection."[7] This annoyed Dudley Wolfe, and eventually the main boom was somewhat shortened and a smaller, more conventional boomkin installed.

Both *Highland Light* and *Vamarie* participated in a major coastal race from New London, Connecticut, to Hampton, Virginia, sponsored by the Storm Trysail Club in 1941. In *Nowhere Is Too Far,* Parkinson wrote that "The U.S. Naval Academy made its first impressive showing."[8] *Vamarie* was the first boat to finish, correcting to second in class A behind fleet winner *Blitzen,* and *Highland Light* was third in the competitive class. *Yachting*'s August editorial stated, "It is doubtful if their [the navy's] *Vamarie* ever sailed a better race."

Freedom: The same year that *Highland Light* arrived on the Bay, the large handsome schooner *Freedom* was acquired by the Naval Academy. She was the first of two well-known academy yachts designed by the renowned Boston firm, the John G. Alden Company; the second was the yawl *Royono.* Built by the Great Lakes Boat Building Corporation in 1931, *Freedom* was donated by Sterling Morton of Chicago. Her great length of 89 feet overall precluded her from most races (those with size limitations) but she was fast and also had luxurious accommodations. They included such posh amenities as a tiled heating stove, serpen-

Facing page: The Alden schooner *Freedom* viewed from her bowsprit. Photograph by Marion E. Warren.

CHESAPEAKE SAILS

tine handrails, and a bathtub. Her draft of 10 feet had been kept moderate to allow passage through the Erie Canal, but she was deep enough to teach midshipmen the importance of accurate piloting along with occasional lessons on extricating a heavy vessel from a soft bottom. *Freedom* was used a great deal for training cruises, and a number of times she competed in the Skipper Race, which had no upper size restrictions. Stiff as a church, the big schooner could carry sail when most others had to shorten down. In one heavy-weather Skipper Race she trounced a fleet of the top ocean racers not only on elapsed time but on corrected time as well.

Royono: In 1950 the 71-foot *Royono* was donated to the academy by John B. Ford. A sleek yawl, her lines were drawn by William McNary of the Alden Company. *Royono* was beautifully built with double mahogany planking over steel frames by the Herreshoff Manufacturing Company in 1936. Originally named *Mandoo II* by her first owner, D. Spencer Berger, she made a very respectable showing in the 1938 Bermuda Race rigged as a cutter. Then, under the ownership of John Ford, she was raced very successfully as a yawl with enlarged foretriangle, winning the 1947 Chicago-Mackinac and taking a fleet second in the Bermuda Race the following year. She continued her successful ways after arriving at the academy by taking a class third in the 1950 Bermuda Race. In that prestigious contest two years later, she won her class and was second in the fleet. Her skipper in those races was Lieuten-

ant Commander Frank Siatkowski, known far and wide as "Ski."

A noted teacher of seamanship and greatly admired by his crew, Ski was a tough little man who once told a seasick midshipman to throw up through his teeth because the solid matter would be needed for energy later on. Ski was again *Royono*'s skipper in the rough Bermuda Race of 1966 when the yawl was thirty years old. This time the old hard-driven boat developed serious leaks (among other troubles) and had to withdraw, but the irrepressible Ski said the experience had provided valuable lessons in seamanship. Not much later, after seventeen years in the navy, *Royono* was sold off the Chesapeake, and was used as a charter boat and then a drug smuggler. While in Annapolis, she had been seen and greatly admired by John F. Kennedy during a visit to the academy. Reportedly, he took a cruise on her while he was president.

Apart from Ski, the most colorful of the many talented Naval Academy skippers was Professor Alden R. "Hap" Hefler. He was often in command of *Vamarie*, and a friendly rivalry existed between his boat and *Royono*. In his privately published autobiography *Jack of All Trades*,[9] Hap tells of skippering the engineless *Vamarie* home from an ocean race when Ski on *Royono* passed close by under power. Since *Vamarie* was becalmed, Hap requested a tow, and Ski

Facing page: The Alden yawl *Royono* carrying her two staysails to good effect. Courtesy United States Naval Academy Archives.

agreed on the condition that *Royono* be supplied with some (illegal) beer. After the tow line had been passed, Ski streamed astern a heaving line made fast to a net sack that would hold the beer. The sack was brought aboard *Vamarie* and partly filled with cans—one empty (for a joke), the others full. When Ski hauled the sack back aboard *Royono*, he reached for a cold beer and withdrew the empty can that was by then partly filled with seawater. In disgust he threw the entire sack overboard and could never be convinced that there were some full unopened cans in the sack. Ski promptly cast off the tow line and powered away but later reconsidered and turned back to resume the tow.

Those were the times when it was generally considered acceptable to throw overboard anything that would sink, and most yachtsmen did so. According to an

The crew of *Royono* with Ski at the helm. This photo was probably taken before the Skipper Race of 1967, her last race at the Naval Academy. Courtesy United States Naval Academy Archives.

CHESAPEAKE SAILS

article in the *Chesapeake Skipper* (August 1950) by Harrison Roberts, there was a tradition that midshipmen returning from their first cruise would throw their shoes overboard, one to port and one to starboard, after rounding Tolley's Point (at the entrance of the Severn River) homeward bound.[10]

Another anecdote told by Hap Hefler in his *Jack of All Trades* concerns an afternoon sail aboard *Highland Light,* which he skippered in a number of ocean races. On that day, sailing with a mostly green crew, Hap was steering and noticed that the wheel had come loose on its shaft due to a slipped-out locking key. He asked a green plebe, "Would you like to take the wheel?" Upon the plebe's enthusiastic acceptance, Hap pulled the entire wheel off its shaft and presented it to the surprised and then hysterical midshipman.

According to Hap, there was only one experienced midshipman aboard *Highland Light* that day. This was Alexander Grosvenor, who in 1975 became the commanding officer of the Naval Station and commodore of the Naval Academy Sailing Squadron, making a major contribution to the sailing program. I knew Alex when he was a young boy at Gibson Island and a talented sailor in Cap Kenney's Junior Fleet. Later he was most helpful to me in preparing a new edition of *Sail and Power,* a manual of seamanship used at the academy. As a midshipman, Alex raced a Star in the Internationals at Chicago, making an impressive showing against some of the world's top racing sailors. This is understandable, since his father, Melville Grosvenor, had been a

Chesapeake Bay Star champion with Alex's mother as the expert crew. Incidentally, Alex's daughter Sandy is now a top race official and match racing expert. Bob McNitt described Alex's arrival at the academy as a tropical storm blowing into town and added that the cyclone gathered strength the following three years.[11] Of the many improvements Alex made to the sailing program, one of the most important was the hiring of civilian talent in yacht maintenance and the teaching of sailing skills by nationally prominent coaches such as Graham Hall and Gary Jobson.

Hap Hefler skippered many of the academy yachts but had a special affection for *Vamarie.* In 1954, the lovely ketch sank at her home base during hurricane Hazel. She broke loose from her mooring and was crushed between a seawall and a tug that was attempting a rescue. When her destroyed hull was raised, Hefler was sufficiently moved to write the following verse, entitled *Vamarie,* which appeared in the *Skipper* (May 1955)[12]:

Here before me, a sun-lit picture of
 Vamarie
gliding along on the Bay under jib-tops'l.
Push back that image of her lying crushed
 and broken
on that make-shift cradle across the River,
lying there down-by-the head in a
 dejected aspect.
Let us see her in her glory, carrying her
 many
skippers and crews in the many cruises
 and races
in the Bay and on the Ocean, in fair
 weather and foul.
Did you know that a man can love a ship?

The crushed hull of *Vamarie* being raised from the bottom of the Severn River, a sight that helped to inspire the accompanying poem by Hap Hefler. Courtesy United States Naval Academy Archives.

During that hurricane Hefler was driving to New York in a Volkswagon "bug," and he ran out of gas. Being the consummate sailor, he fully opened the car doors on each side and with a 70-knot tailwind sailed wing-and-wing to the next gas station. In his own words, "This was about 10 miles, and since the station was on my starboard hand, I managed to close the starboard door and then luff up beside the gas pump."

In 1974, the Naval Academy Sailing Squadron gave a surprise party banquet for Hefler and Siatkowski, in appreciation of their lengthy service and contributions to sailing.. The elaborate affair, hosted by Bob McNitt, was called the "Hap-Ski Night."[13]

Later navy yachts: After the departure of *Vamarie, Highland Light, Freedom,* and *Royono,* numerous yachts were donated to the academy, many of them famous racing cruisers. Among those donated later, craft kept for the longest periods of time and/or having significant racing or cruising achievements under navy management were *Maredea, Rage, Jubilee III, Alliance, Mistral, Astral* and *Constellation. Maredea,* a 61-foot centerboard yawl acquired in 1967 from Dr. Homer Denius, was an enlarged development of Charles Morgan's SORC champion *Paper Tiger.* Under the command of Stephen Van Dyck, she finished a close second in class (fleet third) in the stormy Annapolis-Newport Race of 1967 in

CHESAPEAKE SAILS

which thirty-four boats withdrew and one sank. The most remarkable thing about her near-win was that in the thrash to windward in heavy seas during the latter part of the race, she lost her centerboard and made considerable leeway.[14] Later that year she won the Skipper Race, beating some very competitive yachts. Dr. Denius later donated another Morgan design, this time a deep-keel racing cruiser, the 53-foot sloop *Rage*. Soon after being donated, she won the AYC Fall Series with Van Dyck in charge. In 1972 she did very well in the SORC with such talent as Richard du Moulin as skipper and Anthony Parker and Scott Allan as crew. Later *Rage* participated in the 1972 Bermuda Race and the closely following Transatlantic Race.

Also racing in the latter two events was the 73-foot ketch *Jubilee III,* donated to the academy in 1968 by Francis D. Wetherill. At that time referred to as "the queen of the navy's fleet," *Jubilee III* was an innovative design by MacLear and Harris. She had tandem centerboards for regulation of balance and wetted surface and a tall mizzenmast from which a huge staysail and spinnaker could be flown. Her luxurious accommodations included three heads.[15] Commanded by Howard Randall but skippered by her designer Frank MacLear in the 1972 Transatlantic Race, the big ketch took a northern route around the calm mid-Atlantic high and caught favorable westerly winds. She was the second boat in the fleet to finish, winning first place in her class.

Alliance, formerly named *Charisma,* is a Sparkman and Stephens–designed 56-

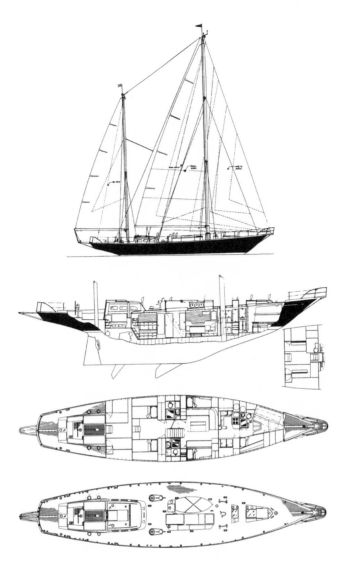

Plans of the MacLear and Harris–designed *Jubilee III*. Courtesy MacLear and Harris, Inc.

foot sloop donated to the zcademy in the late 1970s by Jesse Philips. I met Philips at Cowes in England in 1975 before the Dinard Race. When I asked who was crewing for him on *Charisma* he replied, "Dennis Conner, John Marshall, Steve Van Dyck, Olin Stephens, and some deck apes." *Alliance* had a particularly

The Sparkman and Stephens–designed *Alliance* flying her spinnaker on the Severn River. Courtesy United States Naval Academy Archives.

eventful year in 1979 under the command of Captain Edwin A. "Ned" Shuman III. First, she sailed in the Transatlantic Race that year, a mostly downwind affair, and won not only her class but the fleet award as well, sailing against some of the very best ocean racers. Then she competed in the infamous stormy Fastnet Race previously mentioned, in which fifteen sailors drowned and numerous boats capsized and/or were abandoned. In *Sailing at the U.S. Naval Academy*, Bob McNitt tells how Ned Shuman arrived at the boat before the

start of the Fastnet Race and "found that *Alliance*'s sailing master, trusting in the light wind forecast, had started to off-load the storm sails to save weight. Knowing the history of this race, Shuman had the sails put back on the boat." McNitt added, "This soon turned out to be a very critical decision."[16]

The track of the storm, a summer "weather bomb," was made erratic and more difficult to predict by what meteorologists call a Fujiwhara effect, whereby two lows rotate around a point between them. *Alliance* was hit hard not long before rounding the Fastnet Rock. After blowing out a number three jib, she ran off under bare pole, and then made good use of the nearly-left-behind storm sails, a trysail and a spitfire that was hanked to an inner forestay. At one time a midshipman's tether broke and he was thrown against the steering pedestal with enough force to bend the wheel almost double. The crew did a superb job of finishing the race and bringing their boat into port with minimal damage and injuries. She won the Inter-Regimental Service Trophy.

After the untimely death of Alex Grosvenor, Ned Shuman was selected to take Alex's place, and he did an excellent job of carrying on the Grosvenor-improved sailing program. In a sense, Ned followed in the footsteps of his father, Commander Arthur Shuman, formerly a designer of Marblehead racing yawls, who was the commanding officer of the academy's small craft facility in the early 1950s. Art Shuman had been a talented skipper of Naval Academy yachts, most notably *Highland Light*. He had crewed on her when she set the record in the 1932 Bermuda Race, being the first boat to sail the course in less than three days.[17] Presently, Ned Shuman is a prominent Chesapeake yachtsman. In recent years he has raced his Tartan 41 *Snow White* with consistent success.

A number of the yachts donated to the Naval Academy were raced only occasionally in special events such as tall ship races. Primarily they were used for training cruises and/or U.S. Navy representation in commemorative celebrations or festive occasions. Two such craft were the classic 64-foot schooner *Mistral,* designed by L. Francis Herreshoff, and the 98-foot Rhodes ketch *Astral.* The latter is, I think, the largest yacht used by the academy. *Astral* is a counter-stern development of the Philip Rhodes landmark design *Tamaris.*[18] Although these boats have been called motorsailers, Rhodes preferred to call them heavily powered sailers because of their superior ability under sail. Donated to the academy by Cornelius Vanderstar in 1979, *Astral* was cruised across the Atlantic that year and the next. The midshipmen trainees were forbidden to use her extensive electronic equipment; instead, they were instructed to hone their skills in celestial navigation and dead reckoning. If any trainee questioned this policy, he soon learned why it was so necessary—the big ketch had encountered a storm during which five major electrical circuits shorted out.[19]

Mistral was built in 1938 and donated to the academy by Robert Scarborough in 1976. The following year she was sailed across the Atlantic to participate in the Queen of England's Silver Jubilee. It is interesting that both *Mistral* and *Astral* have been commanded by an army general, Robert Tabor, who was an accomplished seaman in addition to being an expert in a number of fields. His assistant coach was a skilled woman, Louise Burke, who the midshipmen affectionately called "Mother Burke." A handsome vessel with her well-raked masts, graceful sheer, and clipper bow with trailboards, *Mistral* was also able and steady with her old-fashioned long keel and large rudder far aft. I might only question a companionway which, if I remember correctly, was located on the side of her cabin trunk.

Two craft given to the academy were interesting but didn't prove entirely practical; these were the boats previously owned by America's most famous modern singlehanders, Philip Weld and Dodge Morgan. Weld's boat was a 51-foot Newick-designed trimaran named *Moxie,* which won the 1980 transatlantic race for singlehanders, setting a course record for that respected event. Morgan's boat was a 60-foot Hood-designed monohull sloop named *American Promise,* which had set a record of 150 days for a solo circumnavigation. Of course, neither of these boats were meant for a large crew, and the midshipmen had occasional problems with the jamming of their roller-furling sails. *American Promise* was satisfactorily modified and used successfully for several long-distance training cruises, but she was the victim of a catastrophe in 1991. During a night sail just north of the Patuxent River, she collided with a barge being pushed by a tug and sank.[20] Fortunately her crew was rescued, and several days later she was raised and salvaged.

Most notable of the modern Naval Academy yachts is *Constellation*, the PJ (Swan) 48 that won fleet first (racing division) in the 1992 Newport to Bermuda Race. Although it might be a slight exaggeration to compare her victory with winning the World Series, as did one of her crewmembers, the midshipmen had every right to be proud. They trounced the cream of ocean racing yachts manned by some of the nation's top sailors and did so in a relatively old boat that had been used off and on by the academy for about eighteen years. Under the name *Miss Wick*, she was chartered by the academy for use in the 1974 Bermuda Race. A few years later she was donated to the Navy by her owner, Tad Stanwick, a Naval Academy graduate. Prior to her Bermuda win, the Sparkman and Stephens–designed *Constellation* had been greatly admired by the midshipmen and naval personnel who sailed her, and she served as a benchmark boat in planning the Navy 44s that have replaced the Luders yawls.[21]

During her victorious Bermuda Race, *Constellation* was skippered by Ensign Kyle Weaver, who was only twenty-two years old. He was ably assisted by coach-navigator Commander Charles "Chip" Barber, who had been the navigator aboard *Alliance* during the notorious Fastnet Race of 1979. Weaver learned much of his racing skill from excellent coaches at the academy, one of whom was my old friend Jack Quinn from Gibson Island.

The PJ 48 *Miss Wick*, many years later a Bermuda Race winner under the name *Constellation*. Behind the semitransparent genoa, her crew can be seen preparing to set the spinnaker. Photograph by Joe Fuller.

Another sailor who contributed to the victory had a past association with Gibson Island—ex-Star sailor John Jenkins made *Constellation*'s sails. Although there is at least a small element of luck that affects any boat's performance in the Bermuda Race, *Constellation* was painstakingly prepared, her strategy was sound, and she was sailed to her near optimum every minute. Barber gave a lot of credit to Karl Kirkman for introducing him to the utilization of polar diagrams, which show speed curves for all different points of sailing in various strengths of wind. With the advent of the International Measurement System and Velocity Prediction Programs, boats rated under the IMS can obtain polar diagrams that will show optimal headings on all points of sailing. Most racing yachtsmen, including myself, seldom take full advantage of this useful information, but *Constellation* utilized her speed curves with considerable effectiveness.

The Navy 44s: The beautiful 44-foot Luders yawls—the original wooden boats and the fiberglass sisters that replaced them—were used by the academy for nearly half a century. For competitiveness on the race course as well as other reasons, it was inevitable that they be replaced by newer, faster, and more practical modern boats of similar overall length. A great deal of careful thought went into the planning of the replacement boats, formally designated as 44-foot OSTC (offshore sail training craft) but commonly called Navy 44s. As said earlier *Constellation* had been an inspiration long before her Bermuda Race win, but a great many ideas during the planning stage were supplied by the Fales Committee, a group of prominent and highly experienced yachtsmen serving as advisors to the Naval Academy sailing program. Over the years some of the most respected names in yachting have served on the committee such as DeCoursey Fales (for whom the committee was named), Rod Stephens, Sherman Hoyt, Irving Pratt, and Emil "Bus" Mosbacker, just to mention a few. Civilian Chesapeake members have included Clayton Ewing, Karl Kirkman, Newbold Smith, Jack King, Gary Jobson, Victor Romagna, Oliver Reeder, Henry Morgan, and Gaither Scott.[22] Carleton Mitchell was an advisor before the committee was formed. A key figure and twice chairman was prominent local yachtsman Charles Ill, who has contributed much to Naval Academy sailing for a long period of time. I understand that

Constellation under spinnaker in 1981, eleven years before her Bermuda Race victory. Courtesy United States Naval Academy Archives.

many of Ill's ideas were incorporated into the design of the Navy 44s.

Under the leadership of Captain John Bonds, commanding officer of the Naval Station and director of navy sailing, and with advice from Karl Kirkman, a design firm was selected (following a design proposal competition) to create finished plans for the Navy 44s. The chosen firm was McCurdy and Rhodes, headed by James McCurdy, who had previously been

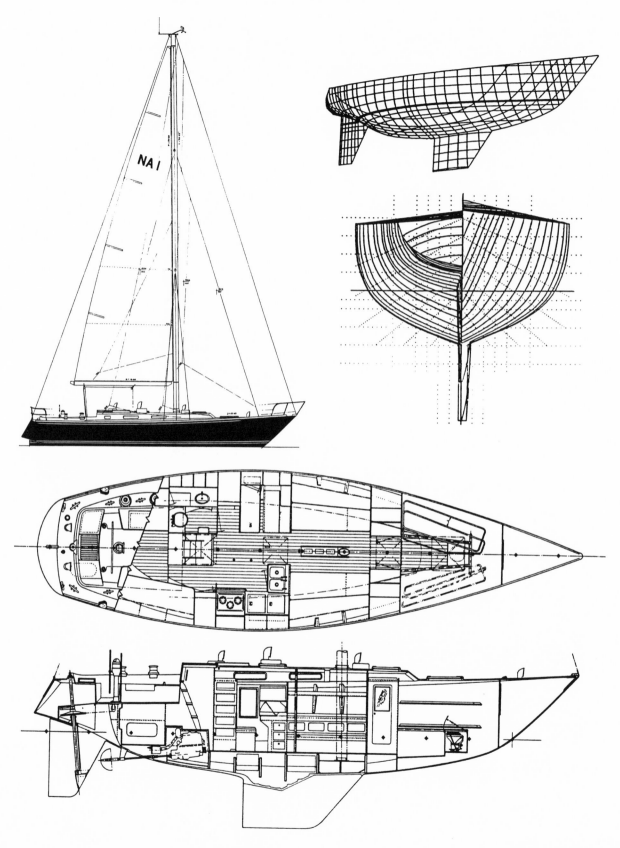

one of the top designers employed by Philip Rhodes. Incidentally, Jim McCurdy's daughter Sheila, with whom I had the pleasure of working on a boat evaluation project, is, so far, the only female member of the Fales Committee. (She served after the Navy 44 contract had been awarded to her father's company). Charlie Ill and Jack Reynolds of the academy's small craft repair department assisted Bonds in selecting a builder. After thirteen leading boatbuilders were invited to submit bids, Tillotson-Pearson was selected. This company specializes in the fiberglass sandwich construction that utilizes a core of end-grain balsa, but the navy, with advice from the Fales Committee, specified a core of Airex foam to ensure against degradation from water penetration. The Navy 44s were built to the highest specifications.[23]

The prototype 44 named *Audacious* was completed in 1987 and thoroughly tested in trials of over one thousand miles offshore under the supervision of John Bonds. His conclusions were submitted in a written report and included such words as "exceptionally able, tractable, predictable, and controllable." Off the cuff he said, "This is the sweetest sailing boat I've ever sailed."[24] *Audacious* also proved fast and comfortable. While her stability range of 130 degrees is less than that of a Luders yawl, it is ample and far in excess of most yachts that capsized in the Fastnet

storm. Her initial stability is much greater than that of the Luders yawl, giving her greater ability to carry sail in a blow. Her displacement is sufficiently heavy to provide a seakindly motion and to allow ample supplies to be added without undue sacrifice of speed for long cruises. A novel feature is molded-in flotation marks to discourage overloading. The cutter rig is a strong one with double lower shrouds; the mast does not need check stays, but there are runners to steady the mast and oppose the pull of a staysail in heavy weather. Accommodations were very thoughtfully planned for offshore use by a crew of nine or ten.

All in all, *Audacious* proved more than satisfactory, and seven sisters were soon ordered. Those Navy 44s that followed *Audacious* did well in many important races including Block Island Race Week and the Annapolis-Newport Race. In the latter event in 1993, Navy 44s finished first, second, third, and fourth in their class. First in class and the PHRF Division was *Swift*, skippered by Ara Barton. Later a photograph of *Swift* was used as a reference for the artwork on the postage stamp that commemorated the 150th anniversary of the Naval Academy.

Aside from the yachts already discussed, many others have been donated to the Naval Academy. Some of the better known are listed at the end of the chapter, along with donors' names.

The Naval Academy's location at Annapolis has proven most beneficial to yachting on the Chesapeake. Not only has it brought large numbers of first-class yachts to the Bay, but it has

Facing page: Plans of the McCurdy and Rhodes–designed Navy 44s that replaced the Luders yawls. Courtesy Ian A. McCurdy of McCurdy and Rhodes, Inc.

Photo of the Navy 44 *Swift* used as the model for the painting on the postage stamp commemorating the 150th anniversary of the Naval Academy. Photograph by Diane Olmstead, courtesy United States Naval Academy Archives.

also sponsored races and produced many programs of interest to civilian yachtsmen. These programs, open to all yachtsmen, include the Sailing Yacht Symposia (sponsored by the U.S. Naval Academy Sailing Squadron, the Chesapeake Yacht Racing Association, and the Society of Naval Architects and Marine Engineers) and the popular Safety at Sea Seminars (initiated in 1979 by Ned Schuman). It is indeed fortunate that the academy's policy has been to unite and cooperate with civilian yachtsmen and whenever possible to combine sailing-related activities. Of course, this spirit of cooperation is mutually beneficial, as civilian yachtsmen have contributed a great deal to navy sailing through advising, coaching, sponsoring races, and of course, donating yachts.

Selected Yachts Donated to the U.S. Naval Academy

Boat name	Size and type	Donated by
America	95½-foot schooner	Eastern Yacht Club
Robert Center (formerly *Medusa*)	60-foot cutter	Mary E. Ludlow
Argo	57-foot yawl	Charles Fitzgerald
Vamarie	72-foot ketch	Vadim Makaroff
Highland Light	69-foot cutter	Dudley Wolfe
Freedom	89-foot schooner	Sterling Morton
Spindrift	55-foot cutter	W. W. Lanahan
Elizabeth	42-foot schooner	Mrs. Henry B. Wilmer
Royano	71-foot yawl	John B. Ford
Annie D (formerly *Windfall II*)	50-foot yawl	F. Nichols
Gypsy (formerly *Blue Water*)	50-foot yawl	Alexander White
Severn Star (formerly *Undine*)	58-foot yawl	Sumner Long
Maredea	61-foot yawl	Homer Denius
Jubilee III	73-foot ketch	Francis Wetherill
Rage	53-foot sloop	Homer Denius
Guerriere	60-foot sloop	Homer Denius
Syren	58-foot sloop	Joseph Wright
Ranger (formerly *Merrythought*)	41-foot sloop	John King
Avenger (formerly *Miss Elaineous*)	40-foot sloop	Dr. Kieth Wold
Fair American (formerly *American Jane II*)	39-foot sloop	George Tooby
Insurgent	48-foot sloop	confiscated for drug running
Mistral	64-foot schooner	Robert Scarborough
Patriot (formerly *Shadow*)	46-foot sloop	Frank Batten
Alliance (formerly *Charisma*)	56-foot cloop	Jesse Philips
Astral	98-foot ketch	Cornelius Vanderstar
Constellation (formerly *Miss Wick*)	48-foot sloop	Tad Stanwick
Spitfire (formerly *Zephyr*)	46-foot sloop	Eugene Sydnor
Cinnabar (formerly *Aries*)	49-foot sloop	Robert Kollar
Bay Bee	50-foot sloop	Mrs. Patrick Haggerty
Moxie	51-foot trimaran	Philip Weld
Enterprise	52-foot yawl	Roy Disney
Rattlesnake (formerly *Inverness*)	68-foot yawl	Robert McCullough
Morning Light (formerly *Scaramouche*)	48-foot sloop	John Ambrose
Elusive	47-foot sloop	William Ziegler
Voyager (formerly *Fun*)	45-foot sloop	Thomas Closs
American Promise	60-foot sloop	Dodge Morgan
Thunderbolt (formerly *Indian River*)	36-foot sloop	Robert McCullough and Emil Mosbacker
Etoile	44-foot sloop	Eugene Sydnor
Congere (formerly *Drum Beat*)	82-foot maxi sloop	Bevin Koeppell

CHAPTER EIGHT

SMALL FRY

Undoubtedly the most widely known small one-design originating on the Chesapeake is the Comet, a 16-foot sloop designed by Lowndes Johnson in 1932. It was created at the request of Maria Dimpfel Wheeler, daughter of the so-called "father of yachting on the Chesapeake," William O'Sullivan Dimpfel, for her two sons. As noted earlier Maria was one of the founders of the Tred Avon Yacht Club. She was an avid Star racer, and she wanted a boat for her young sons that was similar to a Star but smaller and easier to handle. One of them, Tom Martin, wrote me: "Prior to the Star class and later the Comets, the racing was between local sprit-rigged workboat designs di-

vided into two classes: 16′ and 20′. These boats could carry incredible amounts of sail and looked like small canoes! This lack of small one-design classes was the chief reason that mother had Lowndes Johnson design the Comet and started the class. When I first had to race mine in the open 16′ class it was a real David and Goliath match. I used to pray for lots of wind and long weather legs!"[1]

After the Comet's plans appeared in *Yachting* magazine and one of the boats was displayed in the New York Boat Show in 1933, the class was off and running. Two years later, several fleets had been formed, and a national organization for the class was established. Originally the boats were called Crabs and Maria Wheeler's prototype, built by Ralph Wiley at Oxford, was named *Zoea* for the crab larva, but the boat's resemblance to a baby Star suggested the more appealing name Comet. Actually, Comets differ from baby Stars in two major respects: they are centerboarders and have outboard rudders. Obviously they can capsize, but they have the advantage of being easy to beach and put on a trailer.

My limited experience with a Comet occurred soon after World War II when I often crewed for my cousin Ed Henderson. He owned the Comet *Dawn,* which had been rather heavily built of wood by "Skipper" Dixon at Gibson Island. Our good friend Arthur Sherwood, founder of the Chesapeake Bay Foundation, offered to bring *Dawn* home from a regatta in the back of a pickup truck via the Delaware Bridge. In the middle of the bridge, he was hit by a fierce squall that blew *Dawn* halfway off the truck, causing Art to stop and block the bridge traffic. At about the same time, a drunk was walking across the bridge, and he asked for shelter from the rain. Art could not open the door because it was blocked by the boat but he invited the drunk to climb in through the partially open window. The man tried but became firmly stuck when only halfway through. Finally, the police arrived, and the mess was sorted out. It was almost sundown for *Dawn.*

Now, of course, most Comets are built of fiberglass, but a few of them are still built of wood and are surprisingly competitive. Although the class is no longer very active on the Bay, it is very

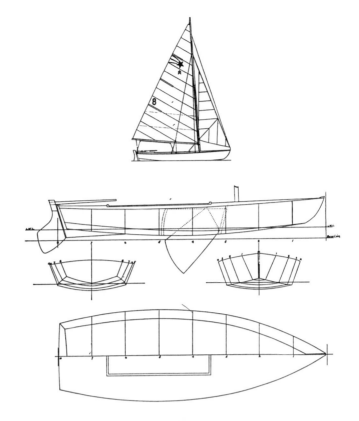

Plans of the most widely known Chesapeake small-boat one-design, the Comet, designed by C. Lowndes Johnson. Courtesy Pete Lesher.

popular nationally, and close to five thousand boats have been built. Class Internationals were held at Oxford, Maryland, in 1994. The most continuously successful skipper in the Chesapeake Comet racing has been John Swaine of the Tred Avon Yacht Club, who won the High Point Championship ten times in a row. The next best record belongs to Elliot Oldak of the Severn Sailing Association, with seven High Point wins.

At about the same time the Comets made their appearance, Ralph Wiley designed and built the Scrappy Cat, a 16-foot hard-chine catboat with lots of sail area. These boats were fast in light air

A Tred Avon Comet owned by J. K. White.
Courtesy Chesapeake Bay Maritime Museum.

The Scrappy Cat *Donna II* well-heeled. Courtesy
Chesapeake Bay Maritime Museum.

and popular in the early 1930s on the Tred Avon River. More than a few went to the Norfolk area. Later, especially in the lower Bay, Scrappys were gradually replaced by a new class of 18-foot sloops called Hampton One-Designs.

Next to the Comet, the Hampton is probably the Bay's best known one-design from a Chesapeake native. To my eye it is one of the prettiest hard-chine daysailers ever built. Its looks are enhanced by low freeboard, a pleasing sheer, a gorgeous stem line, and mahogany cutwater-type coaming. The boat was designed for the Hampton Yacht Club in 1934. Vincent Serio, a self-taught boat designer and expert wooden-boat builder who founded and owned the Hampton Roads Boat Works, created the Hampton One-Design and his associate, Harry Bulifont, drafted the lines. Near the beginning of the decade, Serio had designed and built for his son a miniature boat that in some respects resembled the Hampton. Although the Hampton class never became very popular off the Bay except in the area around Seattle, Washington, it experienced considerable growth around Annapolis and especially in its home waters. Class expansion and Baywide recognition began in 1937 after Vincent Serio, racing his 18-foot Hampton, won against all comers in the 21-foot-and-under knockabout class in the President's Cup Regatta at Washington, D.C.

A key figure in the formation of the Hampton Yacht Club and its one-design class was Harold Jorgensen. As told in the book *Best on the Bay* (edited by Jane and George Webb), Jorgensen kept a

CHESAPEAKE SAILS

stock of high-quality liquor on his yacht moored in Hampton Creek, and one night his prized beverage collection was stolen. The rightfully angry Jorgensen then decided to start a yacht club, "so," he declared, "a man's belongings can be safe." The result was the Hampton Yacht Club, and its clubhouse was built on the site of the then defunct Virginia Yacht Club. After the club became well established and began its own annual regatta, a group of its members, including Jorgensen and Serio, decided it needed a smart attractive one-design, not unlike the Star but with a centerboard suitable for the area's shallow waters. The first Hampton One-Design was built by Serio for naval architect Sydney Vincent, and it attracted great interest at the yacht club. (The fact that the owner of the first Hampton was a naval architect and shared the name Vincent with the boat's designer has sometimes lead to the mistaken belief that Sydney was the designer.) Jorgensen designed the club's burgee, and the flag's symbol, an arrow passing through the letter H, became the sail insignia for the one-design class. (The registered trademark for sailboats and sails was owned by Mr. Serio.) According to *Your New Boat*, edited by *Yachting*, early Hamptons could be bought for as little as "$275 apiece, with a special price to clubs ordering a number of boats."[3]

The class soon began to grow, and most of the Chesapeake regattas gave starts to Hamptons. At times there were as many as fifty of these boats on a starting line. Some of the regatta parties were lively affairs, and on one occasion, ac-

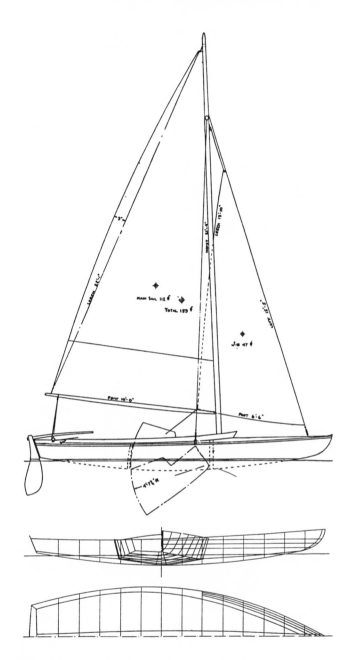

Plans of the sleek Hampton One-Design designed by Vincent J. Serio. Courtesy Vincent J. Serio, Jr., and The Mariners' Museum, Newport News, Virginia.

cording to *Best on the Bay*, "the Hampton fleet was officially removed from the Tred Avon regatta for nearly 40 years as the

Hamptons racing at St. Michaels. Photograph by
Marion E. Warren.

result of destructive behavior brought on
by an overindulgence in alcohol." One of
the most popular regattas was at Cambridge, where the handsome Admiral
Byrd trophy was awarded to the winning
Hampton sailor. One year the famous polar explorer himself flew to the regatta in
an amphibious plane to award the trophy.
Byrd's ship had been fitted out for an Ant-
arctic exploration by Sydney Vincent,
owner of the first Hampton One-Design.

There have been a number of successful Hampton sailors, three of the

most consistent being William P. Hunt,
Robert N. Harrell, and Charles H.
McCoy. My friend and former rival in big
boats, Sunny Smith, was the first Hampton sailor to win the National Championship three times. He also won the
Admiral Byrd Series four times. During
one race in this series, Sunny broke a
spreader but managed to finish after his
crew climbed the mast and rigged a jury
spreader with a paddle.

Hampton hulls are now made of fiberglass and have aluminum spars. Since
1962 their crews have been using tra-
pezes to control heeling. Although these
handsome boats are not now as popular
as they once were, they are still being
raced actively and number close to one
thousand.

Another native design coming from
the southern Bay is the Mobjack, a 17-foot
sloop-rigged one-design created by Roger
Moorman of Gloucester, Virginia. In addition to being a talented boat designer,
Moorman is an avid racing sailor who once
sailed his Mobjack 130 miles from Gloucester to Annapolis to compete in a regatta.[4] He won High Points in that class
three times. Named after its home waters
of Mobjack Bay, the boat has what might
be considered at first glance a rather baf-
fling sail insignia: a jack-tar superimposed
on the letter M. The hull is interestingly
shaped with a shallow V-bottom but soft
well-rounded chines, and just below the
gunwale, there is pronounced flare for
spray deflection and efficient hiking. Designed in 1954, the Mobjack prototype was
well tested and modified before it went
into fiberglass production four years later.

One desirable feature is the shallow air chamber located between the boat's bottom and the cockpit sole; this provides flotation and makes the cockpit self-bailing. The aluminum mast also has flotation to help prevent the boat from turning turtle in the event of a capsize. An international association was formed in 1958, and national championships began the next year. The most consistent Chesapeake Bay champion has been Mark Arnold of the Broad Bay Sailing Association, who won High Points in the class ten times.

Along with Harry Sindle of Gloucester, Virginia, Roger Moorman also had a major hand in designing the Skipjack dinghy, a 14½-foot one-design that has been called a little sister of the Mobjack. Having a self-bailing cockpit and flotation in her spar and fiberglass hull, the Skipjack is easily self-rescued. Her mainsail has full-length battens that hold out a considerable roach. One nice feature is a choice of mast steps so the boat may be rigged as a sloop or a catboat. The Skipjack was only sanctioned for two years by the CBYRA, but for a while the class was used quite a lot for intercollegiate racing. In fact, the U.S. Naval Academy had a fleet of twenty-six Skipjacks in 1967.[5]

An Olympic sailor, Harry Sindle also designed the Newport Holiday, an attractive 19-foot dinghy-type centerboarder with a cuddy shelter and sizable cockpit. Both the Skipjack and Holiday were built at Gloucester, Virginia. This is also the venue of an interesting 15½-foot swing-keel boat called the Gloucester 16.

The 16 is somewhat unique in that she is a sporty dinghy type with a flexible

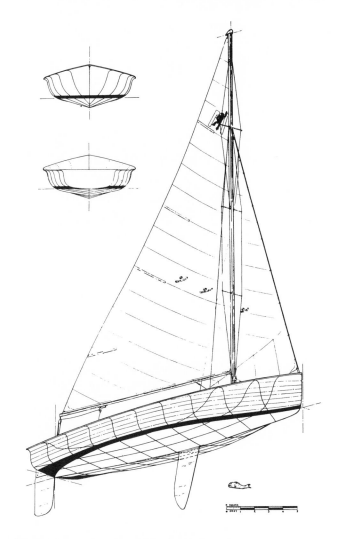

A fish-eye perspective of the Mobjack. Courtesy Roger Moorman, designer; drawing by Joseph F. Gregory.

rig but also has a tiny cabin that houses a portable head and two bunks. A write-up of the boat in *Small Boat Journal* (September 1983) recommended installing a roller-furling jib to avoid going forward to hand the hanked-on jib, but from my experience in sailing the slightly larger Cape Dory Typhoon, I have found that a downhaul led back to the cockpit also obviates the need to go forward. The

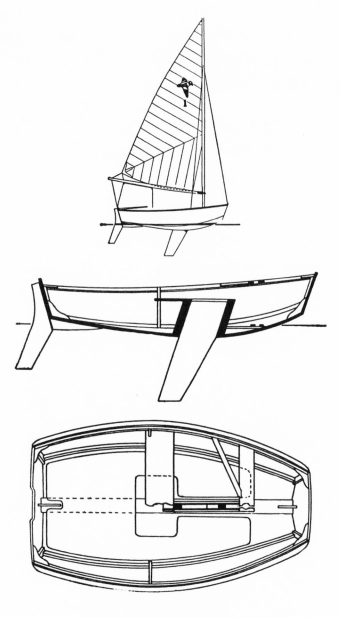

Plans of the Butterball. Design and plans courtesy Richards T. Miller.

Gloucester 16 is not really a native boat, since she was created by the designer of Cal boats, William C. Lapworth, when he lived in California. However, in the late 1980s Bill retired to the Chesapeake, and his waterfront home is not far, as the gull

flies, from where the Gloucester 16 was built.

As mentioned earlier, in the northern Bay, Lowndes Johnson donated an 11-foot cat-rigged scow for junior training at Gibson Island in 1934. In gratitude, Gibson Islanders named the class LJ after the designer's initials. The prototype LJ *Curlew* was built by the Rogers and Townsend yard just north of the island, and it was the lightest fastest boat in the fleet. My Lusby-built *Swift* was fast too, but she was a bit heavier and had quite a tussle with *Curlew* throughout the summer of 1935. The latter's skipper, Gamble Baldwin, started the season as a greenhorn, but under the expert tutelage of the Junior Fleet director, Cap Kenney, he got better with every race. In the climactic last race of the season, held annually in honor of the Gibson Island Club's founder Stuart Symington, the two leading LJs, *Curlew* and *Swift,* were reaching toward the finish neck-and-neck. An anchored yacht blocked the course to the finish line, and Gamble elected to take the most direct route to leeward of the yacht. This caused his sail to be blanketed momentarily, allowing *Swift* to win by just a few feet. Incidentally, a Symington award is more meaningful to me now, as the community's founder was the great-uncle of my wife. Years later our son Rip won a Symington cup sailing a Penguin, and our grandson Ned Cramer did the same sailing an Optimist last summer. As the old expression tells us, "what goes around comes around," and there are often reminders of "the good old days."

Another cat-rigged scow designed for junior sailing by a local naval architect is the Butterball class. Designed by Richards T. Miller in 1958, this boat was first intended for junior training in Charleston Harbor, South Carolina, but has been used in a dozen more states, including Maryland, and in Canada, Australia, and New Zealand as well. An open 9½-foot dinghy of plywood construction, the Butterball is a versatile boat that can serve as a yacht's tender also.

Two native-designed junior trainers with pointed bows are the 12-foot sloop-rigged We-Sort designed by William H. Sands and the 14-foot cat-rigged Oxford Sailer designed by Bob Henry, who also created the Oxford 400. (Bob collaborated with the Butterball's designer Dick Miller on an excellent little book derived from a technical paper, called *Sailing Yacht Design.*) Both the Oxford Sailer and the We-Sort are undecked boats that can be rowed, and they are large enough for adults. Each is made of plywood and weighs 150 pounds. Sands designed the We-Sort for the junior program at the Indian Landing Boat Club on the Severn River. Although she has a pointed bow, the stem is well flattened so novice sailors would cause little if any damage during overly fast head-on landings. We-Sorts are currently being used for junior training by the Chesapeake Bay Maritime Museum at St. Michaels, Maryland.

The Severn River also produced a sportier decked-over 17-foot sloop called the Severn One-Design. Created by Richard C. Bartlett in 1938, this boat was a

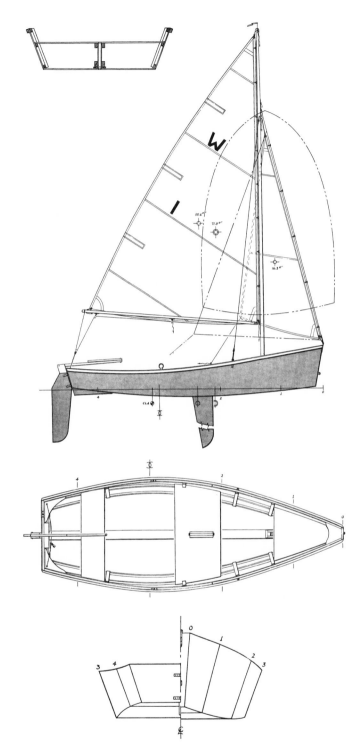

Plans of the We-Sort by William H. Sands.

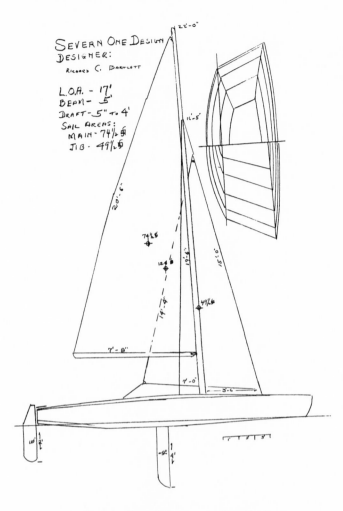

Sketch plans of the Severn One-Design by Richard C. Bartlett. Courtesy Chesapeake Bay Maritime Museum.

speedy arc-bottomed daggerboarder with a tall tri-stay fractional rig and an overlapping genoa. Although never sanctioned by the CBYRA, the class was active and popular at one time but was mostly limited to the Severn.

A couple of large cabinless daysailers by local designers have already been mentioned: the Indian Landing 20 and the Raven. Although neither boat was sanctioned for CBYRA races, the Raven found some

modest popularity off the Bay, especially in New England and Long Island Sound. Both these boats inspired larger versions in the form of racing cruisers with cabins, the Cruisken being a development of the IL 20, and the light-displacement *Dirigo* being an outgrowth of the Raven. The latter, a 24-foot round-bottom centerboard sloop with large mainsail, is intended to have a crew of three. The desirability of extra crew weight was impressed on me after helping to rescue no less an expert sailor than Bob Henry when he capsized a Raven on the Choptank River in the early 1960s. The chine-built IL 20, designed by Jim Speer, has a smaller mainsail but carries an enormous masthead overlapping jib. She is said to be stiff, but could use a coaming to keep water out of the cockpit.

The small craft described thus far are considered true one-designs, with sisters being exactly or almost exactly alike, but other native daysailing boats were called "open" or restricted development classes. The latter boats must meet certain specified measurement limits, such as length and sail area, but some leeway is allowed in hull shape. Two of the most popular of this class created by native designers are the Chesapeake 16 and 20.[6] In the mid-1930s, when there were hardly any sailing yachts on the West River, Ernest H. "Cap'n Dick" Hartge designed and built a 20-foot V-bottom double-ended sloop named *Albatross*.

After more than a dozen boats of the Albatross class had been built, Cap'n Dick designed a transom-stern version of the Chesapeake 20 that became the Sea Witch class. In the early "free-for-all"

CHESAPEAKE SAILS

races there was no limit on sail area. A photograph published in the *Chesapeake Bay Magazine* (February 1989) shows the original *Sea Witch* carrying, in addition to her working sails, a boomed-out single luff spinnaker plus an enormous square sail. This class and the Albatross class were probably the 20-foot racers referred to at the beginning of this chapter by Tom Martin when he said, "These boats could carry incredible amounts of sail and looked like small canoes!"

As a result of being shoal-draft centerboarders with lofty rigs, the Chesapeake 20s could easily capsize. I was told by Bob McLaughlin, who helped the Hartges build these boats, that on one occasion during a squall, thirteen Chesapeake 20s capsized. He also said that Cap'n Dick, an avid racer as well as designer and builder, once capsized twice in the same race but was so adept at righting his boat that he managed to finish in third place. On another occasion, however, during an evening sail, I was told that Cap'n Dick could not right his boat (perhaps the mast had become lodged in the mud), and he was forced to sit on her inverted bottom most of the night while rescuers searched for him.

After a round-bottom 20-footer designed by New Yorker Charles Mower (co-designer of the Sea Bird yawl) began to dominate the class, Cap'n Dick designed a series of round-bottom 20s, each one being a bit faster than her predecessor. The first was the double-ended Challenger, then the square-stern Defender, and finally the Ranger model, a bit more wedge-shaped (finer forward

Perspective view of a Raven, designed by Roger McAleer. Courtesy Time Life Books, illustrated by Jack J. Kunz.

and fuller aft), that was often able to whip the Mower design especially when skippered by John Harding. Since 1990 a number of fiberglass 20s of the Ranger model have been built by the Hartge yard at Galesville, Maryland. Incidentally, one of the early competitive 20s was a boat designed by Norman Owens, later the creator of the Owens cutter.

Several members of the Hartge clan were active racers in this class. In 1994

An Indian Landing using her large masthead jib to good advantage in light weather. Courtesy Chesapeake Bay Maritime Museum, Fred Thomas Collection.

Laurence Hartge's brother Buddy won the Chesapeake 20 distance race from West River to Annapolis. Then seventy-three years old, Buddy was suffering from a lung ailment requiring that he be on oxygen full time, but that didn't stop him from competing and winning! Aside from the Hartges, two of the most consis-

tent winners in the class were Robert Orme and J. Thomas.

Chesapeake 16s are smaller versions of the 20s.[7] The first one was a scaled-down Sea Witch named Mischief built by Fred Davis. A Chesapeake 16 organization headed by Laurence Hartge was formed in 1938, and the class was sanctioned by the CBYRA for ten years, from 1948 to 1958. Two of the most consistent winners of this class were Hugh Wallis and J. E. Vieth.

The Chesapeake 20s were sanctioned for a longer period, from 1942 until 1970. Although they are not now scored for CBYRA High Points, these swift craft are still raced enthusiastically in less formal special regattas. With their shallow draft of only 8 inches (board up) and their large sail areas (to catch the Bay's midsummer zephyrs), the 16s and 20s are well suited for the Chesapeake.

Though the Penguin is usually considered a native class, the boat was actually designed by Philip Rhodes, who was not a native, and its prototype was created for Rhode Island boatbuilder William Dyer for frostbite (cold weather) racing north of the Bay in 1933. Nevertheless, the official history of the class, expressed in the International Penguin Class Dinghy Association Handbook, states: "In 1938–39 a small group of Potomac and Chesapeake Bay sailors, near Alexandria, Virginia, wrote to the leading naval architects for plans of a dinghy which could easily be built by an amateur. Philip Rhodes came up with the 11½-foot dinghy, which could be built of waterproof plywood." The prototype Penguin designed for Dyer was

CHESAPEAKE SAILS

raced and proved very fast, but it did not produce any orders for sisters, because frostbiters of those times were partial to round-bottom designs,[8] and many of the sailors were owners of large yachts who wanted a more versatile boat that could double as a tender.

The design was shelved by Rhodes for five years, then revived after the request from the Chesapeake yachtsmen. It proved ideal for the developing method of simple construction utilizing sheet plywood. After plans were published in *Yachting* in 1940, the boat attracted nationwide interest and a national class was formed headed by William Heintz, a prominent Chesapeake yachtsman and chart publisher. A few months before America's entry into World War II, the first national Penguin regatta was held in Annapolis, and the racing was won by Walter Lawson of the Potomac River fleet. Other local champions include Charles and Vance Strausburg, William McClure, Thomas Kauffman, William Bolger, and Leonard Penso, who won High Points thirteen times. The boat gradually grew in popularity all over America and internationally as well. The class was especially popular for frostbiting: hence its name. For many years the Penguin was used extensively as a junior trainer on the Chesapeake (my son Rip learned to sail in a Penguin named *Ripple,* of course), but then it was replaced by boats such as Lasers and Optimist prams. Recently, however, there has been a revival of interest in Penguin racing, both for juniors and adults, and indications are that the class is making a real

The Chesapeake 20 *Step Aside,* a High Point winner. Courtesy Chesapeake Bay Maritime Museum.

comeback. Some of the Bay's top racing sailors such as Charlie Scott, John White, John Aras, and Jonathan Bartlett are currently racing Penguins with their children.

Outside of the Penguin and Star, little has been said about small-boat classes used on the Bay that were not designed by Chesapeake designers. The separate list of small-boat classes designed off the

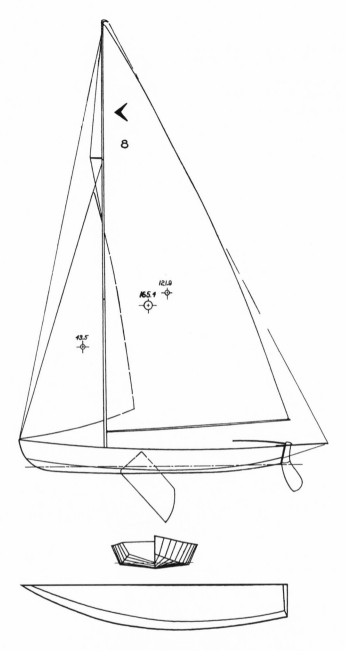

Plans of a Chesapeake 16, designed by Ernest H. Hartge. Courtesy Totch Hartge.

Bay (facing page) shows which are, or have been, sanctioned for five years or more by the CBYRA for racing on the Bay. (An asterisk indicates those classes

that are *currently* sanctioned.) For each class, the boat's overall length is noted, along with the names of some of the most outstanding skippers—generally those with the greatest number of High Point wins.[9]

The granddaddy of the one-designs that came to the Chesapeake is the Star, first appearing at Gibson Island in 1923. This famous design and some of its early champions were discussed in chapter 1. Later champions include Dink Doeller, Mason Shehan, Melville Grosvenor, Henry Wilmer, David and Robert Dunigan, William Myers, the Lippincotts (Howard, Robert, and Richard), James Allsopp, Stanley Ogilvy, John Jenkins, Robert Thompson, Elliott Oldak, David Gaillard, Craig Coltharp, Jonathan Bartlett, and John Sherwood III (who won High Points six times). A number of the one-design sailors later became outstanding skippers of racing cruisers.

This chapter wouldn't be complete without mentioning the northern Chesapeake's answer to the southern Bay's DYs (depression yachts) mentioned in chapter 1. In the early 1950s, a group of avid sailors who sorely missed yacht racing during the winter months formed a frostbite organization in the general vicinity of Baltimore and the Magothy River. The unique aspect of this organization was that their plywood boats were extraordinarily inexpensive (like the DYs), and every racing participant built his own boat from a standardized kit. Dubbed "Shrimp Boats," these 8-foot craft were Hagerty Seashells, and the kit cost thirty-five dollars.

266   CHESAPEAKE SAILS

Small Boat Classes Designed off the Bay That Have Been Sanctioned by CBYRA for Five Years or More

Class	Length	Skippers (High Point leaders)
*Albacore	15 feet	D.L. Wallerstein
Celebrity	19 feet, 9 inches	James Landerman, Richard Kerper
*El Toro	7 feet, 11 inches	Michael Brown, Paul Muma, Geoffrey Schneider
Flying Dutchman	19 feet, 10 inches	Robert James, Robert Daniel
*Flying Scot	19 feet	Jeffrey Stamper, David and Robert Neff
International 14	14 feet	Stuart Walker, Robert Empey, Frank Lawson, Robert Reeves
International 420	13 feet, 9 inches	Jonathan Bartlett
*International 470	15 feet, 5 inches	Peter Mignerey, Gordon Cutler
*International 505	16 feet, 5 inches	Donald Heath, Gary Bodie, Macy Nelson, Henry Amthor
*Jet 14	14 feet	Albert and Celeste Simonds, Gary Smith
*J/22	22 feet, 6 inches	Peter McChesney
Jolly	18 feet	Lloyd Emory, Lloyd Griffin
*Laser	13 feet, 10 inches	Brad Squires
*Lightning	19 feet	Barney Meade, Marbury Fox, Robert Purnell, Stephen Bachman, Fred Mertes
Moth	11 feet	C. Coupland, B.W. Cabell
National One-Design	17 feet	Peter Geis, Michael Phillips
*Optimist	8 feet	John Torgerson, Scott MacMullen, Steve Miernicki
*Penguin	11 feet, 6 inches	Leonard Penso, Thomas Kauffman, William Bolger, Charles Krafft
*Rainbow	24 feet, 2 inches	Raymond N. Brown, John Graham, Peter Gookin
Shark Catamaran	20 feet	James Hagwood
*Snipe	15 feet, 6 inches	John Reckord, William Rushlow, George Brown, Fred Thurston, Griff Hall
*Star	22 feet, 9 inches	Skippers noted in chapters 1 and 8
Tempest	22 feet	Edgar Hoyt, James O'Hara
*Thistle	17 feet	Donald Moore
Windmill	15 feet, 8 inches	Allen Chauvenet, Eric Legstrom

* currently sanctioned by CBYRA for racing on the Chesapeake Bay

A parade of boats associated with Lowndes Johnson: two Johnson designs—the Comet and LJ—and a Star, a Chesapeake champion named *Escape,* built by Lowndes for Melville Grosvenor. Photograph by John Earle, courtesy Chesapeake Bay Maritime Museum).

Popular venues for racing were Blackhole Creek on the Magothy River, Stoney Creek on the Patapsco River, and Lake Roland just north of Baltimore. Most of the participants were big-boat owners who raced in the cruising, racing, or Delta divisions of the CBYRA in the spring, summer, and fall. During those seasons the Shrimp Boats were often used as dinghies

for the big boats. Among the prime movers in the group were prominent sailors mentioned earlier in this book: Buzz White, Larry Newark, Marshall Duer, Martin Alvey, Dick Jablin, Tom Closs, and Ron Ward. Keen racing was combined with a good deal of hoopla and (sea) horseplay. There were informal ceremonies, ridiculous costumes, and practical jokes; in general, a party atmosphere prevailed. The top award was a galvanized garbage can partially filled with shrimp.[10]

It seems to me that racing in those times, even in big boats, was less serious and therefore more fun than it is today. There was less professionalism and greater camaraderie of competitors through corinthianism. Less money was spent on racing, and yachts were truly dual-purpose vessels that could be used for comfortable cruising as well as racing. Pure enjoyment was the primary objective rather than to win at any cost, often for business reasons. Many of the greatest competitors of those times seemed to love cruising on the Bay as much as they did racing. Take, for example, Carleton Mitchell's portrayal of the Wye River, ". . . in its own way worthy of comparison with the Aegean, the Baltic, the Caribbean, the Pacific—a rambling few miles of solitude which seep into the soul, quiet green lanes of peace after the boisterous blue wastes of ocean *Finisterre* and I had known together."[11]

Although those times might be considered by many of my contemporaries as "the dear dead days," the Bay is still an idyllic place to sail. For most of the year, its waters offer beauty, protection, and

variety for racing or cruising. Except for summertime squalls, there are few of the hazards found in other boating areas such as strong currents, extreme tides, frequent fog, dangerous rocks, and exposed anchorages. Despite the fact that certain parts of the Bay are becoming more than a little congested, there are still a number of open areas adjacent to yacht clubs for interesting racing. For the cruisers, there are an infinite number of snug creeks to find and meandering rivers to explore. Lowndes Johnson once remarked that during his seventy-plus years of sailing the Chesapeake, he had not come close to seeing it all.

I know of no better way to end this book than to quote a letter written to the editors of the *Skipper* (October 1967) by Francis L. Koenig of McLean, Virginia. He wrote: "Happiness is your wife snoozing in the sun on the leeward cockpit cushions; forward, the jenny full and drawing under started sheet; abeam, Maryland's Eastern Shore peeking under the boom; from the bow, the soft slap of wavelets against the topsides; in your hand, the firm feel of the tiller with a slight weather helm; on the rail close by, a cold beer. *That's* what happiness is."

NOTES

Chapter 1

1. Chapelle, *American Sailing Craft*, 188.
2. Chapelle, *The Baltimore Clipper*, 10.
3. Stephens, *Traditions and Memories of American Yachting*, 269.
4. Wallace, *The Macmillan Book of Boating*, 13.
5. Stephens, *Traditions and Memories of American Yachting*, 269.
6. Webb and Webb, *Best On The Bay*, 31.
7. C. P. Kunhardt, *Forest and Stream* (March 25, 1886): 174.
8. *Rudder* (July 1906): 460.
9. Brewington, *Chesapeake Bay: A Pictorial Maritime History*, 221.
10. Frederick Tilp, *The Chesapeake Skipper* (February 1952): 14.
11. Maryland Archives, Charter Record Book No. FAP 20, 547.
12. Kunhardt, *Small Yachts*, 282.
13. Tom Martin, letter to author, May 3, 1997.
14. Frederick Tilp, "Capital Y.C.," *The Chesapeake Skipper* (January 1950): 19.
15. *The Chesapeake Skipper*, vol. 1 (August 1947).
16. *Rudder* (August 1905): 461.
17. *Rudder* (June 1905): 378.
18. Hoyt, *Sherman Hoyt's Memoirs*, 59, 60.
19. Miller and Pearre, *Fifteenth Anniversary Record of the Chesapeake Bay Fleet*, 12–17.
20. Ibid, 35–43.
21. Webb and Webb, *Best On The Bay*, 37.
22. H. L. Stone, "Gibson Island Race Brings Out Record Fleet," *Yachting* (August 1929): 98.
23. Fox, *Racing, Cruising and Design*, 304.
24. L. Corrin Strong, log of *Narada* (typed diary), 1939.
25. Tom Martin, letter to author, May 3, 1997.
26. Malcolm Lamborne, Jr., "CBYRA," *The Chesapeake Skipper* (June 1952): 7.
27. Captain Charles G. Halpine, "Annapolis Yachting—Old and New," *The Chesapeake Skipper* (May 1949): 5.

Chapter 2

1. "Synopsis—History of Urbanna YC–Fishing Bay YC," author unknown.
2. John Wilbur, "The U.S. Coast Guard's Coastal Picket Patrol," *The Log of Mystic Seaport* (Spring 1991): 7.
3. H. M. Cadwalader, "Out to Spot Subs in Racing Yachts," *Baltimore Sun* (August 2, 1942).
4. John Trumpy & Sons contract list, courtesy of Sigrid Trumpy.
5. Melinda Berge, *Annapolis to Newport Race, A Brief History*, Annapolis Yacht Club (June 1997).
6. Ibid.
7. Ibid.
8. *The Skipper* (August 1967): 22.

271

9. *PHRF of the Chesapeake,* 1985 Yearbook.

10. Tucker, *Half Pint,* 73, 85.

11. Karl Kirkman, letter to author, July 1997.

12. Anne Hays, "Regional Report—Great Ocean Race," *Rudder* (May 1983): 9.

13. Dr. William Peach, letter to author, May 4, 1998.

14. Steve Callahan, "Gentlemen Do Sail to Windward," *Cruising World* (April 1998): 48.

15. *Practical Sailor* (May 1998): 11.

Chapter 3

1. L. Corrin Strong, log of *Narada,* 1939.

Chapter 4

1. Rothrock and Rothrock, *Chesapeake Odysseys,* 50.

2. Frank Moorshead, conversation with author, December 14, 1996.

3. Ibid.

4. *The Sun Magazine,* December 3, 1972.

5. L. F. Herreshoff, letter to Robert Johnson, October 17, 1966.

6. Edwin Schoettle, editor, *Sailing Craft* (1943): 212.

7. Schult, *Sailing Dictionary,* 329.

8. Tom Vesey, "Experts Speculate on *Pride*'s Dangers," *Washington Post* (May 22, 1986): A37.

9. Gillmer, *Pride of Baltimore,* 161.

10. Linton Rigg, letter to George Bahen, January 11, 1973.

11. Robert Brennan, letter to author, March 9, 1974.

12. Brindze, *The Experts Book of Boating,* 2.

13. Taylor, *Good Boats,* 106.

14. Norman G. Owens, letter to author, May 17, 1995.

15. Norman G. Owens, letter to author, July 26, 1995.

16. Roger Taylor, letter to author, April 28, 1988.

17. *The Capital* (October 25, 1996): A10.

18. Steve Temple, "Four Decades of Dickersons." *Chesapeake Bay Magazine* (December 1987): 48.

19. Neville Lewis, letter to author, July 22, 1994.

20. Ferenc Maté, *The World's Best Sailboats* (New York, W.W. Norton, 1986): 88.

21. Alexander Gifford, "Chesapeake Craft Sweep Race on Bridge Course," *The Baltimore News-Post* (September 22, 1952).

22. Laurence Hartge, "Quadrant," *Chesapeake Bay Magazine* (September 1989): 56.

23. Sunny Gibbons-Neff and Henry Gibbons-Neff, conversation with author, September 27, 1995.

24. Ibid.

25. Thomas E. Colvin, letter to author, May 22, 1997.

26. Thomas E. Colvin, *Steel Boatbuilding* (Camden, Maine: International Marine, 1985).

27. Colvin, *Coastwise and Offshore Cruising Wrinkles,* 37.

28. Thomas E. Colvin, letter to author, May 22, 1997.

29. Ibid.

30. Karl Kirkman, "Ramblings for Jud Henderson," received July 1997.

31. *The Dickerson Story* (advertising brochure).

32. Robby Robinson, "Farrs Down the Line," *Sail* (May 1985): 121.

33. *Yachting* (November 1984): 93.

34. *Cruising Club News* (December 1994): 35.

35. Roger Taylor and Dale B. Lewis, "The Mathis-Trumpy Story," *Wooden Boat* (February 1997): 64.

36. *The Skipper,* design section (March 1959): 4.

37. Henderson, *53 Boats You Can Build,* 126.

38. Benford, *Cruising Yachts,* 9.

39. Jay R. Benford, letter to author, November 27, 1984.

40. Henderson, *Sea Sense,* 3rd ed., 301–2.

41. Charles Lucke, Jr. "Eastern Shore Slants." *The Skipper* (September 1955): 40.

42. Phil Bowie, *"Lady June." Sail* (October 1978): 186.

Chapter 5

1. N. T. Kenny, "Rounding the Buoy," *Baltimore Sun* (August 21, 1947).

2. Snediker and Jensen, *Chesapeake Bay Schooners,* 61.

3. Slack, *In the Wake of the "Spray."*

4. Chesapeake Bay Maritime Museum, newspaper article (no date) by "Old Timer."

5. Sherwood, *The Sailing Years,* 3, 4.

6. L. Corrin Strong, log of *Narada,* 1936, 1937, 1938.

7. Jack Strickland, letter to author, September 28, 1984.

8. Carrick and Henderson, *John G. Alden and His Yacht Designs*, 67.
9. Henderson, *Philip L. Rhodes and His Yacht Designs*, 84.
10. L. Corrin Strong, log of *Narada*, 1936, 1937, 1938.
11. Henderson, *Philip L. Rhodes and His Yacht Designs*, 251.
12. Carrick and Henderson, *John G. Alden and His Yacht Designs*, 184.
13. Ibid.
14. George H. Engeman, "Yacht Racing on the Rolling Deep," *The Baltimore Sun* (October 25, 1931).
15. Carrick and Henderson, *John G. Alden and His Yacht Designs*, 402.
16. Loomis, *Ocean Racing*, 162.
17. Carrick and Henderson, *John G. Alden and His Yacht Designs*, 181.
18. Robert Henry, letter to author, December 1969.
19. Paul Adamthwaite, letter to author, September 28, 1984.
20. "Antigua Race Week," *Islands* (April 1990): 97.
21. Footner, *The Last Generation*, jacket cover.
22. Harriet Hazeleton, "The *Manitou*, Spirit of Camelot," *Chesapeake Bay Magazine* (October 1974): 19.
23. Richards Miller, letter to author, March 7, 1996.
24. Hoyt, *Sherman Hoyt's Memoirs*, 211.
25. James Tazelaar, "An Interview with Jean Gau," *Chesapeake Bay Magazine* (November 1974): 14.
26. Cedric Egeli, telephone conversation with author, February 9, 1995.
27. Mary Corddry, "Gau, Gallant Sailor Rests in South France." *The Baltimore Sun* (January 12, 1974).
28. Borden, *Sea Quest*, 27.

Chapter 6

1. Kinney, *You Are First*, 173.
2. Carleton Mitchell, letter to author, January 31, 1980.
3. Charles Iliff, Jr., from the eulogy of Dr. Charles Iliff; sent to the author by Dr. Nicholas Iliff, December 17, 1997.
4. Robinson, *Legendary Yachts*, 237.

5. Mitchell Gibbons-Neff, letter to author, October 16, 1995.
6. Rod Stephens, Jr., letter to author, November 5, 1969.
7. Robby Robinson, "SORC Standouts," *Sail* (April 1985): 73.
8. John Danly, *North News* (Summer 1985).
9. Charles Iliff, Jr., from the eulogy of Dr. Charles Iliff; sent to author by Dr. Nicholas Iliff, December 17, 1997.
10. Ibid.
11. Ibid.
12. Dan Winters, "*Alaris*—A Winner from the Past," *The Chesapeake Skipper* (August/September1986).
13. Zantzinger, *The Log of the "Molly Brown."*
14. Holm, *The Circumnavigators*, 361.
15. Carl Alberg, letter to author, January 18, 1984.
16. Henderson, *Choice Yacht Designs*, 81.
17. John F. Zanks, letter to author, August 20, 1995.
18. Ibid.
19. Gloria Barry, "The Rough Log," *The Skipper* (July 1967): 30.
20. Hanks, *"Muskrat," A Surprise Bid for the America's Cup.*
21. Henry Kilburn, "The Magnificent *Gesture*," *The Skipper* (December 1965): 37.
22. Howard Fawcett, letter to author, September 28, 1995.
23. Dr. William Peach, letter to author, May 4, 1998.
24. Tom Hunnicutt, telephone conversation with author, August 18, 1995.
25. Pat Brown Fitzgerald, telephone conversation with author, August 3,1995.
26. Gifford Pinchot, letter to author, September 27, 1977.
27. Pinchot, *"Loki" and "Loon."*
28. Ibid.
29. Kinney, *You Are First*, 114.
30. Richard C. McCurdy, Clayton Ewing's obituary. *Cruising Club News* (June 1981): 32.
31. Ibid.
32. Crawford, *Count the Cats in Zanzibar*, 78.
33. Ibid, 20.
34. *Cruising Club News* (June 1981): 31.
35. Newbold Smith, letter to author, December 11, 1995.

36. Ibid.
37. Smith, *Down Denmark Strait,* 6.
38. Ibid.
39. Richard Henderson, *Sea Sense,* 2nd ed. (Camden, Maine: International Marine, 1979): 54.
40. Bill Wagner, "Romagna, Hall of Fame Crewman," *The Capital* (June 15, 1994).
41. *Rudder* staff. "Closeup: Boats to Note." *Rudder* (June 1971): 32.
42. Frederick Hecklinger, letter to author, December 18, 1995.
43. Frederick Hecklinger, letter to author, January 14, 1996.
44. Mrs. Raymond N. Brown, letter to author, May 19, 1995.
45. Frederick Hecklinger, letter to author, January 14, 1996.
46. Garden, *Yacht Designs II,* 31.
47. Kathy Trossbach, review of *The Mooneshine Logs* by Francis Stokes, *Cruising Club News* (June 1994).
48. Ron Trossbach, telephone conversation with author, May 25, 1995.
49. Henderson, *Essential Seamanship,* 249.
50. Barbara Lloyd, "Francis Stokes," *Nautical Quarterly* 24 (Winter 1983).
51. Bill Homewood, letter to author, October 1987.
52. Karina Paape, *The Capital* (June 5, 1986).
53. Bill Wagner, "White Makes Most of MORC Chance," *The Capital* (August 24, 1995).

Chapter 7

1. McNitt, *Sailing at the U.S. Naval Academy.*
2. Ibid.
3. Herreshoff, *An L. Francis Herreshoff Reader,* 4, 5.
4. Norman Owens, letter to author, May 23, 1995.
5. Hefler, *Jack of All Trades,* 96.
6. A. E. Luders, Jr., letter to author, December 2, 1977.
7. Parkinson, *Nowhere is Too Far,* 74.
8. Ibid, 151.
9. Hefler, *Jack of All Trades,* 97.
10. Harrison Roberts, "Prize Crew," *Chesapeake Skipper* (August 1950): 30.
11. McNitt, *Sailing at the U.S. Naval Academy,* 141.

12. Hefler, *Jack of All Trades,* 98.
13. Ibid.
14. Randal Johnson, "The Last Was First," *The Skipper* (August 1967): 32.
15. Henderson, Dunbar, and Brooks, *Sail and Power,* 3rd ed., 376.
16. McNitt, *Sailing at the U.S. Naval Academy,* 162.
17. Parkinson, *Nowhere is Too Far,* 74.
18. Henderson, *Philip L. Rhodes and His Yacht Designs,* 274.
19. McNitt, *Sailing at the U.S. Naval Academy,* 169.
20. Greg Walsh, "Chartroom Chatter," *Ocean Navigator* (July/August 1991): 62.
21. Ian McCurdy and John Bonds, "The Planning, Design, and Construction of the 44-foot Offshore Training Craft for the U.S. Naval Academy," The Ninth Chesapeake Sailing Yacht Symposium (March 1989): 93.
22. McNitt, *Sailing at the U.S. Naval Academy,* 221–222.
23. McCurdy and Bonds, "The Planning, Design, and Construction of the 44-foot Offshore Training Craft for the U.S. Naval Academy": 98.
24. Henderson and Brooks, *Sail and Power,* 4th ed., 139.

Chapter 8

1. Thomas Martin, letter to author, May 3, 1997.
2. Webb and Webb, *Best On The Bay,* 59, and communication with Vincent J. Serio, Jr. (conversation April 22, 1999, and correspondence April 23, 1999).
3. *Yachting* editors, *Your New Boat,* 53.
4. "Chesapeake Chatter." *Skipper* (October 1959): 34.
5. Henderson and Dunbar, *Sail and Power,* 1st ed., 73.
6. Laurence Hartge, "Fifty Years of 20s," *Chesapeake Bay Magazine* (September 1985): 48.
7. Laurence Hartge, "A Memorable Weekend," *Chesapeake Bay Magazine* (February 1989): 59.
8. Mrs. William J. H. Dyer, letter to William L. Henderson, April 21, 1966.
9. CBYRA Yearbooks.
10. *The Sun Magazine* (February 1, 1953).
11. Sherwood, *Understanding the Chesapeake,* 15.

BIBLIOGRAPHY

Anderson, Henry H., Jr., and Robert C. MacArthur. *The Centennial History of the United States Sailing Association.* Sponsored by Rolex Watch U.S.A., Portsmouth, R.I.: U.S. Sailing, 1977.

Barrie, Robert, and George Barrie, Jr. *Cruises Mainly in the Bay of the Chesapeake.* Philadelphia: Franklin Press, 1909.

Barton, Humphrey. *Atlantic Adventures.* Southampton, England: Adlard Coles, 1962.

Beiser, Arthur. *The Proper Yacht.* New York: Macmillan, 1966.

———. *The Proper Yacht,* 2nd ed. Camden, Maine.: International Marine, 1978.

Benford, Jay R. *Cruising Yachts.* Friday Harbor, Wash.: Tiller, 1983.

Blanchard, Fessenden S., and William T. Stone. *A Cruising Guide to the Chesapeake.* New York: Dodd, Mead, 1968.

Borden, Charles A. *Sea Quest.* Philadelphia: Macrae Smith, 1967.

Brewington, M.V. *Chesapeake Bay: A Pictorial Maritime History.* Cambridge, Md.: Cornell Maritime Press, 1953.

———. *Chesapeake Bay Log Canoes and Bugeyes.* Centreville, Md.: Tidewater Publishers, 1963.

Brindze, Ruth, ed. *The Expert's Book of Boating.* Englewood Cliffs, N.J.: Prentice-Hall, 1959.

Burgess, Robert H. *This Was Chesapeake Bay.* Centreville, Md.: Tidewater Publishers, 1963.

———. *Chesapeake Circle.* Cambridge, Md.: Cornell Maritime Press, 1965.

Carrick, Robert W., and Richard Henderson. *John G. Alden and His Yacht Designs.* Camden, Maine.: International Marine, 1983.

Chapelle, Howard I. *The Baltimore Clipper: Its Origin and Development.* Salem, Mass.: The Marine Research Society, 1930.

———. *The History of American Sailing Ships.* New York: Bonanza Books, 1935.

———. *American Sailing Craft.* New York: Kennedy Brothers, 1936.

———. *Notes on Chesapeake Bay Skipjacks.* St. Michaels, Md.: Chesapeake Bay Maritime Museum, n.d.

Colvin, Thomas E. *Coastwise and Offshore Cruising Wrinkles.* New York: Seven Seas Press, 1972.

Crane, Clinton. *Clinton Crane's Yachting Memories.* New York: Van Nostrand, 1952.

Crawford, James W. *Count the Cats in Zanzibar.* Cambridge, Md.: Tidewater Publishers, 1975.

Dixon, Thomas, Jr. *The Life Worth Living.* New York: Doubleday, Page, 1905.

Dodds, Richard J. S., and Pete Lesher, eds. *A Heritage in Wood.* St. Michaels, Md.: Chesapeake Bay Maritime Museum, 1992.

Earle, Swepson. *The Chesapeake Bay Country*. Baltimore: Thomsen-Ellis, 1923.

Eddy, Alan. *So You Want To Sail Around the World Alone*. New York: Allied Boat Company, n.d.

Footner, Geoffrey M. *The Last Generation, A History of a Chesapeake Shipbuilding Family*. Solomons, Md.: Calvert Marine Museum Press, 1991.

Footner, Hulbert. *Soldier of Fortune*. New York: Harper & Brothers, 1940.

———. *Rivers of the Eastern Shore*. New York: Farrar and Rinehart, 1944.

Fox, Uffa. *Sailing, Seamanship and Yacht Construction*. New York: Charles Scribner's Sons, 1934.

———. *Uffa Fox's Second Book*. New York: Charles Scribner's Sons, 1935.

———. *Racing, Cruising and Design*. New York: Charles Scribner's Sons, 1938.

Garden, William. *Yacht Designs II*. Mystic, Conn.: Mystic Seaport Museum, 1992.

Gillmer, Thomas C. *"Pride of Baltimore," The Story of the Baltimore Clippers*. Camden, Maine: International Marine, 1992.

Hanks, Douglas, Jr. *"Muskrat," A Surprise Bid for the America's Cup*. Easton, Md.: privately published, 1987.

Hefler, Alden R. *Jack of All Trades*. Annapolis, Md.: privately printed, 1978.

Henderson, Richard. *Choice Yacht Designs*. Camden, Maine: International Marine, 1979.

———. *Philip L. Rhodes and His Yacht Designs*. Camden, Maine: International Marine, 1981.

———. *53 Boats You Can Build*. Camden, Maine: International Marine, 1985.

———. *Singlehanded Sailing, The Experiences and Techniques of the Lone Voyagers*, 2nd ed. Camden, Maine: International Marine, 1988.

———. *Sea Sense*, 3rd ed. Camden, Maine: International Marine, 1991.

———. *Essential Seamanship*. Centreville, Md.: Cornell Maritime Press, 1994.

Henderson, Richard, and Bartlett S. Dunbar. *Sail and Power*. Annapolis, Md.: U.S. Naval Institute, 1967.

Henderson, Richard, with Bartlett S. Dunbar, and William E. Brooks III. *Sail and Power*, 3rd ed., Annapolis, Md.: Naval Institute Press, 1979.

Henderson, Richard, with William E. Brooks III. *Sail and Power*, 4th ed., Annapolis, Md.: Naval Institute Press, 1991.

Henry, Robert, and Richards T. Miller. *Sailing Yacht Design*. Cambridge, Md.: Cornell Maritime Press, 1965.

Herreshoff, L. Francis. *The Common Sense of Yacht Design*. Jamaica, N.Y.: Caravan-Maritime Books, 1974.

———. *An L. Francis Herreshoff Reader*. Camden, Maine: International Marine, 1978.

———. *"Ticonderoga Letters."* Collected by Max Gwathmey, 1963–1967, n.p.

Hill, Norman Alan, ed. *Chesapeake Cruise*. Baltimore: George W. King Printing, 1944.

Holm, Donald. *The Circumnavigators, Small Boat Voyagers of Modern Times*. Englewood Cliffs, N.J.: Prentice-Hall, 1974.

Hoyt, C. Sherman. *Sherman Hoyt's Memoirs*. New York: Van Nostrand, 1950.

Johnson, Peter. *Boating Facts and Feats*. New York: Sterling Publishing, 1976.

Kinney, Francis S. *Skene's Elements of Yacht Designs*. New York: Dodd, Mead, 1973.

———. *You Are First, The Story of Olin and Rod Stephens of Sparkman and Stephens*. New York: Dodd, Mead, 1978.

Klingel, Gilbert. *The Bay*. New York: Dodd, Mead, 1951.

Kunhardt, C.P. *Small Yachts*. New York: Forest and Stream Publishing, 1885.

Loomis, Alfred F. *"Hotspur's" Cruise in the Aegean*. New York: Jonathan Cape and Harrison Smith, 1931.

———. *Ocean Racing, The Great Blue-Water Yacht Races*. New York: William Morrow, 1936.

McNitt, Robert W. *Sailing at the U.S. Naval Academy*. Annapolis, Md.: Naval Institute Press, 1996.

Middleton, Arthur P. *Tobacco Coast, A Maritime History of Chesapeake Bay in the Colonial Era*. Newport News, Va.: The Mariners' Museum, 1953.

Miller, Robert R., and Aubrey Pearre III. *Fifteenth Anniversary Record of the Chesapeake Bay Fleet*. Baltimore: Hoffman Brothers, 1938.

Mitchell, Carleton. *Passage East*. New York: W. W. Norton, 1953.

Ogilvy, C. Stanley. *A History of the Star Class*. Glenview, Ill.: International Star Class Association, 1991.

Parkinson, John, Jr. *Nowhere Is Too Far*. New York: The Cruising Club of America, 1960.

Pease, Greg, with Thomas C. Gillmer, and Barbara Bozzuto. *Sailing With Pride*. Baltimore: C. A. Baumgartner Publishing, 1990.

Pinchot, Gifford B. *"Loki" and "Loon."* New York: Dodd, Mead, 1985.

Rimington, Critchell, ed. *The Sea Chest*. New York: W. W. Norton, 1947.

Robinson, Bill. *Legendary Yachts*. New York: Macmillan, 1971.

Rothrock, Joseph T., and Jane C. Rothrock. *Chesapeake Odysseys, an 1883 Cruise Revisited*. Centreville, Md.: Tidewater Publishers, 1984.

Schoettle, Edwin J., ed. *Sailing Craft*. New York: Macmillan, 1943.

Schult, Joachim (translated and extensively revised by Barbara Webb). *The Sailing Dictionary*. New York: Granada Publishing, 1981.

Semmes, Raphael. *Captains and Mariners of Early Maryland*. Baltimore: The Johns Hopkins Press, 1937.

Shellenberger, William H. *Cruising the Chesapeake: A Gunkholer's Guide*. Camden, Maine: International Marine, 1990.

Sherwood, Arthur W. *Understanding the Chesapeake*. Centreville, Md.: Tidewater Publishers, 1973.

Sherwood, Donald H. *The Sailing Years*. Baltimore: privately printed, 1971.

Sherwood, John. *Maryland's Vanishing Lives*. Baltimore: The Johns Hopkins Press, 1994.

Shomette, Donald C. *Tidewater Time Capsule*. Centreville, Md.: Tidewater Publishers, 1995.

Slack, Kenneth E. *In the Wake of the "Spray."* New Brunswick, N.J.: Rutgers University Press, 1966.

Smith, E. Newbold. *Down Denmark Strait*. Boston: Little, Brown. 1980.

Snediker, Quentin, and Ann Jensen. *Chesapeake Bay Schooners*. Centreville, Md.: Tidewater Publishers, 1992.

Stephens, William P. *Traditions and Memories of American Yachting*, reprint of articles published by *Rudder*. Camden, Maine: International Marine, 1981.

Strong, L. Corrin. Logs of *Ataloa* and *Narada*. Gibson Island, Md., and Washington, D.C., 1932 through 1947, n.p.

Taylor, Roger C. *Good Boats*. Camden, Maine: International Marine, 1977.

———. *More Good Boats*. Camden, Maine: International Marine, 1979.

———. *Still More Good Boats*. Camden, Maine.: International Marine, 1981.

———. *The Fourth Book of Good Boats*. Camden, Maine: International Marine, 1984.

Tucker, Jane. *"Half Pint."* Cambridge, Md.: Tidewater Publishers, 1975.

Vojtech, Pat. *Chesapeake Bay Skipjacks*. Centreville, Md.: Tidewater Publishers, 1993.

Walker, Stuart H., ed. *The Techniques of Small Boat Racing*. New York: W. W. Norton, 1960.

———. *Wind and Strategy*. New York: W. W. Norton, 1973.

Wallace, William N. *The Macmillan Book of Boating*. New York: Macmillan, 1964.

Waters, John M., Jr. *A Guide to Small Boat Emergencies*. Annapolis, Md.: Naval Institute Press, 1993.

Webb, Jane C., and George R. Webb. *Best On The Bay*. Newport News, Va.: The Sailing Association/Press, 1984.

Wilstash, Paul. *Tidewater Maryland*. Indianapolis, Ind.: Bobbs-Merrill, 1931.

Yachting magazine editors. *Your New Boat*. New York: Simon and Schuster, 1946.

Yacht Racing/Cruising magazine editors with Robert Scharff and Richard Henderson. *Encyclopedia of Sailing*. New York: Harper and Row: 1971.

Zantzinger, Richard C., Jr. *The Log of the "Molly Brown."* Richmond, Va.: Westover Publishing, 1973.

INDEX

Numbers in italic designate illustrations.